F. Bottarelli

Exercises Upon the Different Parts of Italian Speech

With references to Veneroni's grammar

F. Bottarelli

Exercises Upon the Different Parts of Italian Speech
With references to Veneroni's grammar

ISBN/EAN: 9783744717991

Printed in Europe, USA, Canada, Australia, Japan

Cover: Foto ©Thomas Meinert / pixelio.de

More available books at **www.hansebooks.com**

EXERCIS

Upon the different

Upon the different

PARTS of ITALIAN SPEECH;

WITH

REFERENCES

TO

VENERONI's GRAMMAR.

To which is subjoined,

An Abridgement of the Roman History, intended at at once to make the Learner acquainted with History, and the Idiom of the Italian Language.

By F. BOTTARELLI.

LONDON,
Printed for J. NOURSE, Bookseller to His MAJESTY,
MDCCLXXVIII.

PREFACE.

AMIDST the laudable endeavours for the advancement of the Italian language, it is surprising that an easy and expeditious method of teaching it, has been, in a great measure, overlooked; and that beginners have been hitherto left without proper helps. Conscious of its usefulness, I have attempted to write these exercises upon the Italian Syntax of Veneroni's Grammar; with what success I have executed the task, must be submitted to public decision.

These Exercises comprehend all the difficulties, and idiomatical expressions of the Italian Tongue, the rules, and exceptions whereof are exemplified after such a method, that

that he cannot fail to be master of that language, who has gone through them once, or twice.

The examples are of three sorts; the first, that immediately follow the rule, are short, wherein nothing farther is designed than only to exemplify that rule. The second sort are longer, wherein not only the rule, to which they are subjoined, is exemplified, but all the foregoing rules are again brought into practice, the better to impress them on the memory. For, without this contrivance, young scholars would forget one rule while they are learning another. The third sort of examples contain all the foregoing and subsequent rules promiscuously; and for that reason are not to be attempted until they have gone twice through the former part: (for I think it most adviseable they should go through it more than once.)

The roots of the Italian words are interlined; a thing very requisite and useful in

works

PREFACE. vii

works of this nature, to save the trouble of consulting Indexes and Dictionaries, as well as to prevent the use of improper terms, and false spelling, which would be otherwise unavoidable; and those who learn the Italian language will hereby be enabled to make a much quicker progress than they would do, were they to search a Dictionary for the words they want.

I HAVE frequently omitted such words as are the subject of the exercise, which the learner is upon, or have been so often mentioned that it may be presumed there is no occasion for repeating their signification: in order that the scholar may be upon his guard, recollect what he has learnt, and exert both his memory and judgment, or at least be obliged to have recourse to his Grammar when his memory fails him. For these reasons, in the latter part of the Exercises, there is scarce any other Italian but for noun and verb; all the other parts of speech having been already gone through.

There is subjoined, by way of Appendix, an Abridgement of the Roman History. As history is one of the most easy and entertaining part of literature, and that of the old Romans absolutely necessary for a scholar, I hope this addition will be equally useful and agreeable.

ITALIAN EXERCISES.

ON THE

ACCIDENCE OF VERBS.

Regular Verbs of the first Conjugation.

I Love, thou acquirest, he respecteth, we salute,
  amare   acquistare   rispettare   salutare
you speak, ye pass, they walk.
  parlare, passare passeggiare.
I did call, thou didst prattle, he did command,
  chiamare   ciarlare   commandare.
we did begin, you did buy, they did confess.
  incominciare   comprare   confessare.
I confirmed, thou didst deliver, he preserved, we
  confirmare   consegnare   preservare
considered, you advised, they contended.
  considerare   consultare   contrestare.
I have declined, thou hast courted, he has cared,
  declinare   corteggiare   curare;
we have crowned, you have dedicated, they have
  coronare   dedicare
supped.
cenare.
I had wished, thou hadst declared, he had be-
  desiderare   dichiarare   dis-
stowed, we had assembled, you had undeceived,
  pensare   radunare   disingannare
they had wasted.
  guastare
I will expect, thou shalt arrive, he will assault,
  aspettare   arrivare   asaltare
we will assure, you will wish, they shall encrease.
  assicurare   augurare   aumentare.

B   Dance,

ITALIAN EXERCISES.

Dance, let him change, let us walk, sing ye,
ballare   *cambiare*   *camminare*   *cantare*
let them certify.
certificare.

That I may fast, that thou may'st besiege, that
digiunare   *assediare*
he may ride, that we may punish, that they may cause.
cavalcare   *castigare*   *cagionare.*

That we might caress, that thou might'st burn,
accarezzare   *abbruciare*
that he might stoop, that we might accept, that
abbassare   *accettare*
you might embrace, that they might mend.
abbracciare   *accommodare*

I should accompany, thou shouldst accuse, he
accompagnare   *accusare*
should baptize, we should mistrust, you should
battezzare   *diffidare*
venture, they should administer.
arrisicare   *amministrare.*

That I have complained, that thou hast invented,
lamentare   *inventare*
that he has governed, that we have tamed, that
governare   *domare*
you have asked, that they have experienced.
domandare   *esperimentare.*

That I had, should, or could, or would have
formed, that thou hadst, &c. taken away, that he
formare   *levare*
had sent, that we had prepared, that you had
mandare   *preparare*
deprived, that they had resembled.
privare   *rassomigliare*

I should have prolonged, thou shouldst have tried,
prolungare   *provare*
he should have remedied, we should have refused,
rimediare   *rifiutare*
you should have carried back again, they should
riportare
have prayed.
pregare.

I shall

ITALIAN EXERCISES.

I shall, or will have warmed, thou shalt have
riscaldare
transferred, he shall have judged, we shall have
trasportare   *giudicare*
fortified, you shall have inflamed, they shall have
fortificare   *infiammare*
failed.
mancare.

Regular Verbs of the second Conjugation.

I believe, thou receiv'st, he sees, we fret, you
credere   *ricevere*   *vedere*   *fremere*
beat, they drink.
battere bere o bevere.

I did yield up, thou didst owe, he did cleave,
cedere   *dovere*   *fendere*
we did groan, you did feed, they did hang.
gemere   *pascere*   *pendere.*

I enjoyed, thou vomitest, he crop'd, we shone,
godere   *recere*   *mietere*,   *rilucere*
you repeated, they sat down.
ripetere   *sedére.*

I have sold, thou hast crept along, he has shrieked,
vendere   *serpere*   *stridere*
we have glittered, you have shone again, they
splendere   *rilucere*
have received.
ricevere.

The following Verbs of the second Conjugation are irregular.

I had fallen, thou hadst contained, he had held,
calére   *capere*   *tenére*
we had grieved, you had appeared, they had pleased.
dolére   *parére*   *piacére.*

I shall, or will perswade, thou shalt lie in bed, he
persuadere   *giacere*
shall be able, we shall remain, you shall know,
potere   *rimanere*   *sapere*
they shall be accustomed.
solere.

Be silent, let him see, let us hold, be ye pleased,
tacere   vedere   tenere   piacere
let them fall again.
ricadere.

That I may have, that thou may'st owe, that
avere   dovere
he may fall, that we may concern, that you may
cadere   calere
contain, that they may grieve.
capere   dolere.

That I might appear, that thou might'st lie in bed,
parere   giacere
that he might please, that we might persuade, that
piacere   persuadere
you might be able, that they might know.
potere   sapere.

I should be silent, thou shouldst be accustomed,
tacere   solere
he should be worth, we should hold, you should
valere   tenere
see, they should be willing.
vedere   volere.

For a full conjugation of all the verbs in *ere*, see *Gram.* p. 93.

Regular Verbs of the third Conjugation.

I hear, thou follow'st, he opens, we boil, you
sentire   seguire   aprire   bollire
consent, they convert.
consentire   convertire.

I did cover, thou didst sow, he did sleep, we
coprire   cucire   dormire
did fly, you did lie, they did die.
fuggire   mentire   morire.

I departed, thou didst suffer, he repented, we
partire   soffrire   pentirsi
ascended, you served, they went abroad.
salire   servire   sortire.

I have

ITALIAN EXERCISES.   5

I have dressed, thou hast heard, he has con-
  vestire   *udire*   *con-*
sented, we have slept, you have boiled, they have
sentire *dormire*   *bollire*
covered.
coprire.

The following Verbs in ire *are irregular.* See Gram.
      p. 140.

 I had appeared, thou hadst uttered, he had
   comparire   *proferire*
buried, we had dared, you had abolished, they had
seppellire *ardire*   *abbolire*
comprehended.
 capire.
 I shall, or will abhor, thou shalt enrich, he shall
    abborrire   *arricchire*
blush, we shall banish, you shall whiten, you shall
arrossire *bandire*   *bianchire*
strike, they shall bear with.
colpire *compatire.*
 Conceive thou, let him digest, let us finish,
  concepire   *digerire*   *finire*
approve ye, let them bloom.
 gradire *fiorire.*
 That I may suffer, that thou may'st grow mad,
   patire   *impazzire*
that he may languish, that we may dispatch, that
 languire   *spedire*
you may unite, that they may obey.
 unire   *ubbidire*
 That we might colour, that thou might'st go,
  colorire   *ire*
that he might sharpen, that we might inanimate,
 inacerbire   *inanimire*
that you might harden, that they might bellow.
  indurire   *muggire.*
 I should strike, thou shouldst banish, he should
  colpire   *bandire*

abhor, we should abolish, you should enrich, they
abborrire   abbolire   arricchire
should comprehend.
  capire.

For the compound tenses of this mood, see *Gram.* p. 99.

More Verbs of the second Conjugation that are irregular only in some Tenses and Persons.

I belong, thou kindlest, he is frozen, we perceive,
appartenere   accendere,   algere   accorgersi
you kill, they burn.
uccidere   ardere,

I did hide, thou didst arrogate, he did sprinkle,
  ascondere   arrogere   aspergere
we did besiege, you did absolve, they did absorb.
      ossidere   assolvere   assorbere.

I assumed, thou didst, he demanded, we plucked
assumere   facere   richiedere   avellere
up, you shut, they circumcise.
    chiudere   circoncidere.

' I have granted, thou hast run, he has tormented,
    concedere   correre   conquidere
we have believed, you have boiled, they have decided.
    credere   cuocere   decidere.

I had deluded, thou hadst oppressed, he had
    deludere   deprimere
defended, we had expressed, you had sprinkled,
difendere   esprimere   dispergere
they had divided.
dividere.

I shall, or will grieve, thou shalt erect, he shall
         delere   ergere
exclude, we shall require, you shall expel, they
escludere   esigere   espellere
shall extinguish.
   estinguere.

Melt

ITALIAN EXERCISES.

Melt thou, let him drive in, let us feign, break
   fondere   *figgere*   *fingere*   *frangere*
ye, let them kneel down.
     genuflettere.

That I may lay down, that thou may'ſt fry, that
    giacere   *friggere*
he may join, that he may expel, that he may im‑
 giugnere   *impellere*   *impri-*
print, that he may hang, that you may engrave
mere   *impendere*   *incidere*
that they may include.
   includere.

That I might dilute, that thou mightſt intrude,
   intridere   *intrudere*
that he might read, that we might put, that you
    leggere   *mettere*
might bite, that they might plunge.
 mordere   *mergere.*

I ſhould move, thou ſhouldeſt milk, he ſhould
  muovere   *mungere*
conceal, we ſhould neglect, they ſhould hurt.
naſcondere   *negligere*   *nuocere.*

I may have offended, thou may'ſt have oppreſt,
  offendere   *opprimere*
he may have ſtroke, we may have loſt, you may
 percuotere   *perdere*
have pleaſed, they may have wept.
piacere   *piangere.*

That I might have painted, that thou might'ſt
    pignere
have preſented, that he might have curtailed,
 porgere   *precidere*
that we might have taken, that you might have
    prendere
preſumed, that they might have protected.
preſumere   *proteggere.*

I ſhould have redeemed, thou ſhouldſt have re‑
   redimere   *ren-*
turned, he ſhould have reduced, we ſhould have
dere   *ridurre*
laughed

laughed, you should have answered, they should
  ridere   *rispondere*
have suspended.
    sospendere.

When I shall have scattered, thou shalt have
                    spargere
shaken, he shall have risen, we shall have killed,
scuotere   *sorgere*   *uccidere*
you shall have conquered, they shall have lived.
    vincere   *vivere.*

On the RULES of the Italian Language, with References to Veneroni's Grammar.

On the Order of Verbs. *See* Gram. p. 159.

I write three hours every day.
  scrivere tre   *ora ogni giorno.*
Thou art too troublesome to my friends
  essere troppo seccante   *amico.*
He speaks like a Roman orator.
  parlare come *Romano oratore.*
We go out of town every spring.
  andare fuori (a) *città ogni primavera.*
You shew your probity very plainly.
  mostrare probità molto (b) *chiaramente.*
They think it is very fine weather to walk out.
  pensare fare bello tempo passeggiare.
I was extremely glad to see him again.
(b) *rallegrarsi estremamente rivedere.*
Thou wert generously rewarded.
  essere generosamente ricompensare.

    (a) See *Gram.* p. 45, on words in *tà* indeclinable.
    (b) See *Gram.* p. 155, on the formation of adverbs out of adjectives.
    (c) See *Gram.* p. 115, on reflected verbs.

                                      He

ITALIAN EXERCISES.

He bought many things to send abroad.
    comprare molto cosa mandare fuori.
We encouraged all arts and trades.
    incorraggiare (a) *tutto arte mestiere*
You baffled their wicked designs.
    sconcertare scellerato disegno.
They tempted our faithful subjects.
    tentare fedele soggetto.
I have enriched his numerous family.
    avere arricchire (b) *numeroso famiglia.*
Thou hast many accounts to settle.
    molto conto regolare.
He has renewed his promises to us.
    rinnovare promessa.
We have seen the chief curiosities.
    vedere principale curiosità.
You have examined them carefully.
    esaminare attentamente.
They have declared their last will.
    dichiarare ultimo volontà.
I had resolved to get rid of them.
    risolvere disfarsi
Thou hadst determined to tell him plainly.
    determinare dire schiettamente.
He had fixed on that sort of diversion.
    fissare quello sorta divertimento.
We had sworn to love each other eternally.
    giurare (c) *amarsi eternamente.*
You had forsaken his acquaintance.
    abbandonare conoscenza.
They had implored the king's clemency.
    implorare Rè clemenza.
I shall ever commend prudent people.
    sempre lodare prudente gente.
Thou shalt publish this piece of news every where.
    spargere nuove da per tutto.
He will return from France next week.
    tornare Francia prossimo settimana.

  (a) See the declension of *tutto*, Gram. p. 72.
  (b) See *Gram.* p. 53, on adjectives ending in *e*.
  (c) See *Gram.* p. 144, on reciprocal verbs.

ITALIAN EXAMPLES.

We shall travel day and night till we arrive.
    viaggiare giorno e   notte infinchè arrivare.
You will do yourself immortal honour.
    fare   immortale onore.
They will disgrace their noble family.
    disonorare nobile famiglia.
Bring me that bottle and a glass.
(a) *portare fiasco bicchiere.*
Let him gather all his things, and then go.
    radunare tutto roba poi andare.
Let us walk in the garden before dinner.
  Spasseggiare (b) giardino prima pranzo.
Go ye and meet all our friends in the road.
andare rincontrare tutto amico (c) nello strada.
Let them answer all my questions.
    (d) *rispondere domanda.*

On the Articles lo, la, li, le, gli. See *Gram.*
p. 202.

    The study of belles lettres has always been re-
    (e) *studio (belle lettere) (f) essere sempre stato rac-*
commended to the youth of both sexes.
commandare (g) gioventù duo sesso.
    Great events and revolutions followed the death
    grande evento rivoluzione seguire morte
of Cæsar.
  Cesare.
The fear of torments made him fly his country.
  timore tormento fare fuggire patria.
Poland was for many years the seat of domestic
Polonia essere per molto anno seggio domestico

(a) See *Gram.* p. 206.
(b) See rules on the preposition *nello, nella,* &c.
(c) In the p. 42.
(d) *Rispondere* governs the dative case of the thing.
(e) *Lo* before nouns beginning with an *s,* and followed by another consonant. See *Gram.* p. 36.
(f) *essere,* instead of *avere.* See p. 83.
(g) Words in *ù* are indeclinable. See p. 50.

                                            divi-

ITALIAN EXERCISES.

divisions. Portugal is a despotic kingdom. Ava-
divisione. Portogallo despotico regno. Ava-
rice is despicable.
rizia sprezzabile.

My lord the archbishop visited all the clergy.
(a) *signor archivescovo visitare clero.*

My lord the president decreed it in his behalf.
signor presidente decretare favore.

Madam the countess has ordered it.
Signora contessa commandare.

The gentlemen are not yet come to see us.
Signori essere ancora venire vedere.

Women are very fair in the northern countries.
Donna molto biondo settentrionale paese.

The English particle to, *before infinitives, is sometimes rendered in Italian by the Article* il *or* lo. See *Gram.* p. 203.

It is forbidden to do evil.
essere proibire fare male.

It is not convenient to speak always the truth.
convenevole dire sempre verità.

It is permitted to a sick person to complain.
permettere ammalato (b) *lamentarsi.*

It is not polite to interrupt another when he
civile interrompere altro quando
speaks.
parlare.

It is right to correct children when they are young.
giusto correggere ragazzo essere giovine.

It is a great satisfaction to sensible people to hear
grande soddisfazione sensibile gente sentire
their friends are in perfect health.
amico essere perfetto salute.

It is a great pleasure to see brothers well united
piacere vedere fratello bene unito.

(a) The article *il* must be put before *signore*.
(b) See *Gram.* p. 115, on reciprocal verbs.
(c) See *Gram.* p. 203, on words beginning with an *S*.

ITALIAN EXERCISES.

together; but it is a great grief to see them in
  insieme,   *ma*   *grande affanno* *vedere*
discord.
discordia.

    It is not always proper to correct children for the
        sempre convenevole correggere ragazzo
faults they commit; but it is very necessary to
fallo   *commettere ma*   *molto necessario*
make them sensible of them.
rendere   *sensibile.*

    It is easy to give advice, but difficult to execute.
      facile   *dare consiglio, ma* *difficile*   *eseguire.*
    It is easy to perceive you neglect your business.
         accorgersi   *trascurare*   *affare.*
    It was ever commendable to study languages.
      sempre   *laudevole*   *studiare lingua.*

    On the Syntax of Nouns. See Gram. p. 204.

    A dutiful child is a great comfort to his parents.
  ubbidiente figliuolo *grande consolazione* *suo genitore.*
    A good wife is an inestimable treasure.
    buono moglie   *inestimabile* *tesoro.*
    A diligent master instructeth attentive scholars.
   diligente maestro *istruire* *attento* *discipolo.*
    A good action deserves great praise.
   buono azione meritare grande lode.
    A rash counsel is productive of fatal consequences.
inconsiderato consiglio *produttivo* *fatale consequenza.*
    My father and mother are very compassionate.
     padre (a) *madre* (b) *essere molto compassionevole.*
    Their brother and sister are industrious.
       fratello   *sorella*   *industrioso.*
    Your house and garden are excessively beautiful.
     casa   *giardino* *eccessivamente bello.*
    My exercise and my lesson are difficile.
   esercizio   *lezione* *difficile.*

    (a) (b) An adjective with several substantives must agree in gender with that which is the most worthy.

Our

Our man-servant and our maid-servant are good,
 servo   *serva*   *buono*
and therefore they shall have rewards.
 perciò   *avere* *ricompensa.*
You, your master, and your mistress have been
   padrone   *padrona* *essere stato*
civil to me and merit my greatest thanks.
 civile *meritare* (a) *grande ringraziamento.*

On Comparatives. See *Gram.* p. 53.

France is larger, and more powerful than Italy.
Francia *grande*   *potente* *Italia.*
Virgil wrote more than any other poet.
Virgilio scrivere *qualunque altro poeta* (b).
Horace was much more satirical than Juvenal.
Orazio essere *satirico* *Giuvenale.*
Your countrymen are much more richer than mine.
vostro compatriotto (c) *ricco* *mio.*
This water is much clearer than crystal.
questo acqua *chiaro* *cristallo.*
Your sister's hands are whiter than alabaster.
 sorella (d) *mano* (e) *bianco* *alabastro.*
The English are more studious than their neighbours.
 Inglese   *studioso*   *vicino.*
Milton was much more learned than Dante.
Milton essere *sapiente* *Dante.*
The Russians behaved more bravely than the Turks.
 Russo *comportarsi* *valorosamente* *Turco.*
Cicero was less happy than Diogenes.
Cicerone *felice* *Diogene.*

(a) See *Gram.* p. 56, on superlatives.
(b) See *Gram.* p. 45, on words ending in *a* of the Masf.
(c) Words ending *cco* take an *h* in the plural.
(d) *Mano* is of the fem. gender.
(e) Such words as end in *co* take also an *h* in the plural.
See *Gram.* p. 49.

Lewis the Fourteenth was much less admired than
  Luigi   diecimo quarto   ammirare
Henry the Fourth.
  Enrico   quarto.
London is far better paved than Paris.
  Londra   lastricare   Parigi.
Venice is much less populous than Naples.
  Venezia   popolato   Napoli.
Lend me three thousand pounds for a month.
  prestare   tre (a) mille   lira   per   mese.
I have inherited five hundred guineas a-year.
  avere ereditare cinque cento   ghinea   anno.
I have seven brothers and two sisters alive.
       sette fratello   duo sorella vivo.
The tenth of next month I will pay you.
          dieci   prossimo mese   pagare.
Judas was one of the twelve apostles.
  Giuda essere   duodici apostolo.
William the third was a great conqueror.
  Guglielmo   (b) terzo essere grande conquistatore.
Henry the Fourth was a matchless warrior.
  Enrico   quarto   incomparabile guerriero.
Sixtus the Fifth was a barbarous pope.
  Sisto   quinto   barbaro   papa.
Your master has a fine country-house.
     padrone avere (c) bello   villa.
Your brother has six fine dapple-bay horses.
       fratello   sei bello bajo pomellato cavallo.
Your uncle and aunt are my dear friends.
      zio   zia essere   caro amico.
Our general was ever reputed a gallant man.
       generale   sempre riputare galant' uomo.
Solomon was a wise king.
  Salamone   savio Rè.

  (a) Nouns of number ought to be put before the substantive.

  (b) Nouns of order must be after the substantive, when we speak of ecclesiastical, or secular princes.

  (c) Adjectives of quality must be put before substantives.

ITALIAN EXERCISES. 15

King George is a religious monarch.
Giorgio   religioso   monarca.
Nero was a wicked man.
Nerone   cattivo   uomo.
Crœsus was reckoned a rich prince.
Creso   stimare   ricco principe.
The duke of Richmond has six fine grey horses.
duca   Richmond   sei bello (a) *leardo cavallo.*
Spain is a hot country, but Germany is a very cold
Spagna   caldo   paese,   ma Germania   freddo
country.
paese.
Give me some cold water, and red wine.
dare   freddo acqua   rosso vino.
I love better cold weather than hot weather.
amare   freddo tempo   caldo
English ladies are handsomer than Italian ladies.
Inglese   signora   bella   Italiano signora.
I always thought he was a troublesome man.
*sempre   credere   * (b) *seccante   uomo.*
This poor man has crooked legs.
questo povero uomo avere storto   gamba.
Will you have a round hat or triangular?
*   avere   rotondo cappello   triangolare.*
There is a sickly man methinks.
*   ammalaticcio uomo, mi pare.*
You are a thoughtful philosopher.
*   pensieroso   filosofo.*
The industrious are praised, but the slothful are
(c) *industrioso   lodare   ma   pigro*
despised.
sprezzare.

(a) Nouns of colours, elementary qualities, and of nations, must be put after the substantive.
(b) The adjectives of condition, figure, and quantity, must be put after substantives.
(c) Adjectives that have no substantives must be of the masculine gender, because *man* is always understood.

The

ITALIAN EXERCISES.

The righteous find peace, but the wicked feel
        giuſto   trovare pace   *ſcellerato ſentire*
torment.
tormento.

The covetous deſpiſe the poor, but the liberal
        avaro diſpreggiare   povero, ma   generoſo
cheriſh them.
volere bene.

The merciful ſhall find mercy, but the cruel ſhall
     miſericordioſo trovare pietà   crudele
be puniſhed.
caſtigare.

The wiſe man ſeeketh wiſdom, but the fool
     ſavio   cercare ſapienza,   ſtolto
deſpiſeth underſtanding.
ſprezzare intendimento.

Give me ſome bread, ſome wine, ſome butter,
  dare (a) *del pane   vino   butirro*
ſome cheeſe, ſome beef, ſome mutton, ſome veal,
  cacio   aleſſo   caſtrato   vitella
ſome pork, ſome pye, ſome fiſh, ſome muſtard,
  porco   paſticcio peſce   moſtarda
ſome ſalt.
ſale.

Go and fetch me a bit of the white bread.
andare a cercare pezzo   bianco pane.

Send to the market to buy me ten pounds of
mandare   mercato comprare   libra
freſh butter.
(b) *freſco butirro.*

Bring directly ſix pounds of black cherries.
portare ſubito ſei libra   nero   ceraſa

Seven hundred of freſh walnuts, and five pounds
ſette cento   noce   cinque
of hazle nuts.
nocciuola.

(a) When you aſk for ſomething without ſpecifying the quantity of it, uſe the article definite *del, della,* &c. See *Gram.* p. 213.

(b) You muſt uſe the article *di,* when you ſpecify the quantity of the thing.

Have

ITALIAN EXERCISES.

Have you been at Paris? No, but I have been
  essere stato (a)   *Nò, ma*
at Rouen; it is a fine city. Did you see it?
  Rouen   *bello città*   *vedere.*
Did you give your brother the book I lent you?
      dare (b)   *fratello*   *libro*   *prestare.*
No, I gave it to my sister, and she will return it
     dare   *sorella*   *restituire*
to you when she has read it.
          leggere.
Did you tell your father I was in the country?
     dire   *padre*   *essere*   *campagna.*
No, sir, but I told my mother, it is all one.
             dire   *madre (è l'istessa cosa.)*
God demands the pureness of our hearts.
Iddio richiedere   *purità* (c)   *cuore.*
We ought to die for the service of our princes.
  dovere morire   *servizio*   *principe.*

Construction of Adjectives.

The Adjectives betokening desire, knowledge, remembrance, ignorance, forgetting, care, fear, guilt, *or any passion of the mind, require the following noun in the genitive case.*

Those that are desirous of honour, are studious
quello essere   *bramoso*   *onore*   *studioso*
of learning and of good manners.
  scienza   *buono costume.*
He that is not mindful of his own business,
           ricordevole   *proprio*   *affare*
cannot be mindful of others.
(non puol essere)   *altro.*

(a) We put the article *a* before names of cities.
(b) Before the names of men and women, we use *al, allo,* &c.
(c) We use *de'* before pronouns that are joined with substantives. See *Gram.* p. 204.

Thou

Thou and I are guilty of the same crime.
   colpevole *stesso*   *delitto.*
I am ignorant of the fact you mention.
  ignorante   *fatto* *menzionare.*

Adjectives betokening plenty, *or* want, *as* poor, destitute, empty, full, void, *will have the Genitive case after them.*

He whose bags are empty of money, has a house
    sacco *vuoto* *danaro avere casa*
empty of friends, and a coat full of rents.
vuoto *amico*   *abito pieno squarcio.*
The court which is full of flatterers, is pernicious
   corte *essere pieno adulatore* *pernizioso*
to a prince, though he be rich in substance, and
  principe   *ricco* *sostanza*
abundant in honour.
abbondante *onore.*
A journey a hundred miles long wearies a horse
  viaggio *cento* *mile* *stancare cavallo*
that has not his belly moderately full of provender,
       ventre *assai* *pieno* *biada*
for while he is desirous of meat, he goes slowly.
perchè mentre *bramoso* *mangiare andare lento.*
Laziness has need of spurs.
 pigrizia *bisogna sperone.*

These Adjectives worthy, unworthy, adorned, encompassed, content, *will have a genitive after them.*

Those are unworthy of the glory of heaven,
  essere indegno   *gloria* *cielo*
that do not think virtue worthy of love, nor are
che *credere virtù* *degno* *amore*
content with the pleasure that virtue gives.
contento   *piacere* *che* *virtù dare.*
A son endowed with excellent wit rejoices his
 figliuolo dotato   *eccellente spirito rallegrare*
             father

father, whofe good example he imitates, whofe
padre   buono efempio   imitare
commands he obferves, he is never trembling for
comando   offervare   mai tremare
fear, for he provokes not his father's anger, he is
paura perchè irritare   padre collera
always mindful of his duty, he is like a ftaff to
fempre ricordevole   dovere   come baftone
his father's old age.
    padre vecchioja.
He that is endowed with fine qualities, and does
quello   dotato   bello qualità
not behave himfelf well, is unworthy of men's
comportarfi   bene effere indegno   uomo
fociety.
(a) *focietà.*
Thofe who are content with their own condition,
            effere contento   condizione
are worthy of the name of good chriftians, but
degno   nome   buono criftiano
they are very rare.
ma   raro.
If the city of Naples was encompaffed with
fe   città   Napoli   circondare
walls, it would be ftronger than it is.
muro   effere (b) *forte.*
England is adorned with the faireft ladies in the
Inghilterra ornare   (c) *bello fignora (di quefto*
world.
mondo.)
Our country is furrounded with the ftrongeft
    paefe   chiudere   (d) *forto*
bulwarks.
baluordo.
Very few people are fatisfied with the lot that
poco gente   foddisfare   forte
Providence has beftowed on them.
Providenza   concedere.

(a) See *Gram.* p. 45, on words ending in *tà.*
(b) Ibid. p. 53, on comparatives.
(c) (d) Ibid. p. 56, on fuperlatives.

Adjec-

Adjectives governing a Dative Case.

Adjectives betokening submission, relation, pleasure, due, resistance, difficulty, likeness, *will have the following noun in the Dative Case.*

Virtue is pleasant to the righteous, and it is
(a) *virtù   piacevole   giusto*
besides profitable to those that love it.
   oltre . profittevole quello che amare.

Reverence is due to God, the king of all the world.
  riverenza dovuto Dio (b) *Rè, tutto mondo.*

Honour is due to kings, because God has com-
  onore dovuto Rè perchè avere co-
manded that we be obedient to them.
mandare   essere ubbidiente.

It is a lamentable thing that men of excellent
     lamentevole cosa uomo eccellente
wit are prone to wickedness.
spirito dedito malvagia.

A man that lets himself be drawn by the corrupted
  uomo lasciarsi allettare corro.to
pleasures of this world, is more like a beast than a
 piacere questo mondo più simile bestia
christian.
cristiano.

Children are not always like their parents, they
 figliuolo sempre simile genitore.
are sometimes quite different from them.
  talvolta affatto differente.

My father is like my uncle in the shape of his
  padre simile zio forma suo
face, and in the colour of his hair, but he is not
 viso colore capello ma essere
like him in his manners.
  costume.

(a) Words in *ù* are indeclinable. See *Gram.* p. 50.
(b) *Rè* is indeclinable.

ITALIAN EXERCISES.

On Superlative Degrees. See *Gram.* 56.

The most noble of all virtues is charity.
la più   nobile   tutto   virtù   carità.
Those that seem to be the most ingenious, are not
parere essere (a) *più   ingegnoso   essere*
always the most learned.
sempre   sapiente.
The most pernicious of all crimes is slander, it
pernizioso   delitto   calunnia
ruins very often the reputation of the most honest
rovinare (b) *spesso   riputazione   onesto*
people, it puts discord between the most intimate
gente   metere discordia   frà   intrinseco
friends; in short, it is the most abominable crime
amico   in somma   abbominevole delitto
in the world.

The best quality that a man can have, is to be
(c) *buono qualità   uomo potere avere*
civil and obliging.
civile   cortese.
The best friend we can have is money.
amico   danaro.
The best soldiers in the world are sometimes
soldato   talvolta
conquered.
conquistare.
Buy me the best grapes you see in town.
comprare   uva   vedere città.
The greatest men in the kingdom confess it.
grande   uomo   regno   confessare.
The richest people are not the happiest.
ricco   gente   felice.

(a) *The most* is rendered by *il più, la più, i più,* &c. See *Gram.* p. 56.
(b) *Very often,* makes *spessissimo.*
(c) The superlative degree of *buono* is *il migliore.* See *Gram.* p. 53.

The

The moſt virtuous women have been guilty of
         virtuoſo   donna   eſſere ſtato colpevole
coquetry.
civetteria.

We ſhould pay a moſt particular attention to the
     (a) *fare   particolare attenzione*
moral conduct of our children of both ſexes.
morale condotta   figliuolo   duo ſeſſo.

The Pronouns Perſonal io, tu, egli, eſſa, noi, voi, eglino, *being the nominative caſe, ought to be put before the verb, but if there is an interrogation, they ought to be put after the verb.* See *Gram.* p. 205.

I intreat you to grant me that favour.
  ſupplicare voi accordare queſto favore.
What do you deſire of me, madam?
        volere   ſignora.
What do you ſay, ſir? I do not underſtand you.
       dire   capire.
Don't you ſpeak Italian and French?
  parlare Italiano   Franceſe.
I underſtand it pretty well, but when you ſpeak
  comprendere aſſai bene ma quando
ſo very faſt, I cannot underſtand you.
così preſto non poſſo   capire.
I aſk you if you will do me a favour.
domandare   volere fare   favore.
With all my heart, if I can conveniently.
  tutto   cuore   potere comodamente.
Have you an Italian Dictionary?
  avere   Italiano Dizionario
Yes, I have Alberti's Dictionary.

Will you lend it me for two or three weeks?
      preſtare (b)   *due   tre ſettimana.*
It is at your ſervice, if you will ſend for it.
  voſtro ſervizio   (mandarlo a cercare.)

(a) *Pay* is often turned by *fare.*
(b) See *Gram.* p. 206, on pronouns conjunctive.

Did

ITALIAN EXERCISES. 23

Did you see the castle St. Angelo at Rome?
    vedere   castello Sant' Angelo   Roma.
Yes, it is very fine, very rich; in short, I think
    bello   ricco (in somma) credere
it is the finest castle in all Europe.
   (a)   *tutto Europa.*
Do you think the city of Paris is finer than
    credere   città   Parigi bello
London?
Londra.
No, it is not so large, nor so well built as London.
     largo   bene edificata.
I love you with all my heart, and if you will
amare   tutto   cuore
come to morrow to see me, I'll give you what I
venire domani   vedere   dare
promised you.
promettere.
I will not fail, but I am afraid to be too trouble-
  mancare   temere
some to you, and to your family.
       vostro famiglia.
Did Mr. N. give you the book you lent him?
  signor dare   libro   prestare
Not yet; but I believe he will give it me soon.
non ancora, ma credere   dare   presto.
When you get it back, will you bring it me?
   (b) *riavere   portare*
I will do it willingly to oblige you.
  fare volentieri obbligare.
When will you go to see him at his country seat?
 quando   andare vedere suo,   villa.
I believe I shall visit him next month.
 credere   visitare venturo mese.
Bring me to-morrow your grammar.
 portare   domani   grammatica.
Here it is, sir, I brought it with me.
(Eccola quà)   portare   meco.

(a) See *Gram.* p. 56, on superlatives.
(b) This supposes a future; *Quando lo riavrete,* &c.

Shew

Shew me what you have written. That is not
   moſtrare   quel che avere ſcrivere
well, write it over again, and when you have done
bene ſcrivere   di nuovo   (a) *quando   avere fare*
it, give it to your brother.
   dare   voſtro fratello.
Believe me, you are very idle.
  credere   eſſere   pigro.
Forgive me, I will be more diligent.
  perdonare   eſſere più diligente.
Reach me that pen-knife, and a clean pen.
arrecare quello   temperino   pulito penna.
Write an exercife, and then read it to me.
ſcrivere   eſercizio e poi (leggetemelo) (b).

On Pronouns Demonſtrative, and Poſſeſſive.

The Pronouns Demonſtrative queſto, quello, *or* queſti, *and the Pronouns Poſſeſſive,* mio, mia, tuo, tua, ſuo, ſua, *agree with the ſubſtantives in gender, number, and caſe.* See *Gram.* p. 68, *and* 66.

This horſe goes better than any of yours.
queſto cavallo andare   qualunque voſtro.
This man is more honeſt than you think.
   uomo   oneſto   credere.
This woman is not ſo happy as ſhe deſerves.
   donna   felice   meritare.
This houſe ſtands in a moſt pleaſant ſituation.
  caſa ſtare   ameno   ſituazione.
Thoſe gentlemen ſeem to be very cold.
  queſto ſignore pare avere freddo.
Thoſe ladies are very modeſtly dreſt.
  ſignora   modeſtamente veſtire.
My brother is gone into the country for a month.
(c) *mio fratello andare   campagna   meſe.*

  (a) Turn; and *when you ſhall have done it.*
  (b) See *Gram.* p. 65.
  (c) Pronouns poſſeſſive take the article *il, la,* &c. in the nominative. See *Gram.* p. 66.

ITALIAN EXERCISES.

My mother is gone over to France for her health.
    madre   *Francia*   *salute*
My countrymen are very great politicians.
    compatriotto ,   *grande politico.*
My sister loves public diversions to excess.
    sorella amare pubblico divertimento eccesso.
My action is not so blameable as you say.
    azione   *biasimevole*   *dire.*
Your affection for me is false and deceitful.
    affetto   *falso ingannevole.*
Her history has made a great noise in the world.
    Istoria avere fare grande remore , mondo.
Their clock is always out of order.
    orologio sempre in disordine.
Our house is finer than yours.
    casa   *bello*   *vostro.*
Their affairs are more perplext than you imagine.
    affare   *più imbarrazzare immaginare.*

The Pronoun Relative che *is of all genders, and of all numbers.* See Gram. p. 70.

The woman who has a fair face, is loved by all.
    donna che avere bello viso amare tutto.
The girl who brought me my pen-knife, is lovely.
    ragazza portare temperino amabile.
The man who bought me my house, is honest.
    uomo comprare mio casa onesto.
The hat which covers my brother's head, begins
    cappello coprire fratello testa cominciare
to be worn.
    usarsi.
The man who struck my father is a butcher.
    uomo percuotere padre macellaro.
The rewards which are promised shall be given,
    ricompensa essere promettere dare
if the works required be done after to-morrow.
    lavoro richiesto fare dopo domani.
The horse that my father sold, was very good.
    cavallo padre vendere essere buono.

ITALIAN EXERCISES.

The comedy which we acted was pleasant.
    commedia   *rappresentare piacevole.*

The wood that we bargained for was too dry.
    legno   *patteggiare*   *essere*   *secco.*

The wine which you drank yesterday was excellent.
    vino   *bere*   *ieri*   *eccellente.*

The last lesson you gave me, was very difficult.
    ultimo lezione   *dare*   *molto difficile.*

The company you keep is not honest.
    compagnia   *praticare*   *onesto.*

I have found the book that I had lost.
    avere trovare   *libro*   *perdere.*

Note that, he that, *and* she that, *must be turned by* quello che, *and* quella che. *See* Gram. p. 91.

He that does not fear God, does not deserve to live.
    temere Dio   *meritare vivere.*

He that came this morning, has a great regard for you.
    venire   *mattina* *avere gran stima*

He that gave you that counsel, is not your friend.
    dare   *consiglio*   *amico.*

He that lives honestly is esteemed of all honest people.
    vivere onestamente *stimare* *tutto onesto gente.*

He that told you that, did not tell you the truth.
    dire   *verità.*

He that sold you these boots did not cheat you.
    vendere   *stivale*   *ingannare.*

He that is the handsomest is not always the most virtuous.
    bello   *sempre*   *virtuoso.*

He that speaks continually must be very troublesome.
    parlare continuamente deve essere seccante.

She

ITALIAN EXERCISES.

She that told me the news, is your great friend.
   dire *nuova* *grande amico.*
She that is married to Mr. N. is the moſt lively.
   maritare *ſignor N.* *più vivace.*
She that gave me your letter, ſpeaks Italian very
   dare *lettera parlare Italiano*
well.
beniſſimo.
He whom you look for, is gone away this morning.
   cercare *andare* *mattina.*
He whom you hate the moſt, is my intimate
   odiare   *intimo*
friend.
amico.
He whom you have recommended to me, is a
   avere *raccomandare*
great rogue.
birbante.
He whom you ſaw yeſterday is my ſiſter's lover.
   vedere *ieri eſſere* *ſorella amante.*
He whom God loves, is very happy.
   Dio amare *felice.*
She that you ſee, is my eldeſt brother's miſtreſs.
   vedere *primogenito fratello innamorata.*
She that I have recommended to you, is modeſt.
   avere raccomandare *modeſto.*
She whom I loved the beſt is married.
   amare *il più maritare.*
I ſaw to-day the gentleman with whom we dined
 vedere oggi *ſignore* (a) *pranzare*
yeſterday.
ieri.
Here is the lady for whom I have great reſpect.
 Ecco *ſignora* *avere grande riſpetto.*
Let us go and ſee the lady with whom we played
 andare (b) *vedere*   *giuocare*
at cards in the country the other day.
 carta *campagna* *altro giorno.*

(a) We put *chi* after the prepoſitions, ſpeaking of reaſonable creatures. See *Gram.* p. 71.
(b) See *Gram.* p. 209, on verbs of motion.

The gentleman with whom we were the other
  signore   *essere*.   *altro*
day is very sick.
giorno ammalato.

There is the horse for which I offered twenty
   cavallo   *offerire venti*
guineas.
ghinea.

Shew me the watch for which you gave forty
mostrare *oriuolo*   *dare quaranta*
pounds.
lire.

There is the sword for which I offered six guineas.
    spada   *esibire sei ghinea.*

When between two Verbs there is a Noun, we put always che *after the first verb.*

I thought you could speak Italian better than
 credere   *parlare Italiano meglio.*
you do.

I fancy you are not yet twenty years old.
 imaginare (a) *avere ancora venti anni.*

I hope you will not refuse me the favour to re-
sperare   *ricusare*   *favore* *rac-*
commend me to your friends in town.
commandare vostro amico città.

My uncle told me yesterday you was not well,
 zio dire *ieri* (b) *stare* *bene*
but I am very glad to find you are better to-day.
ma rallegrarsi trovare meglio oggi.

You promised to write to me last week, but I
  promettere scrivere passato settimana ma
am very sorry to observe you forgot me.
 rincrescere osservare scordare.

(a) We use the verb *avere* instead of *essere*, talking of age. *Ex.* How old are you? *Quanti anni avete?*

(b) The verb *stare* must be used instead of *essere*, when you talk of health.

We

ITALIAN EXERCISES.

We put always che *instead of* but *in English, with a negation before the Verb.*

I did desire but one favour from you, and you
    chiedere   *favore*
refused it me.
ricusare.

If you would give me but one pistole at once,
         dare   *doppia* *alla volta*
you would oblige me infinitely.
      obbligare *infinitamente.*

When one has but little money, one ought to
quando (a) *avere*   *poco danaro*   *dovere*
spend accordingly.
spendere in consequenza.

I ask you but what others give me.
domandare   *altro*   *dare.*

You do nothing but laugh and play.
   fare (b)   *ridere*   *giucare.*

He does nothing but eat and drink.
               mangiare bevere.

When others laugh, you do nothing but cry.
    altro *ridere*   *fare*   *piangere.*

On the Particles Relative ci *and* vi. *The Particles Relative* ci *and* vi *are put instead of* there; within, *and* in that.

I went yesterday to your house to see you, but
andare ieri   *casa* *vedere*   *ma*
your man told me you was not within.
servo *dire*   *essere*

Indeed I was there almost all the afternoon; at
  in verità   *quasi tutto* *dopo pranzo*
what time did you go there?
che   *time*   *andare.*

(a) *When one has but,* &c. must be turned by, *quando non si ha che,* &c.
(b) *You do nothing but,* &c. turn it, *non fate oltro che.*

30 ITALIAN EXERCISES.

I went there at six o'clock.
     sei *ora.*
He was in the right to tell you I was not within,
 (a) *avere*   *dire*   *essere*
for I was gone to visit a few friends in the square.
   andare visitare qualche amico *piazza.*
My brother and sister are gone in the country.
 fratello *sorella* *andare* *campagna.*
When did they go there, I want to know?
 quando   (*vorrei sapere*)
They went there yesterday morning.
 andare *ieri* *mattina.*
Is it long since you saw our regiment?
 (b)   *vedere* *reggimento.*
It is two months, if I remember well.
 due *mese* *se* *ricordare bene.*
How long is it since you left France?
 essere   *lasciare Francia*
It is five and twenty years, or thereabouts.
 cinque *venti* *anno* *o incirca.*

How to express some of it, *or* of them. *See* Gram. p. 218.

You have three horses, lend me one of them.
 avere tre *cavalla prestare.*
I have but two of them, one for myself, and
 avere *due*   *me stesso*
the other for my man.
    servo.
I thought you had three of them.
 credere *avere tre.*
To shew you that I have but two of them, come
 far vedere *avere* *due* *venire*
with me into the stable, and you won't see any
 meco   *stalla*   *vedere*
more of them.
 più.

(a) To be in the right, is, *avere ragione.*
(b) Long, *molto tempo,* or *un pezzo.*

           I doubt

ITALIAN EXERCISES.

I doubt nothing of it, I believe you.
   dubitare (a)   *credere.*

I fee very fine flowers in your garden, give me
   vedere   *bello*   *fiore*   *giardino*   *dare*
fome of them.

I have not many of them, but what there is, is
   avere   *molto*   *ma*   *quel* (b)
at your fervice.
   servizio.

I have but five or fix of them, as you fee.
   cinque   *sei*   *vedere.*

You may take a dozen of them, if you pleafe.
   potere pigliare dozzina   *piacere.*

What will you have me do with them?
   volere   *fare*

You fhall give fome to your daughters.
        dare   *voftro*   *figliuola.*

Do they talk of the war in your town?
   (c). *parlare*   *guerra*   *città.*

They talk of it all over the ifland.
        tutto   *ifola.*

And what do they think of our neighbour's in-
              credere   *vicino*   in-
tentions?
tenzione.

They know very little about them here.
   sapere   *poco*   *qui.*

Exercifes on the Tenfes of the Verbs.

The prefent Tenfe *is when the Action of which one speaks, is prefent.*

Sir, I come to have the honour to fee you.
Signore venire   *avere*   *onore*   *vedere.*

I am infinitely obliged to you for this favour.
effere infinitamente obbligare   *quefto favore.*

(a) Leave out *nothing*, and turn, *Non ne dubito.*
(b) See *Gram.* p. 148, on the conjugation of *there is*, &c.
(c) See *Gram.* p. 218, on *they, it is,* &c.

How

How does the lady your mother do?
 (a) *ſtare ſignora madre.*
She is very well, ſir, and preſents her compli-
 ſtare beniſſimo preſentare compli-
ments to you.
mento.

✗ I am her moſt humble ſervant, and I am very
 eſſere umile ſervo rallegrarſi
glad to hear ſhe is well.
   ſtare bene.
Will you come and walk with me in the garden?
volere venire ſpaſſeggiare giardino.
I pray you to excuſe me, I cannot ſtay any longer.
pregare ſcuſare potere reſtare.
You are always in great haſte, when you come
 eſſere ſempre grande fretta venire
to ſee me.
vedere.
Not at all, ſir, it is more than an hour ſince I
   eſſere ora che
came here, and my ſiſter is all alone at home.
venire qui ſorella tutto ſolo caſa.
I am ſorry you won't ſtay: I intreat you to
 diſpiacere volere reſtare ſupplicare
preſent my moſt humble reſpects to the lady your
preſentare umile riſpetto ſignora
mother.
madre.

The imperfect tenſe *is when the action of which one
   ſpeaks, is interrupted.*

Sir, we were ſpeaking of you when you came.
Signore parlare quando venire.
What were you ſaying of me, ladies?
che dire ſignora.
We were ſaying that when you was in France
  dire quando eſſere Francia

(a) When we inquire after any body's health, we make
uſe of the verb *ſtare,* inſtead of *fare,* or *eſſere.*
            among

ITALIAN EXERCISES. 33

among the ladies, you was the moſt gallant, the
frà ſignora eſſere galante
moſt courteous, and the moſt complaiſant gentle-
corteſe compiacente ſig-
man in the world.
nore mondo.

  I did not think, ladies, I was ſo happy as to be
penſare ſignora, eſſere felice eſſere
the ſubject of your converſation; and what do you
ſoggetto converſazione
think I am now?
credere.

  We believe that you are ſtill very civil, and very
credere eſſere ancora civile
complaiſant; but not ſo gallant as you was there.
compiacente ma galante eſſere

  Lewis the XIVth was one of the greateſt kings
Luigi (a) grand Rè
in the world, he was a lover of fine ſciences, he
mondo amatore bello lettera]
did not love flatterers, he did follow always his own
amare adulatore ſeguire ſempre
inclinations, and if he could not get the victory
inclinazione e ſe guadagnare vittoria
over his enemies by the force of his arms, he would
nemico forza arma
get it by the number of his Louis d'ors; in a
numero Luigi d'oro in
word, he was a great politician.
ſomma grande politico.

The perfect definite *is a tenſe perfectly paſt, and often determined by an adverb of time paſt.*

Where went you yeſterday, that you was not at
dove andare ieri eſſere
home, when I went to ſee you?
quando vedere.

  (a) We make uſe alſo of the imperfect tenſe, when we ſpeak of the qualities of any body, that is dead.

           C 5   I went

I went to see Mr. N. who is not well.
  vedere il signor   *stare.*
Did you meet with any company there?
 trovare   *compagnia.*
Yes, I met with his uncle and three of his sisters.
       zio   *tre*   *sorella.*
What was the matter of your conversation?
quale essere   *soggetto*   *conversazione.*
We spoke of many different things.
 parlare *molto differente cosa.*
Did you speak Italian with them?
       Italiano
Yes, all our conversation was in Italian.

Did they say you speak it well?
  dire   *bene.*
They said nothing about it.
   niente.
Did they not ask you of whom you learn?
  domandare   *chi*   *imparare.*
Yes, I told them I was learning of you.

Julius Cæsar, the emperor, after he had con-
Giulio Cesare   *imperatore dopo*   *con-*
quered Britain, built a tower at London, but he
quistare Bretagna (a) *edificare torre* *Londra*
continued not there; he appointed rulers in his
restare   *costituire governatore*
stead, and returned from London to Rome.
vece   *ritornare*   *Londra*   *Roma.*
Henry the VIIIth, king of England, regarded
Enrico   *ottavo Rè*   *Inghilterra badare*
not the bulls and threatenings which came from
    bulla   *minaccia*   *venire*
Italy, he violently shook of the papal power,
Italia   *violentemente scuotere*   *papale potere*
though he retained the Roman religion.
     ritenere   *Romano religione.*

(a). We make use also of the perfect definite, when we speak of the stations of dead people.

ITALIAN EXERCISES.

The preterpluperfect is a tense so perfectly past, that it cannot be interrupted.

I am very glad to see you, for your brother told
rallegrarsi   vedere   fratello dire
me you were gone to France.

'Tis true I was resolved to go there, if my father
vero   risolvere   andare (a)   *padre*
had given me money enough to make that journey.
avere dare   danaro   fare   viaggio.

Had he given you leave to go there?
avere dare   permesso   andare.

Yes, and he gave me fifty guineas to make my
sì   dare cinquanta ghinea   fare
journey.
viaggio.

If he had given me thirty more, I should have been
(b) *avere dare   trenta   essere stato*
in Paris now to pass the summer.
Parigi ora   passare   estate.

If you had come to see me, I would have lent
venire   vedere   avere   prestare
you some.

I am much obliged to you for it.
essere molto obbligato.

When you had a mind to go to France, was you
quando   avere voglia, andare Francia
resolved to go away without taking leave of your
risolvere andare via senza   licenziarsi
friends?
amico.

Not at all, I had already taken my leave of several.
niente affatto   digià   molto.

Very well, but you had forgotten me
benissimo   ma   avere scordato.

(a) See *Gram.* p. 209, on *if* before that tense.
(b) See ibid. on the particle *if* before the imperfect indicative.

I am

I am sorry you have so bad an opinion of me.
  dispiacere   cattivo   opinione.

The Future signifies the time to come.

When will you go into the country?
  quando   andare   campagna.
I believe I shall go there to-morrow.
  credere   andare   domani.
Will you stay long there?
           restare   un pezzo.
No, I will stay but two or three weeks.
                     due o tre settimana.
How will you spend your time when you are there?
             passare   tempo quando (a) essere.
I'll go and see my friends, and I will divert my-
  andare vedere   amico   divertire
self with those that receive me kindly.
            (b) ricevere   cortesemente.
Won't you carry some books with you?
           portare   libro.
No, for I am sure while I am there, I shall have
     perchè   sicuro mentre (c)   avere
no time to read.
  tempo leggere.
You will forget all your Italian.
      scordare tutto   Italiano.
I am certain I shall not, for I will not stay long
  certo   dirò   restare
there.
molto.
When once you are there, your friends will not
      una volta (d) essere   amico
permit you to leave them so soon.
permettere   lasciare   così presto.

 (a) *When you are there*, turn, *when you shall be there.*
 (b) *Ricevere*, must be in the future, third person plural.
 (c) Turn, *while I shall be there*, mentre che ci sarò.
 (d) Turn, *when once you shall be there*, quando una volta ci sarete.

You

ITALIAN EXERCISES.

You shall see that I'll be here next Sunday, and
  vedere *essere* *qui prossimo Domenica*
that my friends won't have so much power over me
  amico *avere tanto potere*
as you think.
  pensare.
What will you bring me from the country?
  apportare *campagna.*
I'll bring you some partridges, a hare, and some
  portare *pernice* *lepre*
pheasants.
  fagiano.
I will be obliged to you for it.
  essere obbigato.

The Imperative *is a Mood that commands.*

Go from me to my lady, present my respects to her.
  andare *signora pesentare* *rispetto.*
Give her this letter, and bring me an answer,
  dare *questo lettera* *portare* *risposta*
if she is not at home, stay till she comes back.
  se essere *casa restare* *ritornare.*
Speak Italian with me, pronounce well, begin
  parlare Italiano meco *pronunziare* *ricomin-*
again, read softly, repeat your lesson, get you gone.
  ciare leggere adagio rilegere *lezione andare via.*

On the Construction of the Verbs.

The Auxiliary Verb avere, *requires a Nominative Case:*

You have a son that has the finest qualities in the
  avere figliuolo *bello qualità*
world; he has a sweet countenance, he has a great
  mondo *avere piacevole fisonomia* *molto*
deal of civility, he has very obliging manners, in
  civiltà *cortese* *costume*
short,

short, he has the love of every body, and you are
      affezione tutto   essere
happy in having such a son.
fortunato.

 A man is very happy that has the fear of God,
  uomo molto felice   timore Iddio
and the love of his neighbours, though he has not
   amore   vicino (a) benchè
the riches of fortune.
  ricchezza fortuna.

 Those who have great riches, and no charity for
    avere (b) grande ricchezza carità
the poor, shall not share God's mercy.
povero   partecipare Dio misericordia.

 A man that has wit, and no behaviour, is worse
  uomo   spirito   condotta   peggio
than a beast.
  bestia.

 I have scholars that have sense, and are diligent;
    scolaro   senno   essere diligente
but I have others that are dull, and very idle.
      altro che stupido   pigro.

 If you have good manners, civility, and complais-
    avere buono costume civiltà,   compia-
ance, you will be loved by every body.
cenza   essere amato tutto.

Sometimes we make use of the Verb avere *instead of*
 essere, *especially when we speak of* cold, heat, hun-
 ger, thirst, *and when we speak of the age of any*
 body.

 I was very cold when I came, but I am very
   avere   freddo   venire   avere
warm now.
caldo ora.

 You eat as if you were not hungry.
   mangiare come se avere   fame.

 (a) *Benchè* governs the subjunctive mood.
 (b) See *Gram.* p. 215, on the articles *del, dello, della,* &c.

              I ask

ITALIAN EXERCISES. 39

I afk your pardon, I eat heartily, for I was very
demandare   perdono   mangiare bene   avere
hungry.
fame.
Are you not dry yet?
avere   fete ancora.
Yes, I am very dry, but I won't drink yet, for
fi   avere gran fete ma   volere bere   ancora
if I drink when I am hungry, that hinders me
fe   bevere quando avere fame   impedire
from eating.
mangiare.
How old is your uncle?
quanto anno avere   zio.
He is not feventy years old yet.
avere   fettanta anno   ancora.
You furprize me, I thought he was eighty
forprendere   credere   avere ottanta
years old.
anno.
And you, madam, how old are you?
e   lei   fignora   anno avere
I am not twenty yet, if I remember well.
avere   venti ancora fe   ricordarfi bene.

On the Verb Subftantive *effere.*

The verb fubftantive effere *requires the following noun in the nominative cafe.*

Our mafter is diligent; but I have been hitherto
noftro padrone effere diligente   effere ftato   finora
very idle; I have imitated the drones.
pigro   avere imitare   cacchione.
I have loft my parents love, who always pro-
avere perdere   genitore affezione   fempre for-
vided all things neceffary for me. I have been
nire tutto cofa   neceffario   effere ftato
unworthy of their care; but I will deferve to be
indegno   cura   ma   meritare effere
called

called the most diligent of all our scholars for the
chiamare   diligente   tutto   scolaro
time to come.
(*all' avvenire*).

The lion is accounted the most generous of
  leone   passare   per   generoso
beasts, because he is more placable than others.
bestia perchè   placabile   altro.
The bloody minds of some men are more bar-
       sanguinariamente   uomo essere   bar-
barous than wild beasts. Man is a creature of
baro   fera   Uomo   creatura
upright body; when he is old, his body bends
dritto corpo   quando   vecchio   corpo inclinarsi
downwards towards the earth, and his soul ascends
            verso   terra   anima ascendere
to heaven, which is his habitation for ever.
   cielo   dimora.

How are you this morning? I am very well.
come stare   mattina   stare benissimo.
How do your father and mother do?
(a) *stare   padre   madre.*
I hope my father is well, he was well the last
sperare   padre stare   stare bene   ultimo
time I saw him, but my mother has not been well
volta vedere   ma   madre essere   stato bene (b)
these two or three days. And you, sir, how are you?
        due   tre giorno   signore   stare.
I should be well enough, if I had money.
   stare assai bene   (c) se avere danaro.
I hope your lady is very well.
sperare   signora stare benissimo.
She is perfectly well, at your service.
stare perfettamente bene   servizio.

(a) When we inquire after any body's health, we make use of the verb *stare*, instead of *fare*.
(b) These two or three days, *i. e.* da due o tre giorni in quà.
(c) If I had money, *Se io avessi danari*, and not *avevo*.

I am

ITALIAN EXERCISES. 41

I am very glad to hear she is so well.
rallegrarsi sentire stare così bene.
What weather is it to-day, I want to know?
(a) tempo fare oggi volere sapere.
It is the finest weather in the world.
*   bello   mondo*
Is it hotter in Spain than in Italy?
fare caldo Spagna Italia.
It is hotter there in summer, but it is very cold
fare   estate ma fare freddo
in winter.
in verno.
If it is fine weather to-morrow, we will go in
fare bello tempo domani andare
the country.
campagna.
I believe it won't be fine weather, for it is very
credere fare bello tempo perchè
dark to-night.
oscuro stasera.

Verbs Personal governing a Genitive Case.

The verb avere pietà *governs the Genitive.*

I have no pity on the misery of those, who being
avere pietà del miseria   essere
young and strong, love better to beg from door to
giovine forte amare accattare porta
door, than to work for their bread; but I pity
*   che lavorare   pane ma avere*
much the blind, and old people who are incapable
pietà cieco i vecchi essere incapace
to do any thing for their living.
fare la minima cosa vitto.
I pity my brother, I pity his folly, for he has
avere pietà fratello,   pazzia perche

(a) When we speak of the weather, we use the third person singular of the verb *fare*, instead of the verb *essere*.

wasted

wasted away all the portion my father left him.
spregare   tutto   dote   padre lasciare.

The verb burlarsi governs the Genitive.

Men are very often inclined to laugh at other's
uomo essere   spesso inclinato burlarsi di   altri
misfortunes, instead of having pity on them.
disgrazia   in vece di   avere pietà.
Those that call themselves Christians, and do
quello che   chiamarsi   Cristiano   non
not live according to their religion, mock God
vivere secondo   religione   burlarsi Iddio
and his doctrine.
dottrina.
But God will mock them in his turn.
ma Dio   burlare   sua volta.
Don't jeer at other's poverty, for you do not
burlarsi altro povertà   non
know how long fortune will be favourable to you;
sapere quanto tempo fortuna   essere favorevole
and if you should become poor, every one would
e se   doventare povero ognuno
laugh at you.
ridersi   di.
It is a great mark of folly to laugh at every thing.
essere grande segno   pazzia ridersi di   tutto.

The verb pentirsi governs the Genitive.

If you repent sincerely for the fault you have
se   pentirsi sinceramente   colpa   avere
committed, God will forgive you; for he don't
commesso   Iddio   perdonare   perchè
love the death of a sinner, but he will have him
amare   morte   peccatore   volere
to repent of his sins.
pentirsi   peccato.
It is not enough to say, I repent of my ill con-
non essere abbastanza dire   pentirsi   cattivo con-
duct,

ITALIAN EXERCISES. 43

duct, and of my bad life, if you don't shew the
dotta   cattivo vita se   moſtrare
effects of your repentance by a new and better life.
effetto   pentimento   nuovo   miglior vita.

The verb rallegrarsi *governs the Genitive.*

A good Christian ought never to rejoice at others
buono   Cristiano dovere   mai   rallegrarſi   altro
misfortunes.
diſgrazia.
I rejoice at the good succeſs you had in your
rallegrarſi   buono   riuſcita   avere
businefs.
negozio.
Come and rejoice with me at the good news I
venire   meco   buon nuova
received to-day.
ricevere   oggi.
How will you have me rejoice at a thing I do
come volere   rallegrarſi   coſa
not know?
non ſapere.
Tell me first of all what news I muſt rejoice at:
dire   avanti ogni coſa   nuova   dovere   rallegrarſi.

The verb ricordarsi *governs the Genitive caſe.*

Do you remember the promiſe you made me
ricordarſi   promeſſa   fare
yesterday?
ieri.
I don't remember it at all. Don't you remember
non   ricordarſi affatto
the ſum of money you ſaid you would lend me?
ſomma   danaro   dire   preſtare.
I vow I had forgotten it, I remember it very
proteſtare   avere ſcordato   ricordarſi   beniſ-
well now.
ſimo adeſſo.

Th

The verb languire *requires a Genitive case.*

He that languishes for thirst, gives a man greater
quello languire di sete rendere grande
thanks that offers him water, than if a prince gave
grazia offerire acqua che se principe dare
him a crown.
corona.

The man who languishes for love, ought to be pitied.
uomo languire amore dovere compianto.

The verbs ubbidire *and* disubbidire *will have a Dative case.*

We ought not only to obey our parents, but also
dovere non solo ubbidire parente, ma anche
our superiors, if we would obey God's commands.
superiore se volere ubbidire commandamento.
One sees very seldom a child prosper in this world,
si vedere rare volte figliuolo prosperare mondo
that does not obey his father and mother.
ubbidire padre madre.
When God commanded Abraham to sacrifice
quando Iddio comandare Abramo sacrificare
Isaac, his only son, he immediately obeyed the
Isaaco unico figlio subito ubbidire
Lord's voice; for the angel of the Lord did not
Signore voce ma angelo Signore
permit him to slay the child, and told him his obe-
permettere uccidere ragazzo dire ubbi-
dience had been agreeable to God.
dienza essere stato grato Dio.

The verb parlare *will have a Dative case of the person.*

God speaketh to sinners sometimes most gently,
Iddio parlare peccatore qualche volta benigna-
that he may draw them to obedience, he speaketh
mente trarre ubbidienza parlare

to

ITALIAN EXERCISES. 45

to them of the blessed life which he has prepared
              beato   vita   avere   preparato;
for his servants; sometimes he speaketh to them of
    servo   qualche volta   parlare
the abyss which shall be the reward of sin; yet his
  abisso   essere   mercede peccato. però
promises and threatenings move not stubborn minds.
promessa   minaccia   muovere ostinato spirito.

The verbs pretendere *and* aspirare *govern the Dative case.*

All those that call themselves Christians pretend
tutto quello   chiamarsi   Cristiano pretendere
to everlasting life; but there are few that will suffer
eterno   vita (ma ve ne sono pochi)   soffrire
the least thing to deserve it; if it is a question to
minimo cosa   meritare   (se si   tratta)
aspire to some employment, or to some dignity,
aspirare qualche impiego   dignità
there is none but what would suffer a great deal of
(non vi è nissuno che non soffra)   molto
fatigue, labour, and pain to deserve it.
fatica   lavoro   pena   meritare.

The verb giuocare *(when one speaks of all sorts of game) governs the Dative case.*

I do not love to play at games of chances, as at
         amare giuocare giuoco   sorte   come
cards, or at dice, but I love to play sometimes at
carta   dadi   ma amare giuocare qualche volta
bowls, at billiard-table, at tennis, or at ninepins.
bocce   bigliardo   pallacorda o   sbriglio.
Do you never play at cards, at chess, or draughts?
          mai giuocare carte scacchi o giuoco delle tavole.
I play sometimes at piquet to oblige the company.
  giuocare   picchetto obbligare   compagnia.

Verbs governing an Accusative case of the Person, and a Genitive of the thing.

The verbs accusare, biasimare, avvertire, *and* assolvere, *will have the Accusative of the person, and the Genitive of the thing.*

One boy accuseth another of idleness, the master
    ragazzo accusare altro   pigrizia   maestro
hears their tales; but punishes only those whom he
sentire   storia ma   punire solo   quello
thinks guilty, and worthy of punishment.
credere colpevole   degno   castigo.

Every one blames you for your negligence and
ogn' uno   biasimare   negligenza
ignorance.
ignoranza.

I did often admonish you of your duty, if you
    spesso avvertire   vostro dovere se
do not improve as well as others, it is not my fault.
    profittare come   altro   non è   colpa.

When a judge acquits a man of a crime of which
  quando giudice assolvere uomo   delitto
he is guilty; if he commits again the same fault,
reo   se   commettere di   nuovo   fallo
he is worthy of double punishment.
degno   doppio   castigo.

The verb condannare *governs the Accusative of the person, and the Genitive of the thing; but when it signifies to condemn to death, the name of the torment ought to be put in the Dative case.*

Every one condemns you very much for the action
ogn' uno condannare   molto   azione
you committed the other day.
  commettere   altro giorno.

During

ITALIAN EXAMPLES. 47

During the perfecution in France, many brave
nel tempo del perfecuzione   Francia   molto bravo
gentlemen were condemned, fome to the gallows,
cavaliere   condannare   forca
and fome to the galleys, for the defence of their
              gallera   difefa
religion.
religione.

The verb ottenere *will have an Accufative of the thing, and a Genitive of the perfon.*

A fcholar who obtains his mafter's favour is more
   fcolaro   ottenere   maeftro   favore   più
happy than he that is idle, who lofes his honour,
felice   pigro   perdere   onore
waftes his time, and continues a blockhead; though
fpregare   tempo   continuare ad effere pecorone benchè
play be pleafant to him for a little while.
giuoco effere piacevole   poco tempo.

Verbs governing an Accufative cafe with a Dative.

The verbs invitare, efortare, *will have an Accufative of the perfon, and a Dative of the thing.*

God invites finners to eternal happinefs, he calls
Iddio invitare peccatore   eterno   felicità   chiamare
them to repentance, he fpeaks moft gracioufly to them.
     pentimento   parlare   graziofamente.
He has prepared for penitent finners all things
       preparare   penitente peccatore tutto
that belong to bleffednefs, all things that they can
    appartenere felicità   tutto   quel   potere
defire.
bramare.

Remember your mafter's words, he exhorts you
     ricordarfi   maeftro parola   efortare
to induftry, which is beneficial to yourfelves. Your
     induftria   effere vantaggiofo

pains shall produce a great advantage; he uses his
lavoro produrre grande vantaggio fare ogni
best endeavours for your benefit; be not your own
suo sforzo utilità essere
enemies.
inimico.

Paragonare *requires an Accusative of the first noun,
(either of the person, or of the thing) and the other
in the Dative.*

If we compare the longest life to eternity, it is
se paragonare lungo vita eternità
very short.
corto.
If we compare the happiest condition of this
comparare felice condizione
world to everlasting life, it is miserable, and not
mondo eterno vita miserabile
worthy our desires; if we compare the number of
indegno desiderio paragonare numero
good men to the multitude of wicked, it is small.
buono moltitudine malvagio picculo.

Dare *and* restituire *will have an Accusative of the
thing, and a Dative of the person.*

I'll soon give my mother the money she en-
presto dare madre danaro con-
trusted with me.
fidare.
God will give these men a reward that please
Iddio dare uomo mercede piacere
him, and those whom he has set up governors of
quello che avere costituito governatore
the world.
mondo.
I returned my master the book which I borrowed;
restituire maestro libro imprestare
he lent it to me, and it was my duty to read it, and
prestare essere dovere leggere not

ITALIAN EXERCISES.

not to keep it; though books delight me very much,
tenere   benchè (a) *libro   piacere   moltissimo*
I ought to restore them to those whom they be-
dovere   restituire   quello   che   ap-
long to.
partenere.

These verbs dovere, promettere, *and* pagare, *will have an Accusative of the thing, and a Dative of the person.*

I owe him money, because I promised to pay
dovere   danaro   perchè   promettere   pagare
him another man's debt; but at present I have
altro   debito   ma   adesso   avere
need myself of money, that I may pay what I
bisogno   io   medesimo denaro   pagare
owe to my creditors.
dovere   creditore.

When will you pay me what you owe me?
quando volere   pagare   dovere.
I promise you I will pay it to you next week.
promettere   pagare   prossimo settimana.

Insegnare *requires an Accusative of the thing, and a Dative of the person.*

I have been twelve years in this country, during
(b) *essere stato dodici anno   paese   nel*
which time I have had the honour to teach several
quale tempo avere avuto   onore   insegnare molto
ladies, and gentlemen Italian. Masters ought to
signora   signore   Italiano   Maestro   dovere
teach children not only the things which concern
insegnare ragazzo non solamente   cosa   risguardare

(a) *Benchè* governs the subjunctive mood. See *Gram.* p. 212.
(b) I have been twelve years in this country, turn, *Sono dodici anni che stò in questo paese.*

science; but they ought also to teach them things
scienza   ma   dovere anche insegnare   cosa
which concern their soul and their salvation: for
* risguardare   anima   salvazione perchè*
science without religion is an unprofitable thing.
scienza senza religione svantaggioso cosa.

Of the construction of the Infinitive, with the Article *di*.

When after these verbs attenersi, considerare, *and* avvertire, *follows an Infinitive, it ought to be put with the article* di.

Often rash men propose to do things which are
 spesso temerario uomo proporre fare cosa essere
beyond their capacity. A man that abstains from
superiore capacità Uomo attenersi
eating and drinking to excess, from swearing, and
mangiare bere all' eccesso bestemmiare
keeping bad company, may be called an honest man.
frequentare compagnia, potere chiamare onesto uomo.
I thought to go this morning to see Mr. N. but
  pensare andare sta mattina vedere il signor — ma
one of my friends did admonish me not to go there.
   amico ammonire   andare
I had a mind to advise you not to go in the com-
 avere voglia consigliare andare com-
pany of that man who brought this trouble upon
pagnia uomo causare incomodo
you; but I bethought myself to say nothing of it,
    ma ' considerare dire niente
for fear of disobliging you.
 per timore dispiacere.

These verbs supplicare, consigliare, incaricarsi, *and* costringere, *will have an Infinitive with the article* di.

I have a mind to constrain Mr. N. to pay me
avere voglia costringere il signor — pagare
the money he owes me; nevertheless I would be
danaro dovere nonostante avere
very glad not to put him to trouble, because he has
piacere non dare briga perchè essere
always been my friend: what do you advise me
sempre stato amico consigliare
to do in this case?
fare caso?
I intreat you to have a little patience; I take
supplicare avere pazienza
charge to get you your money.
incaricarsi ricuperare danaro.

These verbs proibire, desiderare, differire, procurare, impedire, sperare, fingere, affrettarsi, *require also an Infinitive with the article* di.

God forbids us to sin, nevertheless we never de-
Iddio proibire peccare nonostante mai de-
sist from offending him, we always defer obeying
sistere offendere sempre differire ubbidire
his voice; we seem to strive to disobey him in every
voce parere procurare disubbidire ogni
thing. If we hope to have share in the merits of
cosa. sperare avere parte merito
our blessed Saviour's sufferings, let nothing hinder
beato Salvatore sofferenza niente impedire
us from beginning this day to use all our endeavours
principiare oggi fare tutto sforzo
to deserve it; let us make haste to begin that great
meritare affrettarsi principiare grande
work of our salvation; let us not feign to be
opera salvazione fingere esser
con

converted, but let us convert ourselves in good
convertito   convertire   da
earnest, for nobody can deceive God.
dovvero   nessuno potere ingannare.

The verbs meditare, parlare, permettere, promettere, proporre, presumere, pretendere, protestare, rifiutare, risolvere, augurare, *will have also after them an Infinitive with the article* di.

Never meditate to do any wrong to your neigh-
mai meditare   fare   torto   pros-
bour. When you speak of undertaking some great
fimo Quando   parlare   intrapprendere   grande
enterprize, permit me to tell you, that you ought
intrappresa permettere   dire   dovere
to consult your friends before you begin it.
amico   prima   cominciare.
Never promise to do any thing, unless you are
mai   promettere fare   cosa   se non   essere
sure you will do it.
sicuro   fare
Never presume to have more wit than those who
presumere   avere   spirito quello
have the care of your conduct.
cura   condotta.
Don't pretend ever to prosper in this world, if
pretendere mai   prosperare   mondo se
you have not the fear of God.
avere   timore   Iddio.
If you protest to God with an humble and sin-
protestare   umile   sin-
cere heart to amend your life, he will receive you
cero cuore   emendare   vita   ricevere
among his children.
fra   figliuolo
Never refuse to do service to your friends, when
rifiutare rendere servizio   amico
it is in your power.
potere.

Do

ITALIAN EXERCISES.

Do you desire to pass for an honest man, endea-
desiderare passare galant'uomo pro-
vour to do all that you can to oblige every body.
curare farè tutto potere obbligare ogn' uno.

When after the verb avere *follows one of these substantives* permissione, desiderio, voglia, cura, costume, bisogno, soggetto, ragione, torto, dritto, occasione, *the following verb ought to be put in the Infinitive with the article* di.

I believe you have a mind to play; but I will
credere avere voglia giuocare ma volere
not give you leave to go out 'till you have done your
dare permissione uscire (a) *infinchè avere fare*
exercise. You are in the right, sir, to believe it,
esercizio (b) *ragione signore credere*
and I am in the wrong to desire it. I have no
    (c) *torto desiderare*
cause to be angry with you, for it is not your
soggetto essere collera essere
custom to be idle.

When after a verb follows one of these substantives l'opportunità, il tempo, il mezzo, la volontà, il cuore, il potere, l'autorità, *the following verb ought to be put in the Infinitive with the article* di.

When I shall have an opportunity to see your
quando avere opportunità vedere
father, I will tell him how much you deserve to
padre dire quanto meritare
be praised for your uncommon diligence.
essere lodato straordinario diligenza.

(a) *'Till* governs the optative mood.
(b) You are in the right, *v. s.* ha ragione.
(c) I am in the wrong, *Io ho torto.*

ITALIAN EXERCISES.

Whilst we have it in our power to acquire know-
mentre   avere   potere   acquistare   cog-
ledge, let us not lose such precious time.
noscere   perdere tale prezioso tempo.

I wonder how men have the heart to hate one
 maravigliarsi   uomo avere   il cuore   odiarsi.
another.

God has given to kings power to command, and
 Iddio   dare   Rè   potere   comandare
judges authority to judge.
giudice   autorità   giudicare.

When after the verb substantive essere *follows one of these nouns* contento, obbligato, in pena, sul punto, in pericolo, *the following verb ought to be put in the Infinitive with the article* di.

I am very glad to hear that you overcame your
 essere contento   sentire   vincere
enemies, and I should have been sorry to have
 nemici   (a) *rincrescere*
heard the contrary.
intendere contrario.

I am obliged to return you thanks for your friend-
 essere obbligato rendere   grazia   ami-
ship, for I was in danger of losing my suit.
cizia perchè essere in pericolo   perdere   lite.

I was in trouble to know what had happened to
         in pena   sapere   succedere
you; and if you had not come, I was on the point
(b)   *se   essere venire   essere sul punto*
of going to see you.
andare   vedere.

(a) I should have been sorry, *mi sarebbe rincresciuto.*
(b) *Se* before the imperfect indicative. See *Gram.* p. 209.

These

These verbs avvezzarfi, impiegare, incorraggire, eccitare, invitare, efibirfi, dilettarfi, tenerfi, pronto, lavorare, *will have after them an Infinitive with the article* a, *or* ad.

We ought to employ the days of our life in pre-
   dovere   impiegare   giorno   vita pre-
paring ourfelves for the other world.
pararfi   altro mondo

Mafters that ufe clemency in teaching their fcho-
Maeftro   ufare clemenza   infegnare   fco-
lars, encourage them more to learn well than thofe
laro incorraggire   imparare bene
that ufe too much feverity. An honeft man takes
  ufare troppo feverità   onefto uomo dilet-
always pleafure in obliging his friends.
tarfi fempre   obbligare   amico.

The love of God invites us to love one another.
  amore   Iddio invitare   amare.

Let us keep ourfelves in readinefs to appear be-
    tenerfi   pronto   comparire in-
fore the living God.
nanzi vivente Dio.

Let us work continually to obtain eternal life.
    lavorare continuamente ottenere eterna vita.

When after vi è, *or* v'è *follows the adverb* niente, *the next verb muft be put in the Infinitive with the article* da, *or* a, ad.

There is nothing to fear in ferving God.
 non vi è niente   temere (a) *fervire Iddio.*
There is nothing to fay to what you have done.
 non v'è niente   dire   avere fatto.
There is nothing to do in that at prefent.
          niente   fare   adeffo.

(a) In ferving God, *nel fervire Iddio.*

There is nothing so easy to learn as the Italian
          niente   *così facile imparare*   *Italiano*
language.
lingua.

When after v'è follows an adverb of quantity, it requires an Infinitive with the article a, *or* ca.

There is a great deal of satisfaction in teaching
V'è   *gran*   (a) *soddisfazione*   *insegnare*
diligent boys, but there is a great deal of trouble
diligente ragazzo   *gran*   *incomodo*
in instructing idle scholars.
    istruire *pigro scolaro.*

There is a great deal to say against the conduct
V'è   *molto*   *dire contro*   *condotta*
of wicked people; but there is nothing to say against
malvagio gente   *non v'è* *niente* *dire contro*
the conduct of honest people.
condotta *onesto gente.*

On the English participle in *ing*.

When the English participle in ing *comes after a verb of motion with a before it, we use the substantive, and sometimes the verb.*

The man that goes a hunting or visiting his
    uomo   *andare* *caccia* (b) *visitare*
friends, when necessary business require his care
amico *quando necessario* *affare richiedere* *cura*
and time, prefers his diversion before his profit,
   tempo preserire   *divertimento*   *profitto*
the company of his friends before the necessary
  compagnia   *amico*   *necessario*
advantage of his family.
vantaggio   *famiglia.*

(a) See *Gram.* p. 217, on *a great deal of.*
(b) Ibid. p. 208, on *verbs of motion.*

ITALIAN EXERCISES.

The boy that goes a playing with his school-
ragazzo andare giuocare condis-
fellows, when he ought to be diligent at the task
cipolo quando dovere essere diligente intorno alla
the master has given him, prefers play to his mas-
parte maestro dare preferire giuoco maes-
ter's love, and his own profit.
tro affetto profitto.

The English particle in ing after from, must be put in Italian in the Infinitive with the article di.

The providence of God keeps us from perishing;
providenza Iddio impedire perire
the power of God hinders us from acting those
potenza Iddio impedire fare
things which displease him; the grace of God
cosa dispiacere grazia Iddio
prevents us from sinning; the goodness of God
impedire peccare bontà
preserves us from suffering afflictions.
preservare soffrire afflizione.

The English participle in ing after a verb importing to cease, to leave, or to give over, must be rendered in Italian by the Infinitive mood with the article di.

He that leaves acting laudable things, and dege-
quello che cessare fare lodevole cosa dege-
nerates into vice, was never truly good.
nerare vizio essere mai veramente buono.
A wise man never leaves learning till he gives
savio uomo mai tralasciare imparare cessare
over living; for he that has great wisdom, has still
vivere perchè avere grande sapienza sempre
need of more knowledge.
bisogno. conoscenza.

58   ITALIAN EXERCISES.

When after the verb substantive essere, *follows the participle in* ing, *the verb substantive ought not to be expressed; but the participle must be put in the same tense, number and person as the verb substantive is.*

A diligent boy is always learning, not only
   diligente ragazzo   sempre imparare non solamente
while the master is instructing, but also while other
mentre   maestro   istruire   ma anche   altro
boys are playing.
ragazzo giuocare.

   Apelles was daily drawing some excellent pic-
Apelle   giornalmente dipingere   eccellente pit-
tures with wonderful art; no day past without
tura   maraviglioso arte nessuno giorno passare senza
a line.
linea.

   Those that don't employ well their time in the
              impiegare   bene   tempo
beginning of their lives; will be perpetually la-
principio   vita   perpetualmente la-
menting their folly, they will be hourly condemn-
mentare   pazzia   ad ogni momento conden-
ing themselves, and saying, Ah! at what a price
narsi   dire Ah!   prezzo
would not I purchase time past!
       comprare tempo passato.

Of the participle of time past.

When one of these pronouns che, il, lo, la, &c. *meets before the compound tenses, the pronoun ought to agree with the particle in gender and number.*

I did receive the books which my brother did
   ricevere.   libro   fratello
send me; I did read them all, they are very good,
mandare   leggere   tutto   essere   buono
and well written.
bene scritto.

The

The letter which my father did write to me is
    lettera   *padre*   *scrivere*   *essere*
very severe, I did shew it to my mother, and she
   severo   *mostrare*   *madre*   (a)
is very sorry for it.
   dispiacere.

When these pronouns mio, me, te, noi, voi, *&c. are the case of the verb, they must agree with the Participle in gender and in number.*

My dear friends, I have always loved you like my
   caro amico *avere sempre amato* *come*
children, I have often admonished you for your own
figliuolo *avere spesso ammonire*
good; I did several times exhort you to practise
bene   *spesse volte esortare*   *praticare*
virtue; if you are not truly virtuous, it is not my
virtù *se*   *veramente virtuoso* *essere*
fault.
colpa.

I met your brother this morning, we did embrace
  rincontrare fratello *mattina*   *abbracciarsi*
one another like good friends, and I rejoice we are
       come buono amico   *rallegrarsi*
reconciled.
riconciliarsi.

The books which I have seen you reading, are
    libro   *avere vedere* *leggere*
not good.
buono.

These are all the copies which you have given
  ecco *tutto*   *copia.*   *avere dare*
me to write.
   scrivere.

Your brothers have done quite contrary to what
    fratello   *fare tutto contrario*
I had advised them to do.
avere consigliare fare.

(a) She is very sorry for it; *gliene dispiace moltissimo.*

ITALIAN EXERCISES.

Of the Adverbs.

Adverbs are generally put after the verb, and in compounded tenses between the verb and the participle.

It is a lamentable thing to see that youths which
        lamentevole cosa   vedere giovane
have much wit, and a great deal of disposition to
avere molto spirito   grande   disposizione
learn well, take but very little pains to answer the
imparare   pigliare   poco   pena (a) *rispondere*
expectation of their parents.
aspettazione   parente.

Adverbs of Interrogation and Question, must always be put before a verb.

From whence come you? Why did you not
 di   dove   venire   perchè
stay for me?
aspettare.
    When will you have done jeering your friends?
    quando   cessare   burlare   amico.
    Why did you say I had promised you to go in
    perchè   dire   promettere   andare
the country?
campagna.
    Where is your father? Is he in town?
    dove   padre essere   città.
    Where did you buy this fine horse?
              comprare bello cavallo.
    I bought it at the last country fair?
    comprare   ultimo campagna fera.
    Where are the ladies your sisters?
        essere   signora   sorella.
    I believe they are gone out to take an airing.
    credere   essere uscito   pigliare l'aria.

(a) *Rispondere*, governs the dative case of the thing.

Where

ITALIAN EXAMPLES.

Where do you go so fast? You are in great haste.
    andare così presto essere gran fretta.
I go to Mr. Clement's house; for I heard my
andare signore Clemente (a) *casa perchè sentire*
brother is there; and I have some business with him.
fratello   avere affare con esso.
You are mistaken, he is not there; for I met
 ingannarsi essere   rincontrare
him just now, and he told me he was going to
 adesso   dire   andare
his sister's house.
 sorella casa.
I was going to your house; but since I meet
  andare   casa ma giacchè rincon-
you, we will go to my house, where we shall
trare andare casa dove
dine.
pranzare.
I pray you to excuse me, indeed I cannot; for
pregare scusare in verità non potere
I must go to my lady Arabella's, to pay a visit to
bisogno andare signora Arabella fare visita
her children.
 figliuolo.
They are not at home, for I saw them going
 essere casa perchè vedere andare
into the park.
 parco.
Let us go then and see if your brothers are at home.
 andare dunque vedere se fratello casa.
They are not in their house, they are gone a-
 essere   casa essere andato
hunting.
caccia.
What is the matter with you, sir? You seem to
 (cosa avete) signor parere
be grieved.
essere afflitto.

(a) *At*, or *to*, before *house*, or *home*, must be rendered by *da, dal,* or *in casa*. See *Gram.* p. 216.

No, sir, I am not, but I come from Mr. Vin-
  (non sono afflitto) venire   Vincent's who is very ill.
cenzio ammalato.

You surprise me, for as I was coming from our
 sorprendere perchè venire
house, I met his brother, who did not tell me of it.
casa rincontrare fratello   dire

Do you know from whence he was coming,
  sapere di dove   venire
when you met him?
quando rincontrare.

I believe he was coming from his own house.
 credere venire   casa.

Can you tell me where he is gone?
potere dire dove essere andato.

I was assured that he is set out for his uncle's
 essere assicurato essere partito   zio
country-house.
casa di campagna.

Which way did you pass, when you were going
 per dove passare - quando   andare
into Italy?
 Italia?

I passed by Rouen, Paris, Orleans, and Lyons.
 passare Rouen Parigi, Orleano Lione.

Which way did you come back to England?
 per dove tornare   Inghilterra.

I returned by Germany and Holland.
 ritornare Germania Olanda.

Of Prepositions.

These prepositions di dietro, vicino, intorno, dirimpetto, infino, *will have a Dative after them.*

Sir, if I knew where you live, I would take the
signore (a) *se sapere dove stare di casa   pigliare*
liberty to go and pay you a visit.
libertà (b) *venire fare   visita.*
Sir, you will give yourself too much trouble,
dare   troppo   incomodo
however, if you do me that favour, you shall be
però se   fare   favore   essere
very welcome; I live near the Temple, over-against
il benvenuto stare vicino   Tempio   dirimpetto
Chancery-Lane.
Cancelleria Strada.
I believe my best way to go to your house is to
credere   via   venire   casa
pass by London-bridge. You are in the right, sir,
passare Londra ponte   avere   ragione
since you live behind the Tower.
giacchè stare di dietro Torre.
A poor labourer that works from morning 'till
povero lavorante   lavorare   mattina infino
night (when he is well paid for his labour) lives
sera quando essere bene pagato   lavoro vivere
more content and satisfied, than those that have
contento   sodisfatto   avere
great riches.
gran ricchezza.
He that shall be constant even to death, shall
essere constante infino morte
have the crown of glory.
avere   corona   gloria.

(a) See *Gram.* p. 209, on *se* before a preterimperfect.
(b) Ibid. p. 210, when we use *venire*, instead of *andare*.

Of Conjunctions that require the Subjunctive after them. See *Gram.* p. 211.

These conjunctions prima che, acciochè, infinechè, per paura che, sia che, benchè, purchè, a meno che, Iddio voglia che, *will have the Subjunctive after them.*

You will speak Italian well, provided you take
   parlare Italiano bene purchè darsi
pains; I tell you so, that you may take courage,
pena dire   acciochè pigliare coraggio
and learn well!
imparare bene.

  I remember that I told you several times that you
   ricordarsi dire parecchie volte
will never write Italian correctly, unless you study
  mai scrivere Italiano correttamente a meno che studiare
the rules.
  regola.

  I'll take so much pains that I hope I shall write
  darsi   pena sperare scrivere
it well before next summer comes on.
   prima che prossimo estate venire.

  You will soon perceive the effects of it, provided
   presto accorgersi effetto purchè
you follow my orders, though you think the Italian
  seguire ordine benchè credere Italiano
tongue is very difficult.
lingua essere difficile.

  Please God it may be as you say; for it would
  Piaccia Iddio essere come dire perchè
be a great satisfaction to me.
essere grande soddisfazione.

  I esteem a man very unhappy that has not the
   stimare uomo molto infelice avere
fear of God, though he should possess all the trea-
timore Iddio benchè   possedere tutto te-
                  sures

ITALIAN EXERCISES. 65

fures in the world, even though he should have all
foro   mondo   benchè   avere
the other fine qualities that can make a man perfect.
altro bello qualità   potere rendere uomo perfetto.
I did always praise you very much before you
*   sempre lodare   molto prima che*
became so idle; and I told you several times that
divenire pigro   dire   spesse volte
you would lose the good opinion every one had of
*   perdere buono opinione tutto   avere*
you, unless you should be as diligent and careful
*   a meno che   essere   diligente   premuroso*
as you were before.
*   essere prima.*
When I corrected you for your faults, it was
quando correggere   colpa   essere
not because I did not love you; on the contrary,
perchè   amare   al contrario
it was to the end you should employ well your
essere   acciochè   impiegare
time, and that you should be a better scholar than
tempo   essere   più   sapiente
you are now.
*   adesso.*
Though you did begin to learn Italian before
Benchè   principiare imparare Italiano prima
me, I hope that I shall speak it soon as well as you.
di me sperare   parlare presto   bene come v.s.
I don't believe so, unless you have learned all
*   credere   a meno che avere   tutto*
the rules of the grammar.
*   regola   grammatica.*
Though I did not learn them, yet I'll take so
benchè   imparare   però pigliare
much pains, that what I told you will prove true.
tanto pena   dire   essere   vero.
It will be some time, before you have read them.
*   tempo prima che   leggere.*
Would to God I had known you sooner, I should
volesse   Iddio   conoscere
                                                 speak

ITALIAN EXERCISES.

speak Italian well now; and although I had learned
parlare Italiano bene ora   benchè   imparare
when I was young, for all that, I knew but very
          essere giovine, con tutto ciò sapere   po-
little of it, when I began with you.
chissimo   quando   principiare.

Perhaps it was not your master's fault; for
forse   essere   maestro   colpa
before I did compose my grammar, I found but
primachè   comporre   grammatica   trovare
few that would learn grammatically, but would
poco   imparare grammaticalmente.
learn by rote.

It is true, I had a very good master, and if I
           vero   avere   buono maestro   se
had believed him, I would have learned by rules,
avere creduto   avere imparato   regola
but I found them too tedious; and would to God
ma trovare   troppo nojoso   volesse Iddio,
I had followed his advice, for I have a great mind
avere seguitato   consiglio perchè avere gran voglia
to speak Italian.
parlare Italiano.

Some verbs signifying will, desire, leave, or fear, *will have the Conjunction* che *after them, and the following verb in the Optative.*

I will leave you to do that.
  volere   fare.
I wish you may be as honest as your father.
desiderare   essere   onesto   padre.
I ordered dinner to be ready immediately.
  ordinare pranzo essere pronto   subito.
That must be done quickly.
     bisogna fare   presto.
God permitted it should happen.
Iddio permettere   succedere.
I am afraid you were mistaken.
   avere paura   sbagliare.

We

We express these two Englicisms, this day se'nnight, this day fortnight, *by* d'oggi a otto, d'oggi a quindici.

I believe I shall go into the country this day
   credere   andare   campagna   d'oggi
se'nnight, but I hope I shall come back this day
 a otto.   sperare   ritornare   d'oggi
fortnight.
a quindici.
   I am sure that when once you are there, you
    essere sicuro   quando   una volta essere
will not return so soon to town.
        tornare così presto città.
   I give you my word that this day fortnight I'll
    dare   parola   d'oggi a quindici
come to see you.
venire vedere.
   When will your brother go to Germany?
   quando   fratello andare Germania.
   He expects to go this day se'nnight, if it is fine
    aspettarsi andare d'oggi a otto se fare   bel
weather.
tempo.

The word people, *when it is taken generally for the people of a whole kingdom, is expressed in Italian by the word* gente.

   The French have the name of being the most
    Francese avere   riputazione essere
civil people in the world.
civile gente   mondo.
   I should not love to live among the Spaniards,
                 amare vivere fra   Spagnuolo
for they are very jealous people, but I should never
perchè essere   geloso   gente   ma   essere   mai
be tired of living among the English, for I believe
stanco   vivere fra   Inglese perchè credere
                                                      they

they are the moſt civil, the moſt courteous, and
    eſſere   *civile*   *corteſe*
the moſt obliging people in the world.
          obbligante gente   *mondo.*

When the word people *ſignifies ſubjects, it is expreſſed in Italian by the word* popolo.

A good prince ſhould prefer the happineſs of his
   buono principe   *preferire*   *felicità*
people to his own. Happy is the people that has
popolo   *felice*   *popolo*   *avere*
a good prince to govern them.
buono   *governare.*

On the Particle *ſi, it is, they, one,* &c. See *Gram.* p. 218.

The Particle ſi *is always put before a verb, and the verb muſt be imperſonal.*

One told me that you ſpeak Italian very well.
   dire   *parlare Italiano beniſſimo.*
They do me more honour than I deſerve, I wiſh
   fare   *onore*   *meritare*   *volere*
it was true.
   vero.
They ſay you are going to be married.
   dire   *andare*   *maritarſi.*
They ſay ſo, indeed ; but they are much miſtaken.
  dire coſì in verità ma   *molto ingannarſi.*
I was aſſured that the lady's father and yours did
   aſſicurare   *ſignora padre*
conclude the articles of marriage.
conchiudere   *articolo*   *matrimonio.*
If they ſay ſo, it is without any foundation.
ſe   *dire coſì*   *ſenza alcuno fondamento.*

ITALIAN EXERCISES.   69

I am very glad to see you, for I was told you
    rallegrarsi   *vedere*   *perchè*   *dire*
were gone to France.
            Francia.
Pray who told you such falsehood? No matter;
di grazia   *dire*   *tale* *falsità*   *non importa*
and we were told too, that you were to go to Italy.
  essere detto   *andare Italia.*

The verb to use in English signifies in Italian servirsi, assuefarsi, accostumarsi; *when it signifies* servirsi, *it is commonly followed by a noun, but otherwise it is followed by a verb.*

He that useth to forget those things which he
    assuefarsi   *scordare*   *cosa*
desires to remember, must use helps to strengthen
desiderare *ricordarsi* *dovere servirsi ajuto* *fortificare*
his memory, or use the greatest diligence and at-
 memoria *o*   *grande diligenza*   *at-*
tention when he is reading, that he may retain
tenzione quando   *leggere*   *ritenere*
profitable instruction; for when they have once
profittevole istruzione *perchè quando* *essere una*
slipt out of the memory, there is need of fresh
volta uscito   *memoria* *v'è* *bisogno* *nuova*
reading to recall them.
lettura *richiamare.*

All men use to desire riches, but all do not use
 tutto uomo   *desiderare ricchezze ma tutto*
riches rightly; when they are come to honour and
richezze bene *quando* *essere arrivato* *onore*
wealth, they still are greedy to heap up more. He
opulenza   *ancora*   *avido*   *accumulare*
that desires nothing, wants nothing; it is a wise
  desiderare niente   *aver* *bisogno*   *savio*
man's part to moderate all his desires.
uomo *dovere* *moderare tutto* *desiderio.*

The verb impersonal importa, *will have a Dative.*

It much concerns young people to avoid bad
   molto   importa   gioventù   schivare cattivo
company, as they would beware of the plague;
compagnia, come   guardarsi   peste
they are more hurtful to the mind, than the most
          nocevole   animo
contagious disease to the body.
contagioso malattia   corpo.
   It concerns me, and all men to look to our-
   importa   tutto uomo   badare
selves; the world is full of knaves and knavery.
       mondo pieno furbo   furberia
It is hard to be known, and he is hard to be found,
  difficile sapere   trovare
who is fit to be trusted.
     confidarsi.
   The greatest caution is to be used in the presence
    grande cautela   adoprare   presenza
of children; masters must behave themselves very
   ragazzo maestro dovere comportarsi
warily, lest scholars learn evil of them; and it
prudentemente per paura che scolaro imparare male
greatly concerns boys to imitate their master's virtue.
molto importa giovane imitare   maestro virtù.

When the word to speak *is joined with* truth, *it is expressed in Italian by* dire.

You promised me several times you would be
   promettere spesse volte   essere
diligent, and that you would never keep bad com-
diligente   mai praticare cattivo company; I perceive that you don't speak always the
pagnia accorgersi   dire sempre
truth, for I met you to-day with a man whose
verità   rincontrare oggi con   uomo
company I did forbid you. A man who does not
compagnia   proibire   uomo
                                          love

ITALIAN EXERCISES.

love to speak always the truth, is unworthy of
amare   dire sempre   verità   indegno
honest people's society.
onesto gente   società.

When there is in English, I wish, I would, *in the beginning of a period, we express it in Italian thus,* vorrei potere, *and the following verb must be in the Infinitive mood.*

I wish I could serve you, I would do it with all
       potere servire   *fare*   *tutto*
my heart.
  cuore.

I wish I could see your sister, I would give her
      vedere   *sorella*   *dare*
something that was sent me for her.
qualche cosa   essere mandato.

I wish I could speak Italian as well as you, it
      parlare Italiano
would be a great satisfaction to me.
    essere grande soddisfazione.

I wish I could do what you desire of me, I would
        fare   *desiderare*
not refuse you.
  ricusare.

I wish I could be reconciled with your brother,
    essere riconciliato   *fratello*
for he is an honest man.
perchè   *galant' uomo.*

I wish I could go into the country with you, I
     andare   *campagna*
would not return soon to town, for I would visit
    ritornare presto   *città*   *visitare*
all my friends.
tutto   amico.

I wish I could follow your example, I would
     seguire   *esempio*
live better than I do.
  meglio.

Ought

ITALIAN EXERCISES.

Ought *and* must *ought to be rendered in Italian by the Present of the Indicative of the verb* dovere, *and are not Imperfonal.*

At church people ought to fit still, not to talk.
 chiefa gente dovere ftare faldo parlare.
At faying leffons, none ought to fpeak but he
 ripetere lezione dovere parlare
that is appointed by the mafter, whofe leave ought
 deftinato   maeftro permeffo dovere
to be afked before the fcholars betake themfelves
 domandare prima fcolare darfi
to play.
 giuoco.
  The boy that is chaftifed becaufe of his flothful-
  ragazzo caftigato a cagione infingardag-
nefs, has no caufe to accufe his mafter of feverity;
gine avere caufa accufare maeftro feverità
he ought to blame himfelf, and to refolve to fhake
 dovere biafimarfi   rifolvere lofciare
off idlenefs for the future.
 pigrizia per l'avvenire.
  The foldier muft fight valiantly, that has a mind
   foldato dovere batterfi valorofamente avere anima
enflamed with a defire to conquer the enemy; his
 accefo defiderio vincere nemico
arm muft procure him the honour which his heart
braccio dovere procurare onore   cuore
wifhes for; but fometimes fecret ftratagems and
defiderare ma qualche volta fecreto ftratagemma
fubtle policy defeat the moft valiant warriors.
aftuto politica fconfiggere valorofo guerriero.
  Children muft be obedient to their parents; thofe
   figlio dovere ubbidire genitore
that grieve their parents, purchafe to themfelves a
 affliggere parente comprare
curfe; they provoke God to deny them that length
maledizione irritare Iddio ricufare lunghezza
of life which he has promifed to the dutiful.
 vita   avere promeffo ubbidiente.

To

To be like, *when followed by a noun, signifies in Italian* rassomigliare, *and will have a Dative case.*

Children are not always like their parents; they
figliuolo   rassomigliare sempre   parente
are sometimes quite different from them.
essere qualche volta   differente.

My brother is not like my father, who is of a
fratello   rassomigliare   padre
good disposition, and rich in good endowments of
buono   indole   ricco   buono   talento
mind, though poor in estate.
animo   benchè povero stato.

Every man loves those that are like him, and
ognuno   amare   rassomigliare
despises those that are hurtful to him; nature
sprezzare   nuocevole   natura
teaches us to love our friends, but religion teaches
insegnare   amare   amico   ma religione insegnare
to love our enemies.
amare   nemico.

To be so kind *in English, must be rendered in Italian by* avere la bontà, *with the following verb in the infinitive mood, with the article* di.

I intreat you to be so kind as to tell me how
supplicare   avere la bontà   dire   come
you call that —— in Italian.
chiamare   Italiano.

If you will be so kind as to grant me that favour,
se v. s. volere aver la bontà accordare   favore
there is nothing but I will do to acknowledge it.
niente   fare   riconoscere.

If your brother would be so kind as to lend me
fratello   prestare
a horse for two, or three days, he would oblige
cavallo   due   tre giorno   obbligare
me infinitely.
infinitamente.

E   I was

ITALIAN EXERCISES.

I was this morning with your friend Mr. N——
 essere mattina con   amico
and he was so kind as to offer me his purse.
   avere   esibire   borsa.

I hope you will be so kind as to recommend me
 sperare   avere   raccommandare
to your friends.
   amico.

Be so kind as to tell me when your sister will
 avere   dire   quando sorella
return from the country, for I make no doubt
ritornare   campagna   dubitare
but she will bring me news from my uncle.
   portare nuova   zio.

The English phrase, there is nothing but, *ought to be rendered in Italian by* non v'è niente che non, *and requires the following verb in the Optative mood.*

There is nothing but I would do to deserve the
non v'è niente   fare meritare
honour of your friendship.
onore   amicizia.

There is nothing but what I would undertake
non v'è niente   intrapprendere
to oblige my friends.
obbligare amico.

There is nothing but what I would suffer wil-
non v'è niente   soffrire vo-
lingly, if I was so unfortunate as to have disobliged
lentieri essere sfortunato   avere disobbligato
you.

There is nothing but what an honest man ought
 non vi è niente   onesto uomo dovere
to do, to deserve every body's esteem.
   meritare ognuno stima.

There is nothing but what a good prince ought
    niente   buono principe dovere
to do, to make his subjects happy.
fare rendere soggetto felice.

This

ITALIAN EXERCISES.

This phrase to be so good as one's word, *must be rendered in Italian by* mantenere la sua parola.

You often promised me to do me service, but I
    spesso promettere   rendere   servizio ma
I will never believe you; it is a very dishonest
   mai   credere   essere   disonesto
thing not to be as good as one's word; for no
    mantenere   la sua   parola perchè nis-
body will credit him afterwards.
suno   dare fede   dopo.

You have often promised me to mend your man-
  avere spesso promettere   emendare   cos-
ners, but you are seldom as good as your word.
tume ma   rare volte mantenere la sua parola.
I confess I have not been as good as my word, but
confessare avere   mantenuto la sua parola. ma
I do promise that for the future, I will be better
  promettere (all'avvenire)   essere
than I ever have been.
  mai essere stato.

So much as, *ought to be rendered in Italian by* tanto.

Your brother seems to have had a better educa-
   fratello parere   avere   educa-
tion than you, though I am sure your father did
zione   benchè   sicuro   padre
not spend so much money for him as he did for you.
spendere tanto denaro.
If we would love God as much as he loves us,
   amare Iddio tanto   amare
we would not offend him so often.
   offendere   spesso.
If we would love our neighbour as much as we
    amare   prossimo   tanto
love ourselves, there would not be so much enmity
                  essere tanto inimicizia
in the world.
  mondo.

ITALIAN EXERCISES.

As long as, *muſt be rendered in Italian, by* infinchè, *or* mentrechè.

As long as you will not be obedient to your pa-
    mentrechè   eſſere ubbidiente   pa-
rents, God will never bleſs you.
rente Iddio   mai benedire.
  As long as you will be idle, you will never learn
   Infinchè   eſſere   pigro   mai impa-
any thing, and you will be ignorant as long as
rare niente   eſſere   ignorante   infinchè
you live.
vivere.
  As long as you are rich, you will not want
              eſſere ricco   mancare
friends. As long as it is in your power to oblige
amico.   eſſere   potere   obbligare
your friends, don't refuſe to do them ſervice.
   amico   ricuſare rendere   ſervizio.

I had rather, *is expreſſed in Italian by* amerei meglio, *or* piuttoſto.

  I had rather loſe ſome ſmall thing, than go to
    amare meglio perdere   piccolo coſa   andare
law with a litigious man.
legge   litigioſo uomo.
  I had rather die than diſoblige you.
    amare piuttoſto morire diſobligare.
  I had rather live all my life-time with you, than
    amare meglio vivere   vita tempo
to ſtay one day with your brother.
  ſtare   giorno   fratello.
  I had rather endure ſome ſmall injury from a
              ſoffrire   piccolo ingiuria
friend, than to fight with him, though I had rather
amico   batterſi   benchè
die than paſs for a coward.
morire   paſſare   poltrone.

When

ITALIAN EXERCISES.

When we enquire for somebody's name, we make use of the verb chiamarsi.

What is your name, pray, friend?
  come chiamare   di grazia amico.
My name is John Baptist.
  Giovanni Battista.
What is your brother's name?
  come   fratello.
His name is George Frederic Augustus.
  Giorgio Frederico Augusto.
What was the late king of France's name?
  Come   defunto Rè   Francia.
He was called Lewis the Fifteenth.
  chiamare   Luigi   diecimo quinto.
What is the young king of France's name?
  come   giovine Rè   Francia.
His name is Lewis the Sixteenth.
  chiamare   Luigi   deicimo sisto.
What was the late regent's name?
  come   defunto regente.
He was called the Duke of Orleans.
chiamare   duca   Orleans.

To entertain *must be turned by* trattare.

If you will come with me into the country, I'll
      venire   campagna
entertain you very well.
trattare   benissimo.
You see I do not entertain you like a stranger,
  vedere   trattare   da   forestiere
but I entertain you like a friend.
ma trattare   da   amico.
I am sure if we were lords, you could not enter-
  essere sicuro   signore   trat-
tain us better.
tare   meglio.

Ciò dipende da voi, *signifies in English*, it lies in your power, *it has all its tenses; and is Impersonal.*

It lies in your power to be a good scholar, for
dipendere   essere   sapiente
you have as much wit as any of your school-fellows.
perchè avere tanto spirito qualunque   condiscipolo.

It is in our power to be happy for ever.
dipendere   essere felice   sempre.

It is in his power to do me that service.
dipendere   rendere   servizio.

It is in your power to go abroad, for your father
dipendere   andar a viaggiare   padre
told me several times that he should be very glad
dire   (sì esse volte)   avere a caro
if you would go on your travels.
andare a viaggiare.

It lies in their power to recommend me to their
dipendere   raccommandare
friends.
amico.

Andare all' incontro d' uno, *signifies* to go and meet somebody.

Sir, I come to beg a favour of you, which I
Signore venire domandare favore
hope you will not refuse me. I heard your uncle
sperare   ricusare   sentire   zio
will come to-morrow to town, you will oblige me
venire   domani   città   obbligare
mightily, if you will lend me your horse to go and
moltissimo   prestare   cavallo andare
meet him, and I assure you that I will take great care
all' incontro   assicurare   avere grande cura
of him.

Sir, I am very sorry I cannot oblige you, for I
rincrescere   non potere obbligare   perchè
must go myself to meet my wife, who is coming
bisogna andare all'incontro   moglie   venire
from

from the country; but at another time, it shall be
  campagna ma altro volta   essere
at your service.
  servizio.

Very often we make use of this expression rincrescere, *when we speak of the misfortune of another, and signifies in English* to be sorry, to be concerned; *and the following word must be in the Genitive.*

 I am sorry for the misfortune that has befallen you.
  rincrescere disgrazia   accadere
 We ought to be concerned at our friends mis-
  dovere rincrescere   amico sven-
fortunes.
tura.
 I was very much concerned at your loss.
  moltissimo rincrescere   perdita.

Mi pare mill' anni *is an Italian expression which signifies* to long; *we make use of it only in the present of the Indicative, and the following verb ought to be in the Infinitive with the article* di.

 I long to see your father, to tell him how much
    vedere padre dire   quanto
you deserve to be praised for your diligence.
  meritare essere lodato   diligenza.
 I long to go in the country, to settle a dispute
    andare   campagna aggiustare disputa
that arose amongst my farmers.
 nascere fra fattore.
 I long to pay what I owe you, for I don't love
    pagare   dovere perchè   amare
to be in any body's debt.
  dovere a nessuno.
 I long to know the Italian language perfectly
     sapere Italiano lingua perfettamente
well.
bene.

Very often we make use of avere gran voglia *for to long, and it requires the following verb in the Infinitive mood.*

I long to go and see Mr. George, to ask him for
        andare vedere   Giorgio   domandare
the money he owes me, but I'll put it off till next
  denaro dovere   ma differire infino venturo
week, that you may go with me.
settimana   potere andare.

I long to go to Italy, for I don't love to live in
      andare Italia   · amare vivere
England.
Inghilterra.

I long to tell you something, nevertheless I do not
      dire   qualche cosa   benchè
know how to tell it you, for fear of disobliging you.
sapere   dire   per paura disobbligare.

I long to learn Italian, and for all that I do not
    imparare italiano   con tutto ciò
know what hinders me from beginning.
sapere   impedire   principiare.

Degnare *is very often used for* to be so kind as, *and requires the following verb in the Infinitive.*

Be so kind as to hear me a moment, and you
  degnare   sentire   momento
will see that what they told you of me is a false
  vedere   dire   essere falso
report.
rapporto.

Be so kind as to grant me that favour, and I will
  degnare   accordare   favore
not trouble you any more.
incommodare.

Posso

Posso appena, I can hardly, *requires the following verb in the Infinitive mood.*

I can hardly believe what you tell me of Mr.
posso appena   credere   dire   signore
Gregory, for I always took him for a very sober
Gregorio perchè   sempre credere   sobrio
and honest man.
onesto uomo.

I could hardly believe my eyes, when I saw you,
potere appena credere   occhio quando vedere
for I thought you were in America.
perchè pensare   essere   America.
I have got such a great cold, and my head is so
essere   raffreddato   testa
heavy that I can hardly read a word.
pesante   potere appena leggere parola.

Scarce, *or* hardly, *must be likewise expressed by* appena.

Scarce were you gone out last night, when your
appena essere   uscito jeri sera   quando
friend sir William Henry came to see me, and was
amico cavaliere Guglielmo Enrico venire vedere
very sorry you did not stay a little longer.
dispiacere   restare poco   più.
There are men in the world who are so much
essere uomo   mondo   essere   tanto
used to do mischief, that hardly they are come out
avezzo fare male   appena   essere   uscito
of one trouble, but fall immediately into another.
impaccio ma cadere subito   altro.
Scarce have you done a good action but it seems
appena avere   fatto buono azione   parere
you repent you have done it; for if it was not so,
pentirsi   avere fatto   perchè   essere   così

ITALIAN EXERCISES.

you would not so soon fall again into your former
     così presto ricadere   *primiera*
bad courses.
cattiva vita.

To have much ado *must be rendered in Italian by*
 stentare, *and requires the following verb in the Infi-*
 nitive with the article a.

  I had much ado yesterday to persuade your bro-
    stentare   *jeri* *persuadere*   *fra-*
ther to stay with me; he would go and sup with
tello *restare*   *andare* *cenare*
Mr. Horace, who killed a man last night.
signor Orazio *ammazzare uomo jer sera.*
  I had much ado to make peace with your mo-
   stentare   *fare pace*   *ma-*
ther, she was fully resolved not to forgive you,
dre *essere affatto risoluto* *perdonare*
therefore take care for the future not to offend her
perciò *badare* *all'avvenire*   *offendere,*
any more.

  I had much ado to engage your uncle to pass
   stentare   *impegnare* *zio* *passare*
his word for a hundred pounds I owe Mr. Clements.
 parola *cento* *lira* *dovere* *Clemente.*

To be quiet *must be rendered in Italian by* star saldo,
 or chetarsi.

  You will not be quiet till you have done some
   stare   *saldo infinchè aver fatto*
mischief.
male.
  Be quiet, or else I'll make you repent it.
  chetarsi *altrimente fare* *pentire.*
  You would not be quiet when I bad you, you
   stare   *saldo quando commandare.*
see now what you suffer for it.
vedere adesso *soffrire.*

               Abbas-

ITALIAN EXERCISES. 83

Abbaſſare gli occhi, *ſignifies* to look downwards.

When you ſpeak to a perſon of great quality,
quando   parlare   perſona   alto   qualità
you ought not to ſtare at him, but you ought
dovere   fiſſare   ma   dovere
ſometimes to look downwards to ſhew him the
qualche volta   abbaſſare gli occhi   moſtrare
reſpect you have for him.
riſpetto   avere.

Upon Interrogations. See *Gram.* p. 70.

From whence had America its name? From
                avere America   nome.
Americo Veſputio, a Florentine, in 1497, though
Americo (a) *Veſpuzio   Fiorentino   benchè*
Columbus was the firſt diſcoverer of it in 1492.
Columbo   eſſere   primo ſcopritore

How large is that country? How is that empire
grande   paeſe   imperio
divided? What is the produce of it? What is
diviſo   prodotto
worthy of notice in that country? Are there any
degno   notizia   paeſe
European colonies in that part of the world?
Europeano   colonia   parte   mondo.

Who ſubdued the greateſt part of the univerſe
ſoggiogare   grande parte   univerſo
in twelve years time? Alexander, king of Mace-
duodici   anno   Aleſſandro   Rè   Mace-
donia.
donia.

To whom do the Canary Iſlands belong, what
Canari Iſola   appartenere
number is there of them, and how do they lie?
numero (b) *eſſere   eſſere   ſituato.*

(a) See *Gram.* p. 212, upon the conjunction *Though.*
(b) See ibid. p. 150, upon the conjugation of the verb impersonal *there is.*

E 6   Upon

Upon the irregular Constructions of the Pronouns personal and Possessive. See *Gram.* p. 61, and 66.

Most men worship love, to it they sacrifice their
la più parte uomo adorare amore   sagrificare
finest days, and from it they expect their greatest
bello   giorno   aspettare   grande
happiness.
felicità.
Glory makes the whole ambition of heroes; they
gloria fare   tutto   ambizione   eroe
gape after nothing else; they seek for nothing else;
respirare altro   cercare   altro
they apply to it alone; 'tis for it alone they make
indirizzarsi solo   solo   fare
vows.
voto.
Self-love is our primum mobile; 'tis it rules our
amore proprio   primo   mobile   regolare
passions, and to it men are indebted for most of
passione   uomo essere debitore
the services which they reciprocally render one
servizio   reciprocamente rendere
another.
Is that the tree of which you were speaking?
essere   albero   parlare
Yes, that's it.
It looks very fine, but its fruit is good for nothing.
parere bello   ma   frutto   (non vale niente.)
This on the contrary has no appearance: 'tis a
contrario avere   apparenza
peach-tree, and its peaches are charming good.
persico   persica essere delizioso.
When general G. saw himself pursued so close, he
quando generale G. vedere   seguitato   vicino
reached the river, and threw himself in it (on horse-
arrivare   fiume   gettarsi   a ca-
back)

back) with a defign to crofs it over, tho' it was fo rapid-
vallo   intenzione attraverfare (a) *benchè   rapido*
When he came to the ftream, for all that he did
quando   venire   corrente   tutto   fare
to refift it, he could not conquer it; he then re-
refiftere   potere   foggiogare   allora ri-
folved to go down with it, and let himfelf be car-
folvere   feguire   lafciarfi   por-
ried away by it; but his horfe was too tired to be
tare via   ma   cavallo effere troppo ftanco
able to fwim long; and as he endeavoured to quit
potere nuotare molto   come   sforzarfi   lafciare
the ftream, his horfe, that had loft all his ftrength,
corrente   cavallo   avere perfo tutto   forza
fell under him. He expected it, and therefore did
cadere   afpettarfi   perciò
not wonder at it. He ftill fwam (for a while) with
maravigliarfi   ancora nuotare (per un pezzo)
the ftream, but not being able to leave it, he was
corrente   ma   potere   lafciare   effere
drowned in it.
affogato.

The water which you have recommended him to
acqua   avere raccomandato
drink is not fit for him; I know all its qualities,
bere effere proprio   conofcere tutto   qualità
and will never recommend it in fuch a cafe. Of
mai raccomandare   tale   cafo.
thefe two rivers, one has its fpring in the Alps,
quefto due fiume   avere   forgente   Alpi
and the other has it in the Pyreneans.
altro avere   Pirenei.
I have bought a new fword, the hilt of it is fil-
avere comprato nuovo fpada   guardia   effere ar-
ver, but I don't like its fhell; I will not part with
gento ma   amare   coccia   disfarfi
the old one; it has done me much fervice, I have
vecchio   avere refo   molto fervizio   avere

(a) See *Gram.* p. 212, upon the conjunction *though.*

owed

86 ITALIAN EXERCISES.

owed twice my life to it. Only I will get it
dovuto due volta vita   solo   fare
cleaned, and put a new hilt to it, and it will be of
ripolire   mettere nuovo guardia   servire
service still to me by night.
ancora   nottetempo.

Keep from the wall, do not go near it.
allontanarsi muro   appoggiarsi.

If you sit in that (easy chair) take care not to
sedere   sedia a bracciuoli   badare
hurt yourself, for the back and elbows are broken.
farsi male, perchè dosso bracciuolo essere rotto.

His house is fine, I like its situation, but the
casa   bello amare   situazione ma
rooms are not well contrived. He has spent a great
stanza essere bene regolato   avere fatto gran
deal of money upon it; he has altered the roof,
spesa   avere fatto cambiar tetto
and made a stately stair-case; it costs him much,
fatto superbo scala   costare   molto
(but upon the whole) he owes his health to it; he
ma per altro   dovere   salute
lives there all the year. His gardens are very fine;
vivere tutto anno   giardino essere bello
he has added groves, and water-spouts to it; there
aver aggiunto boschetto   getto d'acqua
are fine meadows round it. He designs to make
essere bello prato all'intorno   intendere fare
alterations to it.
cambiamento.

Upon the verb to play, with the particles at, and upon.

Do you never play at cards? I play sometimes
mai giuocare carta   qualche volta
at picket, and at quadrille, to oblige the company.
picchetto   quadriglio obbligare   compagnia.

Let us play for a crown. I never play so high;
giuocare scudo   mai   grosso giuoco
I don't care to play so much money: I don't love
curarsi   tanto danaro   amare
to

ITALIAN EXERCISES.

to play at games of chance, as at dice, or even at
giuoco di sorte come dado anche
cards; but I like to play sometimes at bowls, at
carta. piacere qualche volta boccie,
billiards, at tennis, or nine pins. My cousin and
bigliardo pallacorda birillo cugino
I play at chess every night. Can you play upon
scacchi ogni sera sapere suonare
some instrument?
qualche stromento.

I can play a little upon the German flute. I
potere suonare poco Fagotto
thought you could play on the fiddle too. No;
credere suonare violino
but I know that you play on the (bass-viol) very
ma sapere suonare (basso di viola)
well. If you please to come to our house, we will
piacere venire casa
make a little concert. My sister will play on the
fare piccolo accademia sorella suonare
harpsichord, you will play on your bass, and I will
clavecembalo suonare basso
sing.
cantare.

We use the verb avere *instead of* essere, *when we speak of being* hungry, dry, cold, hot, *and* old.

You eat as if you were hungry. Excuse me, I
mangiare avere fame scusare
eat heartily, but I am not very hungry. I am
di buon appetito avere grande fame avere
more dry than hungry. I have been thirsty all
sete fame aver avuto sete tutto
the day.
giorno.

I am very cold, and very hungry. Are you cold?
avere freddo fame avere freddo
on the contrary, I am very warm, but I am tired.
al contrario avere gran caldo ma stanco.

My hands are so cold that I cannot write.
　　mano avere　freddo　　　　potere scrivere.
I believe your head is always cold, for you sel-
　credere　　　testa　sempre freddo　perchè ra-
dom pull off your hat.
ramente levare　cappello.
How old is your sister? She is not fifteen yet.
quanto anno avere sorella　　avere　quindici anno.
I thought she was twenty, how old are you?
　credere　　avere venti anno　　avere.
I was very cold this morning when I came; but
　avere　freddo　mattina. quando venire　ma
I am very warm now. You don't look so. You
　　caldo. adesso　　　parere
eat as if you were not hungry. I am more cold
mangiare　　avere　fame　　　　　fete
than hungry. I have been thirsty all the day.
　fame　　essere stato assetato　　giorno.

The verb impersonal must, *sometimes it is turned by* dovere, *and sometimes by* bisognare.

To make war, plenty of money must be had.
　　fare guerra molto　danaro bisogna　avere.
Men must love virtue to be happy. One must be
si dovere amare virtù　felice　　　bisognare
mad to think that men can be happy without
matto credere　uomo potere　　　senza (a)
loving virtue.
amare　virtù.
Men should learn first the duties belonging to hu-
　　dovere imparare prima dovere appartenente　uma-
man nature.
no　natura.
A woman must have a good deal of circum-
　donna　bisogna avere　　　　　　circo-
spection not to speak of herself. One must not
spezione　　parlare　　　　　bisognare

(a) *Senza* governs the infinitive mood.

　　　　　　　　　　　　　　　　　hope

hope that men can be cured of the ill habit they
sperare   uomo potere   guarirsi   cattivo abitudine
have of speaking always of themselves, their adven‑
avere   parlare sempre   avven‑
tures, and wealth, than which nothing is more
tura   opulenza   niente
tedious. One should impose a law upon one's self,
seccante   dovere   farsi   legge
never to speak of one's self, neither one way, or other.
mai   parlare   (a)

We must not sillily believe those who flatter us; nei‑
dovere facilmente credere   lusingare   nè
ther must we reject rudely the compliments that are
rigettare incivilmente   complimento
paid us, when we think we deserve them; that
fare   quando   credere   meritare
false modesty is hardly less shocking than a foolish
falso modestia   poco meno spiacevole   sciocco
vanity. Much art and nicety are requisite to season
vanità   arte   delicatezza necessario   condire
praises well. But there is also a way of receiving
lode   ma   anche modo   ricevere
them, when they are lawful, which don't hurt
quando   leggitimo   offendere
modesty. Praises are like a sort of tribute that is
modestia   lode   come   specie   tributo
paid to true merit. We must neither reject them
rendere vero merito   dovere   nè rigettare
through affectation, nor hanker after them too
per   affettazione nè   ambire   (con troppa
eagerly.
premura.)

Upon the negative Particles and Adverbs.

None knows the sufferings of lovers unless he
nissuno sapere   sofferenza   amante   se non
has loved.

(a) *Neither one way, or other,* i. e. *nè in bene, nè in male.*

I have

I have always loved her very much.
sempre amato   molto.
To love but little in courting, is a sure means
amare   poco   corteggiare   vero mezzo
to be loved. I have seen nobody of your sentiment.
amato   avere veduto nessuno   sentimento.
I by no means believe what he says; nor I neither.
in conto nessuno credere   dire   nemen'io.
She always comes unseasonably, as well as her
sempre venire fuor di stagione   come   anche
sister.
sorella.
He has not received an answer yet.
avere   ricevuto   risposta ancora.
Is there any thing more wonderful than the
niente   ammirabile
virtue of the loadstone?
virtù   calamita.
Did he ever mention any thing of it?
mai menzionare   niente.
We have done nothing that ought to make you
avere fatto niente   dovere
angry.
stizzire.
I am going there, lest he should come.
andare   per paura venire.
I tell you that if henceforth I perceive that you
dire   se da qui innanzi accorgersi
attempt to play any trick to hinder me from marry-
tentare   fare   furberia impedire   mari-
ing my son, I will send you directly to the castle,
tare   figliuolo   mandare   subito   castello
for all your life. I promise you I'll never do it.
tutto   vita   promettere   mai fare.
She is indifferent to me; and I neither love nor
indifferente   amare
hate her. [*odiare.*]
They behave very prudently, now they are
comportarsi   prudentemente ora   essere
under my care.
sotto   cura.

She

ITALIAN EXERCISES.

She has neither relations nor friends.
avere   nè   parente   nè   amico.
I will never forgive you, unless you promise to
mai perdonare   se non   promettere
see her. She is so ill that she can take nothing,
vedere   stare male   potere pigliare
but she throws it up presently.
che   rendere   subito.
I will not take a purge before the winter is
pigliare medicina prima   Inverno
quite out.
affatto passato.
Why don't he boldly tell her his reasons?
perchè   liberamente dire   ragione.
He knows not where to meet her now.
sapere   dove   rincontrare adesso
I ask nothing but what is just; I cannot pay
domandare   che   giusto   non potere pa-
others, if I am not paid what is due to me.
gare altro   pagare   essere dovuto.

Upon the Conjunctions.

Although I have no money, I cannot resolve to
benchè   avere   danaro non potere   risolvere
borrow any of my friends. Obey, or else you shall
imprestare   amico   ubbidire altrimente (a)
be whipped.
staffilate.
When I punish you for your faults, you think
quando   punire   fallo   credere
I hate you; whereas 'tis only because I love you,
odiare   in vece che   perchè   amare
I take that trouble.
prendere   incomodo.
Your brother came to see me yesterday as soon
fratello venire   vedere   ieri   subito

(a) Turn, *voi avrete le staffilate.*

as

as you was gone. If he comes again, be so good
che   partire   ritornare   avere   bontà
as to tell him that I have waited for him 'till now.
   dire   avere aspettato   fin' ora.
Though I used my utmost endeavours, and neg-
  benchè   fare   tutto il suo possibile   tras-
lected nothing to please him, yet he was constantly
curare niente   piacere   nientedimeno continuamente
scolding at me.
sgridare.
That Adrian, whether she is Pamphilus's wife,
  Adriana   che   Pamfilo   moglie
or whether she is but his mistress, is with child.
o   che   amorosa   gravida.
Either through taste, or reason, or caprice, she
    sia   per   gusto   ragione   capriccio
has married him.
    sposare.
Wars are not so bloody since gunpowder is used.
guerra   sanguinoso dacchè polvere a cannone in uso.
Unless a book is instructive or entertaining, I
  a meno libro   istruttivo   piacevole
don't care to read it.

Whether she is writing, or reading, she will
  che   scrivere   leggere   volere
have her parrot with her.
avere pappagallo.
Since you have forbidden him, he does it no more.
 dacchè   avere. proibito   fare
If he should call at my house, and I was not at
           passare   da me   essere
home, my people would tell him where I am.
casa   gente   dire   dove.
Whether he wins, or loses, he is always the same.
  sia guadagnare perdere   sempre   l'istesso.
I will not go thither, unless you go along with me.
          andare   a meno   meco.
You must not play before you can say your lesson.
    dovere   giuocare prima   sapere   lezione.

He

ITALIAN EXERCISES.

Why don't you learn it then, instead of losing
perchè   imparare   dunque in vece   perdere
your time? He is so far from being forward, that
tempo   in vece   essere avanzato
he knows nothing at all. Far from following my
sapere   niente affatto   in luogo   seguire
advice, he does not mind what I say to him.
consiglio   badare   dire.

I will rather consent to lose all, than give up
piuttosto acconsentire perdere   rinunziare
my right.

Though you were a king, I would not marry you.
se   essere Rè   sposare
Would to God I was under his tuition still, and
volere   essere sotto   condotta ancora
my father had never removed me from his school.
padre   avere mai   ritirato   scuola.

It avails nothing to a girl to be young, without
servire niente   ragazza   giovine   senza
being handsome, nor to be handsome without be-
bello   nè   essere   senza
ing young.
giovine.

After you have done your exercise, you must
dopo   fare   esercizio   dovere
read it over two or three times, to correct the faults
leggere   due   tre   volta   correggere   errore
you may have done in it.
potere   fare

Remember what I told you several times, that
ricordarsi   dire   parecchie volte
you will never be able to speak, or write Italian,
*   mai   potere   parlare scrivere Italiano*
unless you are master of your rules.
a meno   possedere   regola.

I will take so much pains that I hope I shall speak
pigliare   tanto pena   sperare
it before it is long, though I am convinced it is very
frà   peco   benchè   convinto
difficult to learn the Italian tongue perfectly well.
difficile imparare   Italiano lingua perfettamente.

You

You will not find it so hard, if you learn well
．．．．．．．．．trovare．．．．．．difficile．．．．．．．．．．bene
your principles.

The narrowness of the mind, ignorance, and
．．．bassezza．．．．．．．．．．．．．anima．．ignoranza
presumption, make stubbornness; because obstinate
．presunzione．．fare．．ostinazione．．perchè．．．ostinato
people will believe nothing but what they appre-
．．gente．．．．．．credere．．．．．．．．che．quel．．．comp ren-
hend, and they apprehend but very few things.
dere．．．．．．．．．．．．．．．．．．．．．．．．．．．poco．．．．cosa.

Upon most Prepositions.

I rather chuse to live in the country than in
．．．．．．amare meglio．．vivere．．．．．campagna
town, especially at Florence. Therefore I intend
città．．．．sopra．．．．tutto Firenze．．Perciò．．．．fare
to set out to-morrow for my castle, and then I will
conto partire domani．．．．．．．．castello．．e．．poi
send my eldest son to Sicily, for the summer.
mandare．．primogenito figlio Sicilia．．．．．．．estate.

Where will you go to-night? To the play.
．．dove．．．．．．andare stasera．．．．．．．commedia.

When shall I dance, sir? You shall dance in
quando．．．．．．．ballare
your turn, and not before.
．．volta．．．．．．．prima.

Where do you live, sir? I live in St. James's-
．．．．．．．．．vivere．．．．．．．．．．．．．．San Giacomo
street, near a fruiterer's, over-against a taylor's,
strada vicino．．fruttajuolo．．dirimpetto．．．．．sartore
at the sign of the Queen's-head. The best way to
．．．．．insegna．．．regina testa．．．．．．．．．．via
go to my house, is to pass through the Park, since
andare．．．casa．．．．passare attraverso Parco giacchè
I live behind it. I design to travel first all over
．．．．．di dietro．．．．．intendere．．viaggiare tutto
England, and France, then to Germany, and
Inghilterra．．．Francia．．poi．．．．．Germania
．．．．．．．．．．．．．．．．．．．．．．．．．．．．．．．．．．．Italy;

ITALIAN EXERCISES. 95

Italy; from Italy to Spain, where I shall embark
Italia   Spagna   dove   imbarcarsi
a board a ship to return to Great Britain.
a bordo   nave   ritornare   Gran Bretagna.
   I'll go to Scotland in six months, or thereabouts.
    andare   Scozzia fra sei   mesi   o   incirca.
I will call upon our partners within twelve days;
    passare   compagno   fra   duodia   giorno
and I will wait upon them as far as their seat, which
   accompagnare   infino   villa
is magnificent; was you ever there? The walls
   magnifico   essere   mai   parete
are built with marble; the stair-case is painted in
  fabbricato   marmo   scala   depinto
oil; all the furniture is worked with the needle,
oglio tutto   fornimento   fatto   ago
nothing richer can be seen.
    ricco   potere   vedere.
   I should be mighty glad to spend a few days at
    avere a caro   spendere poco giorno
that wonderful seat. How far is it?
meraviglioso villa   lontano.
It is a great way off; it is about forty leagues off.
  molto lontano di qui   incirca   lega.
The most uneasy situation is to be between fear
    incommodo situazione   fra   timore
and hope. Heroes formerly sacrificed themselves
speme   eroe anticamente sacrificarsi
for their country, and their mistress; now-a-days
   patria   amata   oggi   di
nothing is done but for fortune and pleasure.
 niente   fare   fortuna   piacere.
   A woman can please without beauty and sense,
   donna   potere piacere senza   bellà   senso
but she can hardly do it without wit and agreeableness.
ma   appena   spirito   piacevolezza.
   There is no less eloquence in the tone of the voice,
    meno   eloquenza   tuono   voce
the eyes, and the countenance, than in the choice
 occhio   aspetto   scelta
of words.
  parola.   Europe,

Europe, in relation to the other parts of the
Europa   relazione   altro   parte
world, lies northward. It is bounded on the eaſt
mondo eſſere ſituato ſettentrione   confinato   oriente
by Aſia, and the Black Sea, which communicates
Aſia   Nero Mare   communicare
with the Mediterranean by the ſtreights of Con-
Mediterraneo   ſtretto   Co-
ſtantinople; on the ſouth by Africa, and the Me-
ſtantinopoli   mezzogiorno Africa
diterranean Sea; on the weſt by the Atlantic ocean,
mare   occidente   Atlantico oceano
and on the north by the Arctic Pole, and the great
ſettentrione   Artico Polo
icy sea; its length taken from Cape St. Vincent to
glaciale   lunghezza miſurato   Capo San Vincenzio
the frontiers of Muſcovy, is about 3600 Engliſh
confine   Muſcovia   incirca   Ingleſe
miles; and its breadth from Sweden to Greece is
mila   larghezza   Svezzia   Grecia
about 2200 miles.

France has Spain towards the ſouth, from which
Francia   Spagna   verſo   mezzogiorno
nature has divided it by the Pyrenean mountains,
natura   diviſo   Pireneo
which are of a ſurpriſing height, and extend from
ſtupendo   altezza   ſtenderſi
the Mediterranean to the great ocean, which is a
Mediterraneo   oceano
tract of 300 miles, or thereabouts.
tratto   mila   incirca.

AN

ABRIDGEMENT

OF THE

ROMAN HISTORY.

CHAP. I.
Of the ORIGIN of the ROMANS.

ALL [a] nations [b] seem [c] willing to [d] derive [e] merit from the [f] splendour of their [g] originals, and [h] where [i] history is [k] silent, they [l] generally [m] supply the [n] defect with [o] fable. The [p] Romans were [q] particularly [r] desirous of being [s] thought [t] descended from the [v] Gods, [u] as if to [x] hide the [y] meanness of their [z] real [a] ancestry. [b] Æneas, the [c] son of [d] Venus and [e] Anchises, having [f] escaped from the [g] destruction of [h] Troy, [i] after [k] many [l] adventures and [m] dangers [n] arrived in [o] Italy, [p] where he was [q] kindly [r] received by [s] Latinus,

a *nazione* b *parere* c *desideroso* d *trarre* e *merito* f *splendore* g *originale* h *dove* i *istoria* k *tacito* l *generalmente* m *sovvenire al* n *difetto* o *favola*. p *Romano* q *particolarmente* r *desideroso* s *creduto* t *disceso* v *dio* u *come se* x *nascondere* y *bassezza* z *vero* a *pro sapia* b *Enea* c *figlio* d *Venere* e *Anchise* f *scampare* g *distruzione* h *Troja* i *dopo* k *molto* l *avventura* m *pericolo* n *arrivare* o *Italia* p *dove* q *cortesemente* r *ricevuto* s *Latino.*

F king

ITALIAN EXERCISES.

ª king of the ᵇ Latins, who ᶜ gave him his ᵈ daughter ᵉ Lavinia in ᶠ marriage. Italy was ᵍ then, ʰ as it is ⁱ now, ᵏ divided into a ˡ number of ᵐ small ⁿ states, ᵒ independent of ᵖ each other, and, ᑫ consequently, ʳ subject to ˢ frequent ᵗ contentions ᵘ among themselves. ᵛ Turnus, ˣ king of the ʸ Rutuli, was the ᶻ first who ª opposed Æneas, he having ᵇ long ᶜ made ᵈ pretensions to Lavinia himself. A ᶜ war ᶠ ensued, in which the ᵍ Trojan ʰ hero was ⁱ victorious, and ᵏ Turnus ˡ slain. In ᵐ consequence of this, Æneas ⁿ built a ᵒ city, which was ᵖ called ᑫ Lavinium, in ʳ honour of his ˢ wife; and ᵗ some time after, ᵘ engaging in another ᵛ war, ˣ against ʸ Mezentius, one of the ᶻ petty kings of the ª country, he was ᵇ vanquished in ᶜ turn, and ᵈ died in ᵉ battle, after a ᶠ reign of four ᵍ years.

ʰ Ascanius, his ⁱ son, ᵏ succeeded to the ˡ kingdom, and to him, ᵐ Silvius, a ⁿ second son, whom he had by Lavinia. It would be ᵒ tedious to ᵖ recite a ᑫ dry ʳ catalogue of the kings that ˢ followed, and of whom we ᵗ know ⁿ little more than their ᵛ names; it will be ˣ sufficient to ʸ say, that the ᶻ succession ª continued for ᵇ near ᶜ four ᵈ hundred

a *rè* b *Latino* c *dare* d *figliuola* e *Lavinia* f *matrimonio* g *allora* h *come* i *ora* k *diviso* l *numero* m *piccolo* n *stato* o *independente* p *l'uno dall' altro* q *conseguentemente* r *soggetto* s *frequente* t *contesa* u *fra* v *Turno* x *rè* y *Rutuli* z *primo* a *opporsi* b *molto tempo* c *fare* d *pretensione* e *guerra* f *nascere* g *Trojano* h *Eroe* i *Vittorioso* k *Turno* l *ucciso* m *conseguenza* n *edificare* o *città* p *chiamato* q *Lavinio* r *onore* s *moglie* t *qualche tempo dopo* u *attaccare* v *guerra* x *contro* y *Mesenzio* z *regolo* a *paese* b *vinto* c *volta* d *morire* e *battaglia* f *regno* g *anno* h *Ascanio* i *figlio* k *succedere* l *regno* m *silvio* n *secondo genito* o *nojoso* p *raccontare* q *insipido* r *catalogo* s *seguire* t *sapere* u *poco* v *nome* x *bastante* y *dire* z *successione* a *continuare* b *vicino* c *quattro* d *cento*

years

years [e] in the [f] family, and that [g] Numitor was the [h] last king of Alba.

CHAP. II.

THE [a] twelfth [b] king of the [c] Latins after [d] Æneas, was [e] Amulius, who [f] circumvented his [g] brother [h] Numitor, to whom the [i] right of [k] succession [l] appertained, upon the [m] account of his [n] age. Numitor had an [o] only [p] daughter [q] called Sylvia, whom Amulius [r] made a [s] vestal nun, that there might be no [t] hopes of any [u] posterity by her, but she ([v] by whom she was [w] pregnant is [x] uncertain) was [y] brought to-bed of [z] twins, [a] Romulus and [b] Remus; who being [c] exposed by the [d] king's [e] order, and [f] privately [g] educated by one [h] Faustulus, a [i] shepherd, when they were [k] grown up, they [l] slew [m] Amulius, restored their [n] grandfather to his [o] kingdom, and [p] built [q] Rome 753 years before [r] Christ was [s] born.

Romulus having [t] put his [u] rival brother to [v] death, [w] was [x] proclaimed king by his [y] followers; and having [z] settled the [a] state of [b] affairs, [c] being in want of women, he [d] seised upon all the [e] young women that [f] came to [g] see the [h] public [i] games

 e *anno*   f *famiglia*   g *Numitore*   h *ultimo.*

a *duodecimo*   b *rè*   c *Latino*   d *Enea*   e *Amulio*   f *ingannare*   g *fratello* ,   h *Numitore*   i *dritto*   k *successione*
l *appartenere*   m *cagione*   n *età*   o *unico*   p *figlia*   q *chiamare*   r *fare*   s *vestale*   t *speranza*   u *posterità*   v *dachè*
w *gravida*   x *incerto*   y *partorire*   z *gemello*   a *Romolo*
b *Remo*   c *esporre*   d *rè*   e *ordine*   f *segretamente*
g *educare*   h *Faustulo*   i *pastore*   k *crescere*   l *uccidere*
m *restituire*   n *avo*   o *regno* ,   p *edificare*   q *Roma*
r *Cristo*   s *nascere*   t *mettere*   u *emolo*   v *morte*   w *essere*
x *proclamare*   y *seguace*   z *regolare*   a *stato*   b *affare*
c *avendo bisogno*   d *pigliare per forza*   e *giovane*   f *venire*
g *vedere*   h *pubblico*   i *giuoco.*

ITALIAN EXAMPLES.

at Rome; upon which a [a] terrible and long [b] war with the [c] Sabines [d] ensued.

The [e] Cæninenses, [f] Antemnates, and [g] Crustumini were [h] conquer'd; and [i] at last the [k] Sabines, under the [l] conduct of [m] Tatius, [n] bearing hard upon the Romans, by the [o] interposition of the [p] Sabine women that had been [q] detained at Rome, it was [r] agreed upon [s] betwixt both [t] parties, [u] that they should [v] jointly [w] inhabit Rome, and Romulus and Tatius should [x] reign [y] together. Tatius being [z] slain six [a] years after, Romulus reigned [b] alone, and [c] completed the [d] term of 38 years, having conquered the [e] neighbouring cities. At last [f] a great [g] tempest [h] arising, as he [i] held an [k] assembly at the [l] lake of Caprea, [m] he was no where to be found, being [n] tore in pieces by the [o] senators, (as it was [p] generally [q] thought) to whom he was [r] now [s] grown [t] odious upon the [u] account of his [x] cruelty. He [y] first [z] divided the city into [a] thirty [b] curiæ, and [c] three [d] tribes. The [e] poor he [f] put [g] under the [h] protection of the [i] great ones, whom he [k] named [l] patricii. He [m] triumphed [n] three times over his [o] vanquished [p] enemies; [q] first,

a *terribile* b *guerra* c *Sabini* d *seguire* e *Ceninensi* f *Antennati* g *Crustumini* h *conquistare* i *alla fine* k *Sabini* l *comando* m *Tazio* n *trattando i Romani troppo rigorosamente* o *interposizione* p *donne Sabine* q *ritenere* r *convenire* s *frà* t *partito* u *che* v *unitamente* w *abitare* x *regnare* y *insieme* z *uccidere* a. *anno* b *solo* c *compire* d *termine* e *vicino* f *grande* g *burrasca* h *sopravvenire* i *tenere* k *assemblea* l *logo* m *non si potette trovare in nissun luogo* n *sbranare* o *senatore* p *generalmente* q *credere* r *allora* s *divenire* t *odioso* u *a cagione* x *crudeltà* y *al principio* z *dividere* a *trenta* b *curie* c *tre* d *tribù* e *i poveri* f *mettere* g *sotto* h *protezione* i *grande* k *chiamare* l *patrizio* m *trionfare* n *tre volte* o *vinto* p *nemico* q *prima*.

over

over the Cæninenſes, and Antemnates, in which ᵃ war having ᵇ killed their ᶜ king ᵈ Acron with his own ᵉ hand, he ᶠ conſecrated his firſt ᵍ ſpoils to ʰ Jupiter Feretrius; ⁱ ſecondly, over the ᵏ Camerini; ˡ thirdly, over the ᵐ Fideŋates, and ⁿ Veientes.

ᵒ After an ᵖ interregnum of a ᑫ year's continuance, ʳ Numa Pompilius, a Sabine, ˢ born at ᵗ Cure, was ᵘ choſen king by the Romans, 714 years before ᵛ Chriſt was ʷ born; ˣ who ʸ applying himſelf to the ᶻ preſervation of the public ᵃ quiet, ᵇ inſtituted all the ᶜ religious ᵈ rites of the Romans. He ᵉ made an ᶠ addition of two ᵍ months to the year, which ʰ till that time had ⁱ conſiſted of ᵏ ten, and ˡ reigned forty-three years.

ᵐ The third king of the Romans was ⁿ Tullius Hoſtilius, a ᵒ man, of a ᵖ reſtleſs temper, and ᑫ fit for nothing but war. He ʳ conquer'd the Albans, and ˢ deſtroyed their city, after he had firſt ᵗ removed the ᵘ inhabitants, and all their ᵛ ſubſtance to Rome, and ʷ tore to pieces, ˣ tied ʸ betwixt two ᶻ chariots, ᵃ Metius Fufetius, ᵇ dictator of the ᶜ Albans, ᵈ convicted of ᵉ treachery. He ᶠ triumphed ᵍ three times over the Albans, the ʰ Fidenates, and the Sabines. He ⁱ reigned thirty-two years, and ᵏ periſhed with

a *guerra* b *uccidere* c *rè* d *Acrone* e *mano*
f *conſacrare* g *ſpoglia* h *Giove Feretrio* i *ſecondo*
k *Camerini* l *terzo* m *Fidenati* n *Vejenti* o *dopo*
p *interregno* q *anno* r *Numa Pompilio* s *nato* t *Cure*
u *ſcelto* v *Criſto* w *nato* x *il quale* y *applicarſi*
z *preſervazione* a *pace* b *iſtituire* c *religioſo* d *rito*
e *fare* f *addizione* g *meſe* h *fin allora* i *conſiſtere* k *dieci* l *regnare* m *il terzo* n *Tullio Oſtilio* o *uomo* p *inquieto natura* q *abile* r *conquiſtare* s *diſtruggere* t *traſportare* u *abitante* v *foſtanza* w *ſbranare* x *attaccare* y *fra* z *carro*
a *Mezio Fufezio* b *dettatore* c *Albani* d *convinto*
e *tradimento* f *trionfare* g *tre volte* h *Fidenati* i *regnare* k *perire*

his ᵃ wife, and ᵇ whole family, by ᶜ lightning from ᵈ heaven.

The ᵉ fourth king that reigned at Rome was ᶠ Ancus Martius, ᵍ grandson of Numa Pompilius, by whom the ʰ Latins were ⁱ subdued, and moſt of them ᵏ taken into the city, and ˡ settled in the ᵐ Aventine mount; ⁿ the Janiculum was ᵒ fortified by him, a ᵖ bridge made over the ᑫ Tiber, and Oſtia ʳ built. He reigned 24 years.

The ˢ fifth king of Rome was ᵗ Tarquinius Priſcus, the ᵘ ſon of ᵛ Demaratus, a ʷ Corinthian. He ˣ came to Rome from ʸ Tarquinii, a ᶻ town of Etruria, ᵃ from whence he was ᵇ called ᶜ Lucius Tarquinius. After he ᵈ came to the ᵉ government, he ᶠ augmented the ᵍ senate, ʰ subdued the ⁱ twelve ᵏ nations of Etruria, and ˡ borrowed from them the ᵐ enſigns of ⁿ ſupreme ᵒ power, the ᵖ faſces, the ᑫ trabea, the ʳ curule chair, the ˢ prætexta, and other ᵗ things of that ᵘ kind. He was ſlain by the ſons of ᵛ Ancus, after he had reigned 38 years.

His ʷ ſon-in-law Servius Tullius, the ˣ ſixth in ʸ order, ᶻ began his ᵃ reign in the year 577 before Chriſt. He was for his ᵇ rare ᶜ endowments ᵈ preferred before thoſe of the ᵉ blood royal. He firſt ᶠ inſtituted the ᵍ cenſus, and ʰ ordered it to be

a moglie   b tutta la ſua famiglia · c lampo   d cielo
e quarto   f Anco Marzio   g nipotino   h Latini   i ſoggiogato   k preſo   l ſtabilirſi   m monte Aventino   n Il Gianicolo   o fortificato   p ponte   q Tevere   r edificato   s quinto   t Tarquinio Priſco   u figlio   v Demarato   w Corinteo   x venire   y Tarquinii   z città   a dalla quale   b chiamato   c Lucio Tarquinio   d parvenire   e governo   f aumentare   g ſenato   h ſoggiogare   i duodici   k nazione   l impreſtare   m inſegnare   n ſupremo   o autorità   p faſce   q trabea   r ſedia curulea   s preteſta   t coſa   u ſorta   v Anco   w ſuocero Servio Tullio   x feſto   y ordine   z principiare   a regno   b raro   c talento   d preferito   e ſangue reale   f iſtituire   g cenſo   h lo fece

kept

ITALIAN EXERCISES.

^a kept ^b every five years; ^c divided the ^d people into ^e classes, and ^f centuries, and ^g enlarged the city: and after he had ^h governed the ⁱ kingdom with great ^k applause 44 years, he was ^l murdered by the ^m horrid ⁿ villany of a ^o daughter, and Tarquin his ^p son in-law.

The ^q seventh and ^r last king that reigned at Rome, was Tarquin, ^s firnamed ^t the Proud, whom ^u most of the ^v old Roman ^w authors ^x affirm to be the son of ^y Priscus; ^z but ^a Dionysius ^b will have him to be his grandson. He ^c managed the ^d kingdom he had ^e procured by his ^f wickedness no better than he ^g got it, being ^h cruel to the ⁱ senators, and his ^k other ^l subjects. He ^m conquered the ⁿ Volsci, the Sabines, and Gabii; and having ^o built the ^p Capitol with the ^q spoils of the cities he had ^r taken, he was ^s at last ^t turned out of the city, and his kingdom too, for a ^u rape ^v committed by his ^w son upon ^x Lucretia.

a *osservare* b *una volta ogni cinque anni* c *dividere* d *popolo* e *classe* f *centuria* g *accrescere* h *governare* i *regno* k *applauso* l *assassinato* m *orribile* n *scelleratezza* o *figlia* p *suocero* q *settimo* r *ultimo* s *cognominato* t *l'orgoglioso* u *la più parte* v *antico* w *autore* x *affermare* y *Prisco* z *ma* a *Dionisio* b *vuol che sia il suo nipotino.* c *governare* d *regno* e *procurare* f *malvagia* g *avere* h *crudele* i *senatore* k *altro* l *soggetto* m *conquistare* n *Volsci* o *edificare* p *Campidoglio.* q *spoglia* r *prendere* s *alla fine* t *scacciare* u *ratto* v *commesso* w *figlio* x *Lucrezia.*

CHAP. III.

^a KING Tarquin, with his ^b family, being ^c banished, ^d L. Junius Brutus, and ^e L. Tarquinius Collatinus were ^f made ^g consuls. ^h The former was so ⁱ severe, that he ^k scourged and ^l beheaded his own sons for ^m favouring ⁿ the banished kings, being a ^o greater ^p friend to the ^q public ^r liberty than his own family. A ^s field of the Tarquins, which ^t lay ^u betwixt the city and ^v Tiber, being ^w consecrated to ^x Mars, was ^y from thence ^z called ^a Campus Martius. ^b Brutus ^c died in the ^d war ^e against the Tarquins, who ^f prevailed upon some of the ^g neighbouring ^h nations to ⁱ assist them; ^k amongst the ^l rest, Porsena, king of Etruria, ^m made war upon the Romans, in ⁿ favour of the Tarquins: in which war the ^o bravery of ^p Horatius Coccles was very ^q remarkable, who ^r maintained the ^s fight ^t against the ^u victorious ^v enemy ^w till the ^x bridge was ^y cut down, and ^z then ^a swam the ^b river. Nor ^c must we ^d pass over in silence the ^e noble ^f attempt of ^g Mucius Scævola, who ^h secretly ⁱ entered the ^k enemy's ^l camp with a ^m resolution to ⁿ kill

a *Il rè Tarquino*   b *famiglia*   c *bandito*   d *L. Giunio Bruto*   e *L. Tarquinio Collatino*   f *fatto*   g *console*   h *il primo*   i *severo*   k *flagellare*   l *decapitare*   m *favorire*   n *i rè banditi*   o *grande*   p *amico*   q *pubblico*   r *libertà*   s *campo*   t *stare*   u *frà*   v *Tevere*   w *consecrato*   x *Marte*   y *da questo*   z *chiamato*   a *Campo Marzio*   b *Bruto*   c *morire*   d *guerra*   e *contro*   f *impetrare*   g *vicino*   h *nazione*   i *assistere*   k *frà*   l *resto*   m *fare*   n *favore*   o *bravura*   p *Orazio Coccle*   q *segnalato*   r *mantenere*   s *conflitto*   t *contro*   u *vittorioso*   v *nemico*   w *insinchè*   x *ponte*   y *tagliato*   z *allora*   a *nuotare*   b *fiume*   c *dovere*   d *passare in silenzio*   e *nobile*   f *intrapresa*   g *Mucio Scevola*   h *segretamente*   i *entrare*   k *nemico*   l *campo*   m *risoluzione*   n *uccidere.*

ITALIAN EXERCISES.

the king; ^a but having by ^b miftake ^c flain one of his nobles, he ^d thruft his ^e hand into the ^f fire that was upon the ^g altar; which fo ^h terrified the king that he ⁱ made ^k peace with the Romans, and ^l returned ^m home again. ⁿ After this, the ^o Latins made ^p war upon the Romans, ^q under the ^r conduct of ^s Octavius Mamilius, Tarquin's ^t fon in-law; ^u againft whom ^v Pofthumius being made ^w dictator, ^x vanquifhed them in a ^y memorable ^z battle at the ^a lake Regillus.

^b Afterwards a war was ^c proclaimed ^d againft the ^e Volfci, who had ^f raifed fome ^g troops, to ^h fend to the ⁱ affiftance of the ^k Latins in the ^l former war. The ^m fortune of ⁿ Caius Marcius Coriolanus was ^o remarkable in that war, who being ^p condemned in his ^q abfence, ^r retired amongft the Volfci, and ^s advifed them to ^t renew the war; for the ^u management of which being ^v chofen ^w general with ^x Tullius Accius, after he had ^y routed the Romans in ^z feveral ^a engagements, and ^b advanced up ^c to the very walls of the city, he was fo ^d moved by the ^e prayers of his ^f mother, that he ^g raifed the ^h fiege. After the ⁱ death of ^k Coriolanus, the Volfci ^l went on with the war, and

a *ma* b *fbaglio* c *ammazzare* d *mettere* e *mano* f *fuoco* g *altare* h *fpaventare* i *fare* k *pace* l *ritornare* m *cafa* n *dopo* o *Latino* p *guerra* q *fotto* r *condotta* s *Ottavio Mamilio* t *fuocero* u *contro* v *Poftumio* w *dettatore* x *vincere* y *memorabile* z *battaglia* a *Lago Regillo* b *Dopo* c *proclamare* d *contro* e *Volfci* f *levare* g *truppe* h *mandare* i *foccorfo* k *Latino* l *primo* m *fortuna* n *Caio Marzio Coriolano* o *fegnalato* p *condennato* q *affenza* r *ritirarfi* s *configliare* t *ricominciare* u *condotta* v *fcelto* w *generale* x *Tullio Accio* y *fconfitto* z *parecchio* a *battaglia* b *avanzare* c *infino ai muri* d *commoffo* e *preghiera* f *madre* g *levare* h *affedio* i *morte* k *Coriolano* l *continuare.*

were, ᵃ together with the ᵇ Æqui, and ᶜ Hernici, ᵈ soundly ᵉ beat by ᶠ Spurius Caſſius, that had been ᵍ thrice ʰ conſul, who being ⁱ elevated by his ᵏ ſucceſs, ˡ aſpired to the ᵐ throne, ⁿ but was ᵒ prevented in his ᵖ deſign, and ᵠ thrown headlong from the ʳ Tarpeian rock.

In the year 261 from the ˢ building of the city, the ᵗ common people being very ᵘ much ᵛ in debt, and ʷ provoked by the ˣ cruelty of their ʸ creditors, ᶻ retired ᵃ beyond the ᵇ Anien into the ᶜ ſacred mount, but were ᵈ reconciled by the ᵉ prudent ᶠ perſuaſions of ᵍ Menenius Agrippa; having ʰ firſt ⁱ obtained from the ᵏ fathers, that ˡ officers ſhould be ᵐ appointed to ⁿ ſkreen them from the ᵒ violence of the ᵖ patricii, who were ᵠ called ʳ tribunes of the ˢ common people.

After this, the Romans had a war with the ᵗ Veientes, which the ᵘ family of the ᵛ Fabii ʷ undertook to ˣ manage by themſelves; and having ʸ pitched their camp by the ᶻ river ᵃ Cremera, were ᵇ trepanned by the ᶜ enemy, and ᵈ cut off in one ᵉ day to the ᶠ number of 306.

The war with the ᵍ Volſci ʰ continued. They were ⁱ often ᵏ conquered, ˡ eſpecially by T. ᵐ Quinc-

a inſieme   b Equi   c Ernici   d fortemente   e battuto   f Spurio Caſſio   g tre volte   h conſole   i eſaltato   k ſucceſſo   l aſpirare   m trono   n ma   o impedito   p diſegno   q precipitato   r rupe Tarpeja   s fabbricazione   t plebe   u molto   v indebitato   w irritato   x crudeltà   y creditore   z ritirarſi   a di là   b Anieno   c ſacro monte   d riconciliato   e prudente   f perſuaſione   g Menenio Agrippa   h prima   i ottenuto   k padre   l uffıciale   m coſtituito   n proteggere   o violenza   p patrizj   q chiamato   r tribuni   s popolaccio   t Vejenti   u famiglia   v Falj   w intraprendere   x maneggiare   y accampare   z fiume   a Cremera   b acchiappare   c nemico   d ucciſo   e giorno   f numero   g Volſci   h continuare   i ſpeſſo   k conquiſtato   l ſpecialmente   m Quinzio Cincin-

tius

tius Cincinnatus, who took ᵃAntium, the ᵇ metropolis of their ᶜ nation. ᵈ Afterwards being ᵉ taken from the ᶠ plough, and ᵍ made ʰ dictator ⁱ against the ᵏ Æqui, he ˡ delivered the ᵐ consul ⁿ Minucius, who was ᵒ besieged by them, and ᵖ obliged the ᑫ enemy to ʳ pass under the ˢ yoke.

In the year 303, ᵗ after the ᵘ building of the city, and 451 years ᵛ before ʷ Christ, the ˣ form of the ʸ government was ᶻ changed. ᵃ For ᵇ instead of ᶜ consuls, the ᵈ decemviri were ᵉ set up, with ᶠ supreme ᵍ power to ʰ make ⁱ laws for the Roman ᵏ people, from those which their ˡ ambassadors had the year before ᵐ brought from ⁿ Greece. But ᵒ abusing their ᵖ power, they were ᑫ obliged to ʳ lay down their ˢ authority; and the ᵗ consuls and ᵘ tribunes were ᵛ restored.

In the 315th year of the city, Sp. Melius, in the ʷ time of a ˣ famine, ʸ endeavouring to ᶻ make his way to a ᵃ throne, by ᵇ dividing ᶜ corn ᵈ amongst the ᵉ people, was ᶠ slain by the ᵍ order of ʰ Quinctius Cincinnatus the ⁱ dictator, by ᵏ C. Servilius Ahala ˡ master of the horse. In the ᵐ following year the ⁿ Fidenates ᵒ revolt to ᵖ Lars Tolumnius,

nato   a *Anzio*   b *metropoli*   c *nazione*   d *dopo*
e *preso* f *aratro*   g *fatto*   h *dettatore*   i *contro*
k *Equi*   l *liberare*   m *consòle*   n *Minucio*   o *ossediato*
p *forzare*   q *nemico* r *passare sotto al*   s *giogo*
t *dopo*   u *fabbricazione*   v *prima*   w *Cristo*   x *forma*
y *governo*   z *cambiato*   a *perchè*   b *in vece di*   c *consòle*
d *decemviri*   e *creato*   f *supremo*   g *autorità*
h *fare*   i *legge*   k *popolo*   l *ambasciadore*   m *apportato*
n *Grecia*   o *abusarsi*   p *potere*   q *obbligato*
r *tralasciare*   s *autorità*   t *consòle*   u *tribuno*
v *ristabilito*   w *tempo*   x *carestia*   y *procurare*   z *arrivare*
a *trono*   b *dividere*   c *grano*   d *frà*   e *popolazzo*
f *ammazzato*   g *ordine*   h *Quinzio Cincinnato*
i *dettatore*   k *C. Servilio Ahala*   l *cavallerizzo*
m *seguente*   n *Fidenati*   o *rivoltarsi*   p *Larte Tolunnio*

king

king of the ^a Veientes, and ^b put the Roman ambassadors to ^c death, who had their ^d statues ^e erected in the ^f forum. The ^g Veientes ^h in the next year were ⁱ subdued by ^k Mamercus Æmilius, ^l dictator. ^m Tolumnius was ⁿ slain by ^o Cornelius Cossus, who was the ^p second from ^q Romulus that ^r dedicated the ^s spoils ^t called ^u Opima to Jupiter ^v Feretrius.

^w Censors were ^x set up at Rome in the 311th year of the city, who ^y held their ^z office ^a at first for ^b five ^c years, ^d but were ^e afterwards, in the year 320, ^f reduced by ^g Mamercus Æmilius, ^h dictator, to a year and a ⁱ half. In the year 323, the ^k dictator ^l A. Posthumius, was very ^m successful ⁿ against the ^o Æqui and the ^p Volsci; but ^q stained the ^r victory with the ^s blood of his own ^t son, whom he ^u beheaded for having ^v fought ^w contrary to his ^x orders.

In the year of the city 358, the ^y town ^z Veii was ^a taken by ^b Camillus, dictator, ^c after a ^d siege of ^e ten years. He ^f likewise ^g reduced the ^h Falisci, ⁱ not so much by his ^k arms, as the ^l opinion they had of his ^m justice

But after these ⁿ mighty ^o successes, the Romans were ^p very nigh ^q ruined by the ^r Galli Senones,

a *Vejenti*   b *mettere*   c *morte*   d *statua*   e *eretto*
f *foro*   g *Vejenti*   h *l'anno dopo*   i *soggiogato*   k *Mamerco Emilio*   l *dettatore*   m *Tolunnio*   n *ammazzato*   o *Cornelio Cosso*   p *secondo*   q *Romolo*   r *dedicare*   s *spoglia*   t *chiamato*   u *Opima*   v *Giove Feretrio*   w *censore*   x *stabilire*   y *tenere*   z *ufficia*
a *al principio*   b *cinque*   c *anno*   d *ma*   e *dopo*
f *ridotto*   g *Mamerco Emilio*   h *dettatore*   i *mezzo*
k *dettatore*   l *A. Postumio*   m *fortunato*   n *contro*
o *Equi*   p *Volsci*   q *macchiare*   r *vittoria*   s *sangue*
t *figlio*   u *decapitare*   v *battere*   w *contrario*   x *ordine*   y *città*   z *Vej*   a *preso*   b *Camillo*   c *dopo*
d *assedio*   e *dieci*   f *parimente*   g *ridurre*   h *Falisci*
i *non tanto*   k *arme*   l *opinione*   m *giustizia*   n *grande*
o *riuscita*   p *quasi*   q *rovinato*   r *Galli Senonesi*

who

ITALIAN EXERCISES. 109

who having [a] laid [b] siege to [c] Clusium in Etruria, the Romans [d] sent three of the [e] Fabian family ambassadors to them; who, [f] contrary to the [g] law of [h] nations, [i] marched out into the [k] field with the [l] Clusini against the [m] Gauls, which so [n] incensed them, that [o] leaving [p] Clusium, they marched to Rome. The Romans were [q] routed and [r] put to [s] flight in the very [t] first [u] attack at Allia. After which the city was [v] taken and [w] burnt; the [x] Capitol, [y] whither the [z] flower of the Roman [a] youth [b] retreated, was [c] besieged; and had it not been for Manlius, who was afterwards sirnamed [d] Capitolinus, had been [e] taken by the [f] barbarians in the [g] night time; but he being [h] awakened by the [i] cackling of a [k] goose, and [l] others [m] after him, [n] pushed the [o] Gauls [p] as they [q] came up, headlong down the [r] precipice. [s] In the mean time [t] Camillus, who was [u] then in [v] exile at Ardea, being [w] recalled and [x] made [y] dictator, having [z] raised an [a] army, [b] came to Rome, [c] drove them out, and at [d] about [e] eight [f] miles [g] distance from the city, [h] utterly [i] ruined their [k] whole [l] army.

a *mettere*   b *assedio*   c *Clusio*   d *mandare*   e *famiglia de' Fabj*   f *contro*   g *diritto*   h *nazione*   i *marciare*   k *campo*   l *Clusini*   m *Galli*   n *irritare*   o *lasciare*   p *Clusio*   q *sconfitto*   r *messo*   s *fuga*   t *primo*   u *attacco*   v *preso*   w *abbrucciato*   x *Campidoglio*   y *dove*   z *fiore*   a *gioventù*   b *ritirarsi*   c *assediato*   d *Capitolino*   e *preso*   f *barbaro*   g *notte tempo*   h *svegliato*   i *il gracchiare*   k *oca*   l *altro*   m *dopo*   n *spingere*   o *Galli*   p *secondo*   q *venire*   r *precipizia*   s *nell' istesso tempo*   t *Camillo*   u *allora*   v *esilio*   w *richiamato*   x *fatto*   y *dettatore*   z *levare*   a *armata*   b *venire*   c *scacciare*   d *incirca*   e *otto*   f *mile*   g *distanza*   h *affatto*   i *rovinare*   k *tutto*   l *armata.*

CHAP.

CHAP. IV.

THE city being ᵃ destroyed by the Gauls, the Romans had ᵇ thoughts of ᶜ leaving it, and ᵈ removing to ᵉ Veii; but were ᶠ dissuaded from that ᵍ design by ʰ Camillus; ⁱ whilst ᵏ Marcus Manlius, (who ˡ got the ᵐ surname of ⁿ Capitolinus for his ᵒ noble ᵖ defence of the ᵠ Capitol) ʳ endeavoured by ˢ ambition and ᵗ popular ᵘ favour ᵛ to possess himself of the ʷ supreme ˣ power, he was ʸ thrown from the ᶻ Tarpeian rock, which he had ᵃ defended in the year 370.

In the year 377, there was a ᵇ mighty ᶜ contest ᵈ betwixt the ᵉ nobility and the ᶠ commons. ᵍ C. Licinius Stolo and ʰ L. Sextius, ⁱ tribunes of the ᵏ common people, ˡ proposed a ᵐ law for ⁿ chusing ᵒ one of the consuls out of the ᵖ commons. They ᵠ carried their point at last, in the year 387, and in the ʳ following year ˢ L. Sextius was chosen consul.

ᵗ After this, the Romans had ᵘ war with the ʷ Tiburtes, the Tarquinienses, and ˣ Falisci; and again with the ʸ Gauls, who being ᶻ drawn up ᵃ in order of ᵇ battle, one of them ᶜ sent a ᵈ chal-

a *distruggere* b *idea* c *abbandonare* d *rimovere* e *Vej* f *dissuaso* g *disegno* h *Camillo* i *mentre* k *Marco Manlio* l *ebbe* m *cognome* n *Capitolino* o *nobile* p *difesa* q *campidoglio* r *cercare* s *ambizione* t *popolare* u *favore* v *impadronirsi* w *supremo* x *potere* y *precipitato* z *rocca Tarpeja* a *difendere* b *grande* c *contesa* d *frà* e *nobiltà* f *commune* g *C. Licinio Stolo* h *L. Sestio* i *tribuno* k *popolaccio* l *proporre* m *legge* n *scegliere* o *console* p *commune* q *riuscire* r *seguente* s *L. Sestio fù scelto console.* t *dopo* u *guerra* v *Tiburti* w *Tarquinienfi* x *Falisci* y *Galli* z *mettere* a *ordine* b *battaglia* c *mandare* d *disfida*

lenge

ITALIAN EXERCISES. 111

lenge to the Romans, and was [a] slain by one [b] M. Valerius, a [c] tribune of the [d] soldiers, by the [e] assistance of a [f] crow, who [g] from thence had the [h] surname of [i] Corvinus.

[k] But of all their [l] wars, none was more [m] troublesome, and [n] lasting than that [o] against the [p] Samnites; which the Romans [q] undertook the year of the city 411, at the [r] request of the [s] Campani. It [t] lasted [u] seventy years; [v] though they were [w] several times [x] beaten, as in the year 413, in which the [y] Latins [z] rose up in arms [a] against the Romans, but were the year after [b] conquered by the [c] consuls Torquatus and Decius; the [d] former of whom [e] beheaded his own [f] son for [g] fighting [h] without his [i] order; the [k] other [l] devoted himself to [m] destruction for the [n] army; after which the [o] enemies [p] submitted, but [q] soon after [r] rebelling again, they were [s] at last [t] entirely [u] reduced in the year 416.

[v] About this time the [w] Gauls [x] made a [y] peace with the Romans, which they [z] kept [a] thirty years. But in 450, the [b] Cisalpine, [c] together with the [d] Transalpine [e] Gauls, and the [f] Tuscans, [g] laid waste the [h] Roman [i] territories. The Cisalpine [k] returning [l] home [m] loaden with [n] spoils, [o] fell

a *uccidere* b *M. Valerio* c *tribuno* d *soldato* e *assistenza* f *corvo* g *da ciò* h *cognomine* i *Corvino*
k *ma* l *guerra* m *gravoso* n *durevole* o *contro*
p *Sanniti* q *intraprendere* r *richiesta* s *Campani*
t *durare* u *settanta* v *benchè* w *spesse volte*
x *battuto* y *Latino* z *prendere l'armi* a *contro*
b *conquistato* c *consoli Torquato e Decio* d *primo*
e *decapitare* f *figliuolo* g *battersi* h *senza* i *ordine* k *altro* l *consacrarsi* m *distruzione* n *armata* o *nemico* p *sottomettersi* q *poco dopo* r *ribellare* s *alla fine* t *affatto* u *ridotto* v *incirca*
w *Galli* x *fare* y *pace* z *conservare* a *trenta*
b *Cisalpino* c *assieme con* d *Transalpino* e *Galli*
f *Toscani* g *distruggere* h *Romano* i *territorio* k *ritornare* l *casa* m *caricato* n *spoglia* o *contestare*.

toge-

together by the ears about it. [a] Four years after that, having [b] joined the [c] Samnites and [d] Tuscans, they fell [e] upon the Roman [f] army [g] commanded by [h] L. Scipio, the [i] proprætor, in which [k] battle [l] P. Decius [m] the consul [n] devoted himself.

[o] Ten years after this, the [p] Galli Senones being [q] invited by the [r] Lucani, [s] Brutii, Samnites, and Tuscans, [t] besieged [u] Aretium, and having [v] vanquished [w] L. Cæcilius the [x] prætor, [y] killed 13000 of the Romans; which [z] overthrow the consul Dolobella [a] revenged upon them [b] soon after, and having [c] routed the [d] Gauls, and [e] taken their city Sena, [f] sent a [g] colony tnither. The [h] Boii being [i] moved at the [k] hard [l] fate of the [m] Senones, [n] entered into an [o] alliance with the [p] Tuscans, and [q] engaged the Romans at the [r] lake of [s] Vadimon; in which [t] fight [u] almost [v] all the Tuscans, were [w] slain, and very [x] few of the Boii [y] escaped. That [z] happened in the year of the city 471; but in the [a] following year the Boii were [b] entirely [c] reduced, which was [d] about three years [e] before [f] Pyrrhus [g] came into [h] Italy.

The [i] Palæpolitani [k] likewise, [l] where [m] now [n] Naples is, [o] venturing to make war upon the Ro-

a *quattro* b *unirsi* c *Sanniti* d *Toscani* e *lanciarsi* f *armata* g *comandare* h *L. Scipione* i *propretore* k *battaglia* l *P. Decio* m *console* n *consecrarsi* o *dieci* p *Galli Senonesi* q *invitato* r *Lucani* s *Bruzi* t *assediare* u *Arezio* v *vincere* w *L. Cecilio* x *pretore* y *ammazzare* z *sconfitta* a *vendicare* b *poco dopo* c *sconfiggere* d *Galli* e *preso* f *mandare* g *colonia* h *Bej* i *commosso* k *crudele* l *sorte* m *Senonesi* n *entrare* o *alleanza* p *Toscani* q *venire a giornata con* r *lago* s *Vadimone* t *battaglia* u *quasi* v *tutto* w *ucciso* x *poco* y *scampare* z *succedere* a *seguente* b *assfatto* c *ridotta* d *incirca* e *primache* f *Pirro* g *venire* h *Italia* i *Palepolitani* k *parimente* l *dove* m *adesso* n *Napoli* o *avventurare*.

mans, were [a] subdued the third year [b] after, [c] that is to say, in the year of the city 428, by [d] Publius the proconsul.

The [e] twelve [f] nations of the Tuscans, [g] rising for the [h] utter ruin [i] of the Roman name in the year of the city 442, were [k] routed in a great [l] battle by Fabius the [m] consul, in the [n] year 444, in which were [o] slain, or [p] taken of the [q] enemy, to the [r] number of 60,000.

In the year 472, the [s] Tarentines [t] brought the [u] Romans about their ears [v] by plundering their [w] fleet, and [x] beating their [y] ambassadors, who [z] came to [a] complain of the [b] injury. They, [c] together with the [d] Samnites, and [e] Salentines, were [f] defeated by L. [g] Æmilius Barbula. [h] Terrified at this [i] ill fortune, they [k] sent for [l] Phyrrus to their [m] assistance; who, in the year of the city 474, having [n] brought over an [o] army into [p] Italy, [q] made [r] war with the Romans, which [s] lasted six years. In the [t] first [u] encounter the Romans, [v] headed by [w] Lævinus, being [x] conquered, not so much by the [y] strength of the [z] enemy, as by the [a] strange [b] shape of the [c] elephants, [d] yielded up the [e] day, Phyrrus [f] dismissed all the [g] prisoners [h] without [i] ransom.

a *soggiogato* b *dopo* c *cioè a dire* d *Pubblio il proconsole* e *duodici* f *nazione* g *sollevarsi* h *intiero* i *rovina* k *sconfiggere* l *battaglia* m *console* n *anno* o *ucciso* p *preso* q *nemico* r *numero* s *Tarentini* t *tirarsi addosso* u *Romano* v *saccheggiare* w *flotta* x *battere* y *ambasciadore* z *venire* a *lamentarsi* b *ingiuria* c *insieme* d *Sanniti* e *Salentini* f *sconfitto* g *Emilio Barbula* h *spaventato* i *sventura* k *mandar a cercare* l *Pirro* m *ajuto* n *trasportare* o *armata* p *Italia* q *fare* r *guerra* s *durare* t *primo* u *zuffa* v *comandato* w *Levino* x *conquistato* y *forza* z *nemico* a *strano* b *forma* c *elefante* d *cedere* e *battaglia* f *mandar via* g *prigioniero* h *senza* i *riscatto*.

Soon

ITALIAN EXERCISES.

ᵃ Soon after, having ᵇ made some ᶜ fruitless ᵈ overtures of ᵉ peace by his ᶠ ambassador ᵍ Cyneas, (ʰ for ⁱ Appius Claudius ᵏ obstructed it) he ˡ engaged the Romans ᵐ twice, the ⁿ victory ᵒ both times being ᵖ dubious. He was ʳ then ˢ invited by the ᵗ Syracusans into ᵘ Sicily against the ᵛ Carthaginians; ˣ where ʸ matters ᶻ not succeeding ᵃ according to his ᵇ desires, he ᶜ returned into ᵈ Italy in the year 479; and being ᵉ defeated, ᶠ forced out of his ᵍ camp, and ʰ beaten from ⁱ Tarentum, he returned into ᵏ Epire.

CHAP. V.

ᵃ AFTER this a ᵐ war ⁿ broke out ᵒ betwixt the Romans and the ᵖ Carthaginians, in the year of the city 490, ᑫ occasioned by the ʳ ambition and ˢ formidable ᵗ power of each of them. Hiero, king of ᵘ Syracuse, and ᵛ ally of the Carthaginians, ˣ made war upon the ʸ Mamertini, who had ᶻ seized upon Messana. They ᵃ applied to the Romans for ᵇ help, who ᶜ carrying over an ᵈ army into ᵉ Sicily, ᶠ fell upon Hiero, and the Carthaginians. The ᵍ fortune of the war was for a ʰ long time very ⁱ doubtful; the Carthaginians being ᵏ successful by

a *poco dopo*　　b *fatto*　　c *inutile*　　d *proposizione*
e *pace*　　f *ambasciadore*　　g *Cinea*　　h *perchè*　　i *Appio Claudio*　　k *impedire*　　l *attaccare*　　m *due volte*　　n *vittoria*　　o *due*　　p *dubbioso*　　r *allora*　　s *invitato*
t *Siracusei*　　u *Sicilia*　　v *Cartaginese*　　x *dove*　　y *cosa*
z *riuscire*　　a *secondo*　　b *richiesta*　　c *ritornare*　　d *Italia*
e *sconfitto*　　f *scacciato*　　g *campo*　　h *battuto*　　i *Tarento*　　k *Epiro*　　l *dopo*　　m *guerra*　　n *accendersi*
o *trà*　　p *Cartaginese*　　q *causare*　　r *ambizione*　　s *formidabile*　　t *potere*　　u *Siracusa*　　v *alleato*　　x *guerreggiare*　　y *Mamertini*　　z *usurpato*　　a *indirizzarsi*
b *ajuto*　　c *trasportare*　　d *armata*　　e *Sicilia*　　f *attaccare*　　g *forte*　　h *lungo tempo*　　i *incerto*　　k *fortunato*,

sea,

ITALIAN EXERCISES. 115

[a] sea, and the Romans by [b] land. The most [c] memorable [d] person in all this war was [e] Attilius Regulus, who having [f] brought the Carthaginians very low by [g] two [h] victories [i] obtained over them at sea and land; and [k] refusing to [l] grant them [m] peace but upon [n] hard terms, he was [o] vanquished by [p] Xantippus, the [q] Lacedæmonian [r] general, and [s] taken [t] prisoner with 15,000 [u] men, 30,000 being [v] slain, in the year 498. Being [w] afterwards [x] sent to [y] Rome by the [z] Carthaginians, to [a] treat with the [b] senate upon an [c] exchange of [d] prisoners, he [e] interposed to [f] prevent it, and [g] returning to [h] Carthage, was [i] put to [k] death in the most [l] cruel [m] manner [n] imaginable, as [o] many [p] authors [q] tell us. The [r] first among the Romans that [s] obtained a [t] victory by sea, was C. [u] Duilius, in the first year of this [x] war. C. [y] Lutatius [z] gained [a] another in the 23d and [b] last year; in which he [c] made an end of the war with the Carthaginians, [d] near the [e] island of the [f] Ægates. A [g] peace was [h] concluded upon these [i] terms, that they should [k] quit all the islands which [l] lie betwixt Italy and Africa, and should [m] pay [n] yearly 2200 [o] talents for [p] twenty

a *mare*   b *terra*   c *memorabile*   d *persona*   e *Attilio Regolo*   f *abbattuto*   g *due*   h *vittoria*   i *riportato*   k *rifiutare*   l *concedere*   m *pace*   n *patti rigorosi*   o *vinto*   p *Xantippo*   q *Lacedemone*   r *generale*   s *fatto*   t *prigioniero*   u *uomo*   v *ucciso*   w *indi*   x *mandato*   y *Roma*   z *Cartaginesi*   a *trattare*   b *senato*   c *cambio*   d *prigioniero*   e *interporre*   f *impedire*   g *tornare*   h *Cartagine*   i *messo*   k *morte*   l *crudele*   m *maniera*   n *immaginabile*   o *molto*   p *autore*   q *rapportare*   r *primo*   s *riportare*   t *vittoria*   u *Duilio*   x *guerra*   y *Lutazio*   z *guadagnare*   a *altro*   b *ultimo*   c *terminare*   d *vicino*   e *isola*   f *Egate*   g *pace*   h *concluso*   i *condizione*   k *abbandonare*   l *situato*   m *pagare*   n *annualmente*   o *talento*   p *venti*.

years

116 ITALIAN EXERCISES.

years ᵃ together. This ᵇ happened in the year of the city 513, and 241 before ᶜ Christ.

In the year 519, the ᵈ temple of ᵉ Janus was ᶠ shut, which very ᵍ rarely happened in Rome; but upon the ʰ breaking out of new wars, was ⁱ presently ᵏ open again. The ˡ Ligures, the Sardi, and Corsi were ᵐ subdued; after which the Romans ⁿ had war with the ᵒ Illyrians, and their ᵖ queen Teuta, which was ᑫ dispatched in ʳ three years time. There ˢ happened ᵗ about this ᵘ time a ᵛ dreadful ʷ irruption of the ˣ Gauls. The ʸ Insubres and ᶻ Boii, having ᵃ first ᵇ sent for some ᶜ transalpine Gauls, ᵈ fell upon the Romans, ᵉ upon the account of the ᶠ land in Picene, which had been ᵍ taken from the Galli ʰ Senones; and ⁱ disposed of by ᵏ Flaminius, ˡ tribune of the ᵐ commons, by the ⁿ Agrarian law, which was ᵒ made in the year of the city 522. They were ᵖ several times ᑫ worsted, and the Insubres ʳ entirely ˢ subdued, and king ᵗ Virdumarus ᵘ slain by C. ᵛ Marcellus, the ʷ consul, who was the only person after ˣ Romulus that ʸ consecrated ᶻ Opima Spolia to ᵃ Jupiter Feretrius. In this war Hiero, king of Sicily, ᵇ sent the Romans a ᶜ vast quantity of ᵈ corn, the ᵉ price of which he ᶠ received after the war was ᵍ ended.

   a *di seguito*   b *succedere*   c *Cristo*   d *tempio*   e *Giano*
f *chiuso*   g *raramente*   h *principio*   i *presto*   k *aperto*
l *Liguri*   m *vinto*   n *guerreggiare*   o *Illiri*   p *regina*   q *spedito*   r *tre*   s *avvenire*   t *incirca*
u *tempo*   v *terribile*   w *incursione*   x *Galli*   y *Insubri*   z *Boj*   a *primieramente*   b *mandare*   c *transalpino*   d *attaccare*   e *a cagione del*   f *terra*   g *levato*   h *Senonesi*   i *disporre*   k *Flaminio*   l *tribuno*
m *communi*   n *legge Agraria*   o *fatto*   p *parecchie volte*   q *soprafatto*   r *affatto*   s *vinto*   t *Virdumaro*   u *ucciso*   v *Marcello*   w *console*   x *Romolo*
y *consacrare*   z *Opima spolia*   a *Giove Feretrio*   b *mandare*   c *quantità immensa*   d *grano*   e *prezzo*   f *ricevere*   g *terminato*.

ITALIAN EXERCISES.   117

After this ^a followed a ^b second war with the Carthaginians, four and twenty years after the ^c end of the ^d former; which ^e indeed did not ^f last ^g so long, but was ^h so much more ⁱ terrible for the ^k dreadful ^l slaughter that was made in it, (^m says Florus) that if ⁿ any one ^o compared the ^p losses on each ^q side, the ^r people that ^s proved ^t victorious ^u seemed more ^v likely to be ^w conquered. The first cause of this war was the ^x same with that of the former, ^y ambition, and the ^z impatience of the Carthaginians ^a under their ^b servitude. The first cause of this ^c combustion was ^d Annibal, the son of ^e Hamilcar, who was ^f general of the ^g Carthaginians in the ^h former ⁱ war, and had ^k accepted the ^l conditions of peace with a ^m heavy heart. For after ⁿ affairs were ^o settled in Africa, being ^p sent into ^q Spain in the year of the city 517, he ^r carried Annibal, who ^s was then nine years old, along with him, having ^t first ^u brought him to the ^v altar, and ^w made him ^x swear that he would ^y never be ^z friends with the Romans. Hamilcar being ^a slain about nine years after, Asdrubal his son-in-law was ^b put into his ^c place. He ^d sent for Annibal, and being slain eight years after, was ^e succeeded by him, being in the 27th year of his ^f age.

a *seguire*   b *secondo*   c *fine*   d *precedente*   e *alla verità*   f *durare*   g *cotanto*   h *tanto*   i *più*   k *terribile*   l *orrendo*   m *macello*   n *a quel che dice Floro*   o *paragonare*   p *perdita*   q *parte*   r *gente*   s *essere*   t *vittorioso*   u *parere*   v *probabilmente*   w *conquistato*   x *stesso*   y *ambizione*   z *impazienza*   a *sotto*   b *servitù*   c *incendio*   d *Annibale*   e *Amilcare*   f *generale*   g *Cartaginesi*   h *antecedente*   i *guerra*   k *accettato*   l *condizione*   m *malvolentieri*   n *affare*   o *stabilito*   p *mandato*   q *Spagna*   r *portare*   s *avere allora nove anni*   t *primieramente*   u *presentato*   v *altare*   w *fatto*   x *giurare*   y *mai*   z *amico*   a *ucciso*   b *messo*   c *posto*   d *mandar a cercare*   e *successo*   f *età*.

aAs soon as he was b made general, he c subdued all Spain within the river d Iberus. After that he e fell upon the f town of g Saguntum with all his h forces, and i took it, after a k siege of seven l months. All the m Saguntins having n in vain o waited for p assistance from the Romans, were q destroyed, r partly by the s enemy's t sword, and u partly by their own v hands. This war w broke out in the year of the city 536, and x lasted seventeen years.

Upon the first y coming of Annibal into Italy, both the z consuls were a defeated, P. b Cornelius at c Ticinus, and d Sempronius at Trebia. They e received a greater f overthrow the g following year near the h Thrasymene i lake. k In the mean time, Q. l Fabius Maximus being made m dictator by the n people, o recovered in some p measure the Roman q affairs. But the r bloodiest s stroke was that of Cannæ, in the year of the city 538, t occasioned by the u rashness of one of the v consuls, w Terentius Varro. x Forty thousand Romans were y killed in that z battle: a however, their b courage was not c cast down by this d overthrow; for they would not e redeem those that had been f taken g prisoners, in the battle of Cannæ. In the year

a *subito che*   b *fatto*   c *soggiogare*   d *fiume Ibero*
e *attaccare*   f *città*   g *Sagunto*   h *forza*   i *prendere*   k *assedio*   l *mese*   m *Saguntini*   n *indarno*
o *aspettato*   p *assistenza*   q *distrotto*   r *in parte*   s *nemico*   t *spada*   u *in parte*   v *mano*   w *accendersi*
x *durare*   y *venuta*   z *console*   a *sconfitto*   b *Cornelio*   c *Ticino*   d *Sempronio*   e *ricevere*   f *rotta*
g *seguente*   h *Trasimene*   i *lago*   k *nell' istesso tempo*
l *Fabio Massimo*   m *dettatore*   n *popolo*   o *riparare*
p *modo*   q *affare*   r *sanguinoso*   s *colpo*   t *cagionato*   u *temerità*   v *console*   w *Terenzio Varrone*
x *quaranta mila*   y *ucciso*   z *battaglia*   a *con tutto ciò*   b *coraggio*   c *sgomentato*   d *rotta*   e *riscattare*   f *preso*   g *prigioniero*.

ITALIAN EXERCISES. 119

540, the ᵃconsul ᵇMarcellus ᶜbesieged ᵈSyracuse, which had ᵉdeclared for the Carthaginians; it was ᶠwonderfully ᵍdefended a long time by the ʰcontrivance of ⁱArchimedes, who was an ᵏexcellent ˡastronomer, but more ᵐfamous for the ⁿinvention of ᵒmilitary ᵖengines. It was ᑫtaken ʳat last with ˢmuch ᵗdifficulty, after a ᵘsiege of three years. We are ᵛtold that Archimedes being very ʷintent upon his ˣstudy at that time, and not ʸminding the ᶻhurry, and ᵃnoise of the ᵇarmy, when they ᶜbroke into the ᵈtown, was ᵉkilled by a ᶠsoldier; that Marcellus was much ᵍconcerned for his ʰdeath, having ⁱgiven ᵏstrict ˡcharge to his ᵐsoldiers to ⁿspare his ᵒlife. _

ᵖIn the mean time, ᑫLævinus the ʳprætor ˢstopt ᵗPhilip king of ᵘMacedon, who having made an ᵛalliance with Annibal, was ˣready to ʸcome into Italy, and ᶻforced him to ᵃburn his ᵇfleet, and ᶜretreat into Macedonia, in the year of the city 542. But in Spain, the two ᶜbrothers P. and C. ᵈScipio, who had ᵉhitherto ᶠprevented Asdrubal's ᵍpassage into Italy to his brother Annibal, and had ʰperformed a great many gallant ⁱactions, were both slain, and their ᵏarmies ˡdestroyed.

 a *consolo* b *Marcello* c *assediare* d *Siracusa*
e *dichiarato* f *maravigliosamente bene* g *difeso* h *ingegno* i *Archimede* k *eccellente* l *astronomo* m *famoso* n *invenzione* o *militare* p *macchina* q *preso*
r *alla fine* s *molto* t *difficoltà* u *assedio* v *dire*
w *fisso* x *studio* y *badare* z *confusione* a *strepito* b *armata* c *avventarsi* d *città* e *ucciso*
f *soldato* g *afflitto* h *morte* i *dato* k *preciso*
l *ordine* m *soldato* n *salvare* o *vita* p *nell' istesso tempo* q *Levino* r *pretore* s *fermare* t *Filippo* u *Macedonia* v *alleanza* x *pronto* y *venire* z *forzare* a *abbrucciare* b *flotta* c *ritirarsi* c *fratello* d *Scipione* e *fin' allora* f *impedito* g *passaggio* h *fare* i *fatto* k *armata*
l *distrotto*.

L. Marcus, a Roman knight, being [a] chosen general, by the [b] votes of the [c] soldiers, [d] upheld their [e] tottering [f] cause; by whose [g] conduct in one [h] day, and a [i] night, two [k] camps of the [l] enemy were [m] taken by [n] assault, and about [o] thirty-seven thousand [p] men [q] slain. The [r] same year [s] Tarentum, [t] except the [u] citadel, was taken by Annibal; and Capua [v] besieged by the Romans; and Annibal [x] marched to Rome to [y] draw them from it. But a [z] sudden [a] tempest [b] arising, [c] forced him from the [d] walls, and the [e] sight of it. · Capua was after that [f] surrendered to the Romans, the [g] grandees of which [h] poisoned themselves; the [i] senators were [k] beheaded, and the city [l] deprived of its [m] liberty.

There was a [n] son of that P. Scipio, who, we have told you was [o] killed in [p] Spain, [q] named [r] likewise P. Scipio, who after the [s] death of his [t] father and [u] uncle, was [v] sent into Spain, [x] being but twenty-four years old. There having [y] performed very great [z] things, and [a] vanquished Asdrubal, the son of [b] Giscon and [c] Mago, [d] drove the Carthaginians out of Spain, in five years after he [e] came there; from thence [f] passing over into Africa, he [g] made an [h] alliance with [i] Syphax, king of the [k] Masylians, and after that with Masanissa,

a *eletto*   b *voto*   c *soldato*   d *sostenere*   e *vacillante*
f *causa*   g *condotta*   h *giorno*   i *notte*
k *campo*   l *nemico*   m *preso*   n *assalto*   o *trenta sette mila*
p *uomo*   q *ucciso*   r *stesso*   s *Tarento*
t *eccettuato*   u *cittadella*   v *assediato*   x *marciare*
y *trarre*   z *repentino*   a *tempesta*   b *sollevarsi*   c *forzare*
d *muro*   e *vista*   f *reso*   g *grande*   h *avvelenarsi*
i *senatore*   k *decapitato*   l *privato*   m *libertà*
n *figlio*   o *ammazzato*   p *Spagna*   q *nominato*
r *parimente*   s *morte*   t *padre*   u *zio*
v *mandato*   x *non avendo che 24 anni*   y *fatto*   z *cosa*
a *vinto*   b *Giscone*   c *Magone*   d *scacciare*   e *venire*
f *passare*   g *fare*   h *alleanza*   i *Siface*
k *Masiliani.*

king of the [a] Masasulians. These things were [b] done in the year 548, and the [c] third from the [d] death of [e] Marcellus; who having been [f] successful in [g] several [h] battles with Annibal, was [i] at last [k] trepanned by an [l] ambuscade, and slain. In the [m] following year, Asdrubal was [n] cut off, with his [o] army [p] before he could [q] join his [r] brother, by the two [s] consuls, [t] Claudius Nero and [u] Livius Salinator. Annibal was [v] then in Apulia, [w] opposed by Nero the consul. [x] Livy was [y] encamped in [z] Cisa'pine Gaul [a] against Asdrubal, Nero [b] marched [c] through Italy [d] privately, in six [e] days time, [f] came to the [g] camp of his [h] colleague with a [i] part of his [k] army, and having [l] conquered the [m] enemy, [n] returned to his camp before Annibal [o] perceived that he was [p] gone. There are [q] said to have been 56,000 of the [r] enemy [s] slain in the [t] battle, and 5400 [u] taken [v] prisoners. The head [w] of Asdrubal was [x] thrown before the [y] advanced guards of the Carthaginians by Nero.

P. Scipio [z] resolved to [a] carry the [b] war into Africa, that he might [c] draw Annibal out of Italy: but [d] at first that being [e] looked upon as a [f] rash [g] design, he had neither [h] money nor [i] men from the

a *Masasuliani* b *fatto* c *terzo* d *morte* e *Marcello* f *fortunato* g *molto* h *battaglia* i *alla fine* k *tirato* l *imboscata* m *seguente* n *tagliato a pezzi* o *armata* p *prima che* q *accozzare* r *fratello* s *console* t *Claudio Nerone* u *Livio Salinatore* v *altera* w *opposto* x *Livio* y *accampato* z *Gallia Cisalpina* a *contro* b *marciare* c *attraverso* d *segretamente* e *giorno* f *venire* g *campo* h *collega* i *parte* k *armata* l *conquistato* m *nemico* n *tornare* o *accorgersi* p *andato* q *dire* r *inimico* s *ucciso* t *battaglia* u *preso* v *prigioniero* w *testa* x *gettata* y *la guardia avanzata* z *risolvere* a *portare* b *guerra* c *trarre* d *alla prima* e *considerato* f *temerario* g *disegno* h *danaro* i *uomo*.

govern-

ᵃ government. ᵇ Wherefore having ᶜ raised none but ᵈ volunteers and ᵉ borrowed money, he firſt ᶠ went to ᵍ Sicily, and ʰ from thence to Africa, in the year 550; ⁱ when the ᵏ image of the ˡ Idæan mother was ᵐ brought from ⁿ Peſſinnus in ᵒ Phrygia, to Rome, ᵖ according to the ᑫ advice of the ʳ oracle.

The general ˢ employed ᵗ againſt him by the ᵘ Carthaginians was Aſdrubal, the ſon of Giſcon, who had ᵛ contracted his daughter ʷ Sophoniſba to Maſaniſſa. But the Carthaginians had ˣ given her to ʸ Syphax, (who being ᶻ in love with the ᵃ young lady, ᵇ laid waſte their ᶜ country in the ᵈ abſence of her ᵉ father and ᶠ ſpouſe) to ᵍ take him off from the Roman ʰ alliance: at which ⁱ uſage Maſaniſſa being ᵏ incenſed, he ˡ gave himſelf up ᵐ entirely to the Roman ⁿ intereſt, and was very ᵒ ſerviceable to them in ᵖ reducing the Carthaginians.

ᑫ After a great many ʳ overthrows, the Carthaginians ˢ found themſelves ᵗ obliged to ᵘ recal Annibal out of Italy, to the ᵛ defence of their country, where after a ʷ fruitleſs ˣ overture of ʸ peace, he was ᶻ vanquiſhed by Scipio, and an ᵃ end put to the ᵇ war, after it had ᶜ laſted ſeven years.

The ſecond ᵈ Punic war was ᵉ followed by the ᶠ Macedonian, ᵍ againſt king Philip. What put the

a *governo*   b *perciò*   c *levato*   d *volontario*   e *impreſtato*   f *andare*   g *Sicilia*   h *di là*   i *quando*   k *ſimulacro*   l *madre Idea*   m *portato*   n *Peſſinno*   o *Frigia*   p *ſecondo*   q *conſiglio*   r *oracolo*   s *impiegato*   t *contro*   u *Cartagineſi*   v *promeſſo*   w *Sofoniſba*   x *dato*   y *Siface*   z *innamorato*   a *giovane*   b *diſtruggere*   c *paeſe*   d *aſſenza*   e *padre*   f *conſorte*   g *diſtrarre*   h *alleanza*   i *tratto*   k *irritato*   l *darſi*   m *affatto*   n *intereſſe*   o *ſervizievole*   p *debellare*   q *dopo*   r *ſconfitta*   s *trovarſi*   t *obbligato*   u *richiamare*   v *difeſa*   w *inutile*   x *propoſizione*   y *pace*   z *vinto*   a *terminato*   b *guerra*   c *durato*   d *punico*   e *ſeguito*   f *Macedone*   g *contro*.

ITALIAN EXERCISES.

Romans upon it was the ᵃ former injuries ᵇ Philip had done them, ᶜ as likewise the late ᵈ vexation he had given their ᵉ allies, ᶠ especially the Athenians, who being ᵍ harrassed by the king, ʰ fled to the Romans. ⁱ At length ᵏ Titus Quinctius Flaminius ˡ put an end to the war, four years after it ᵐ began, by the ⁿ conquest of Philip at ᵒ Cynoscephalæ, in ᵖ Thessaly.

After this ᑫ followed the war with ʳ Antiochus, king of Asia, who having ˢ recovered Syria, and ᵗ conquered Scopas, the general of ᵘ Ptolemæus Epiphanes, ᵛ began now to be ʷ formidable to the Romans, ˣ against whom Annibal did not a little ʸ inflame him; who, for ᶻ fear of the same ᵃ enemy, had ᵇ fled to the king. The ᶜ ambassadors of the ᵈ Ætolians too, who were now ᵉ averse to the Roman ᶠ alliance, ᵍ contributed not a ʰ little towards it. Antiochus ⁱ therefore having ᵏ clapped up a peace with ˡ Ptolemy, to whom he ᵐ gave his daughter Cleopatra in ⁿ marriage, and ᵒ granted ᵖ Cœlo Syria, and ᑫ Judea by way of ʳ portion, ˢ made war upon the Romans, which being begun in the year of the city 562, ᵗ lasted in all three years. For in the year 565, L. ᵘ Cornelius Scipio the ᵛ consul, ʷ going over into Asia, with his brother P. Scipio ˣ Africanus, as his ʸ lieutenant, did, by the ᶻ assist-

a *precedente*   b *ingiuria*   c *com' anche*   d *fastidio*
e *confederato*   f *spezialmente*   g *straccare*   h *fuggire*
i *alla fine*   k *Tito Quinczio Flaminio*   l *terminare*   m *principiare*   n *conquista*   o *Cinoscefale*   p *Tessalia*   q *seguire*   r *Antioco*   s *ricuperato*   t *conquistato*   u *Ptolemeo Epifane*   v *principiare*   w *formidabile*   x *contro*   y *infiammare*   z *paura*   a *nemico*   b *fuggito*   c *ambasciadore*   d *Etoliani*   e *contrario*   f *alleanza*   g *contribuire*   h *poco*   i *perciò*   k *fatto una pace finta*   l *Ptolemeo*   m *dare*   n *matrimonio*   o *concedere*   p *Celo Siria*   q *Giudea*   r *dote*   s *fare guerra*   t *durare*   u *Cornelio Scipione*   v *console.*   w *passare*   x *l'Africano*   y *luogotenente*   z *ajuto.*

ance ᵃ chiefly of his ᵇ counsel, ᶜ conquer Antiochus. Livy ᵈ tells us, there were 50,000 ᵉ foot ᶠ slain in one ᵍ battle, and 4000 ʰ horse. A peace was ⁱ granted Antiochus ᵏ upon this condition ˡ amongst others, that he should ᵐ recede from all the ⁿ countries ᵒ on this side ᵖ mount Taurus.

After Antiochus was ᑫ conquered, the Ætolians were ʳ reduced by Fulvius the consul; and the same year the Gallo-Greci were ˢ subdued by the other ᵗ consul, Cneius Manlius.

In the 149th ᵘ Olympiad ʸ died three ʷ famous generals, P. Scipio, Annibal, and ˣ Philopæmen. Scipio was ʸ impeached for ᶻ taking ᵃ money of Antiochus for the peace he ᵇ granted him; after which he ᶜ retired to ᵈ Liturnum in Campania, and ᵉ died there in the year of the city 570. Annibal a year or two after (for ᶠ historians are not ᵍ agreed upon the ʰ matter) being ⁱ demanded of Drusias, king of Bithynia, by the Roman ᵏ ambassadors, ˡ in order to be ᵐ put to ⁿ death, ᵒ poisoned himself. ᵖ About the ᑫ same time Philopæmen, general of the ʳ Achæans, was ˢ taken by the ᵗ Messenians, and ᵘ slain, after he had ᵛ forced the Lacedæmonians to a ʷ submission, who had ˣ thrown off the Achæan ʸ alliance.

In the mean time Philip, being ᶻ checked ᵃ rather

a *sopra tutto*   b *consiglio*   c *conquistare*   d *dire*   e *infanteria*   f *ucciso*   g *battaglia*   h *cavalleria*   i *concesso a*   k *con questo patto*   l *fra*   m *partire*   n *regione*   o *di quà dal*   p *monte Tauro*   q *vinto*   r *debellato*   s *soggiogato*   t *consule Cnejo Manlio*   u *Olimpiade*   v *morire*   w *famoso*   x *Filopemeno*   y *inquisito*   z *prendere*   a *danaro*   b *accordare*   c *ritirarsi*   d *Liturno*   e *morire*   f *istorico*   g *d'accordo*   h *cosa*   i *richiesto*   k *ambasciadore*   l *acciò*   m *messo*   n *morte*   o *avvelenarsi*   p *incirca*   q *stesso tempo*   r *Acheani*   s *preso*   t *Messeniani*   u *ucciso*   v *costretto*   w *sommissione*   x *sbrigato*   y *alleanza*   z *represso*   a *piuttosto*.

than

than ᵃ conquered in the ᵇ former war, was ᶜ very busy in ᵈ making ᵉ preparations for ᶠ another; but before ᵍ matters were ʰ ripe ⁱ enough ᵏ for that purpose, he died, and was ˡ succeeded by his son ᵐ Perseus, who ⁿ went on with the ᵒ preparations of war ᵖ against the Romans; which was ᵠ finished in four years after its ʳ beginning, with the ˢ ruin of him and the ᵗ kingdom of Macedonia ᵘ together, in the year of the city 586. The general ᵛ employed by the Romans in that war, was ˣ Paulus Æmilius, who in one ʸ battle, ᶻ wherein were slain 20,000 ᵃ men, and 11,000 ᵇ taken ᶜ prisoners, ᵈ put a ᵉ final ᶠ period to the Macedonian ᵍ empire in the ʰ 11th year of king Perseus. About the same time, ⁱ Gentius, king of the ᵏ Illyrians, being ˡ trepanned into an ᵐ alliance by Perseus, was ⁿ conquered by ᵒ Amicius the ᵖ prætor.

After the ᵠ conquest of Antiochus, the Macedonians ʳ rebelled again, but were ˢ subdued, and Macedonia ᵗ reduced into the ᵘ form of a ᵛ province.

Some time after a war ˣ broke out with the ʸ Achæans, who having ᶻ pulled down the ᵃ walls of ᵇ Lacedæmon, and ᶜ taken away their ᵈ ancient ᵉ laws, had ᶠ obliged them to ᵍ unite with them; which the Lacedæmonians ʰ complained of to the

a *vinto* b *precedente* c *affaccendato* d *fare* e *preparativo* f *altro* g *cosa* h *maturo* i *abbastanza* k *a questo effetto* l *successo* m *Perseo* n *continuare* o *preparativo* p *contro* q *terminato* r *principio* s *rovina* t *regno* u *insieme* v *impiegato* x *Paolo Emilio* y *battaglia* z *nella quale* a *uomo* b *preso* c *prigioniero* d *mettere* e *ultimo* f *periodo* g *imperio* h *undecimo* i *Genzio* k *Illirj* l *adescato* m *alleanza* n *vinto* o *Amicio* p *pretore* q *conquista* r *ribellarsi* s *soggiogato* t *ridotto* u *forma* v *provincia* x *accordarsi* y *Acheani* z *demolito* a *mura* b *Lacedemonia* c *levare* d *antico* e *legge* f *obbligare* g *unirsi* h *lamentarsi.*

ITALIAN EXAMPLES.

Romans, who [a] sent [b] against the Achæans Metellus the prætor, by whom they were [c] defeated in two [d] engagements at [e] Thermopylæ, and in [f] Phocis; and [g] presently after [h] entirely reduced by the consul [i] L. Nummius, and [k] Corinth, the [l] metropolis of their [m] nation, [n] burnt.

The same year Carthage was [o] taken and [p] destroyed. The [q] occasion of this war was a [r] difference [s] between Masanissa and the Carthaginians [t] about their [u] territories; which [v] controversy being [w] referred to the Romans, they obliged the Carthaginians to [x] give up the [y] country in [z] dispute, and [a] money too, to Masanissa. But the Romans had [b] before-hand [c] resolved [d] utterly to [e] raze Carthage, [f] right or wrong, [g] chiefly at the [h] instigation of [i] Marcus Cato the censor, who, whenever he [k] gave his [l] opinion upon any [m] debate in the [n] senate, [o] used [p] finally to [q] add, Carthage [r] must be [s] destroyed. [t] Wherefore in the year of the city 605, Carthage was [u] besieged by the consuls [v] Manilius and [w] Censorinus. They soon after [x] surrendered to the Romans; but being [y] ordered to [z] demolish their city, and [a] seat themselves at ten [b] miles [c] distance from the [d] sea, they were so [e] inflamed with [f] fury and [g] despair, that they [h] held out

a *mandare* b *contro* c *sconfitto* d *battaglia* e *Termopile* f *Foci* g *poco dopo* h *affatto* i *L. Nummio* k *Corinto* l *metropoli* m *nazione* n *bruciato* o *preso* p *distrotto* q *cagione* r *lite* s *tra* t *rispetto a* u *territorio* v *controversia* w *riferito* x *abbandonare* y *paese* z *disputa* a *danaro* b *anticipatamente* c *risolvere* d *intieramente* e *distruggere* f *bene o male* g *sopra tutto* h *instigazione* i *Marco Catone il censore* k *dare* l *opinione* m *contesa* n *senato* o *solere* p *finalmente* q *aggiungere* r *bisogna* s *distrotto* t *perciò* u *assediato* v *Manilio* w *Censorino* x *arrendersi* y *comandato* z *demolire* a *stabilirsi* b *mila* c *distanza* d *mare* e *infiammato* f *furia* g *disperazione* h *mantenersi*.

even

ITALIAN EXERCISES.

even ᵃ beyond their ᵇ strength, ᶜ till in the fourth year, the ᵈ same in which ᵉ Corinth was destroyed, it was ᶠ taken by ᵍ P. Cornelius Scipio, the ʰ proconsul, who was ⁱ Paulus Æmilius's son, and had been ᵏ adopted by the son of Scipio Africanus. At the ˡ beginning of the war Masanissa, king of the ᵐ Numidians ⁿ died, in the 97th year of his ᵒ age, having ᵖ left behind him forty-four sons, and ᑫ continued an ʳ ally of the Romans near 60 years.

CHAP. VI.

ˢ ABOUT the same time the ᵗ Lusitanians in ᵘ Spain ᵛ beat the Romans most ˣ shamefully ʸ under the ᶻ conduct of ᵃ Viriathus; who of a ᵇ huntsman, ᶜ became a ᵈ highwayman, and of a highwayman, a general, and ᵉ defeated the Roman ᶠ armies several ᵍ times. But that ʰ overthrow was most ⁱ memorable of all ᵏ others, in which, in the year 608, having ˡ routed the ᵐ forces of ⁿ Vetilius the ᵒ prætor, ᵖ he took him prisoner, and ᑫ put him ʳ to death, as ˢ Appian says. Nor was he the ᵗ only one that was ᵘ conquered by Viriathus, but several others ᵛ underwent the same ˣ fate. The first that was ʸ successful ᶻ against him was ᵃ C. Lælius the prætor, in the year 609. After that the proconsul

a clire	b forza	c infino	d stesso	e Corinto
f preso	g P. Cornelio Scipione		h proconsole	i Paulo Emilio
k adottato	l principio	m Numidi	n morire	o età
p lasciato	q continuato	r alleato	s incirca	t Lusitanj
u Spagna	v battere	x ignominiosamente	y sotto	z condotta
a Viriato	b cacciatore	c doventare	d ladro di strada	e sconfiggere
f armata	g volta	h sconfitta	i memorabile	k altro
l rotto	m forza	n Vetilio	o pretore	p prendere
q mettere	r morte	s Appiano	t solo	u vinto
v soffrire	x fato	y fortunato	z contro	a C. Lelio

128 ITALIAN EXERCISES.

^a Quintus Fabius Maximus ^b defeated him. In the year 614, ^c Q. Servilius Cæpio ^d basely ^e procured him to be ^f assassinated by some of his own ^g officers, whom he had ^h bribed ⁱ for that purpose, to the great ^k dishonour of the Roman ^l people.

After this a much more ^m dangerous war ⁿ broke out in Celtiberia. The Numantini having ^o received the ^p Segidenses their ^q allies, that had ^r escaped the ^s hands of the Romans, being ^t commanded by Metellus the proconsul, ^u to deliver up the ^v refugees, and ^x lay down their ^y arms, ^z refused both : and ^a though they were so much ^b inferior to the Romans, in ^c number and ^d strength, they ^e made a ^f gallant ^g resistance for some ^h years. The ⁱ army of ^k M. Popilius the proconsul, was ^l cut off by them, and the year ^m following, ⁿ thirty ^o thousand Romans, under the consul Mancinus, were ^p routed by four thousand of the Numantini; which ^q disgrace was ^r followed by a most ^s shameful ^t peace; but the senate ^u refused to ^v ratify it; ^x wherefore Mancinus was ^y delivered up into their hands, but the Numantini would not ^z receive him. ^a At last they were ^b vanquished in the ^c field by Scipio, who had ^d destroyed Carthage; and being ^e shut up within their own ^f walls, were ^g reduced

---

a *Quinto Fabio Massimo*   b *sconfiggere*   c *Q. Servilio Cepione*   d *vilmente*   e *fare*   f *assassinare*   g *ufiziale*   h *corrotto*   i *a questo effetto*   k *disonore*   l *popolo*   m *pericoloso*   n *accendersi*   o *ricevuto*   p *segidensi*   q *alleato*   r *scappato*   s *mano*   t *commandato*   u *consegnare*   v *rifuggiato*   x *cedere*   y *arma*   z *rifiutare*   a *benchè*   b *inferiore*   c *numero*   d *forza*   e *fare*   f *gagliardo*   g *resistenza*   h *anno*   i *armata*   k *M. Popilio*   l *sconfitto*   m *seguente*   n *trenta*   o *mila*   p *messo in rotta*   q *disgrazia*   r *seguito*   s *vergognoso*   t *pace*   u *ricusare*   v *ratificare*   x *perciò*   y *consegnato*   z *ricevere*   a *alla fine*   b *vinto*   c *battaglia campale*   d *distrotto*   e *rinchiuso*   f *muro*   g *ridotto*.

to that ª desperate condition that they all ᵇ laid violent hands upon themselves; and Numantia was ᶜ levelled with the ground, in the ninth year after their ᵈ revolt, from the Romans, and from the ᵉ building of the city 621.

ᶠ Whilst the Romans were ᵍ still at war with the ʰ Achæans and Carthaginians, Macedonia was ⁱ conquered a third time; which ᵏ Andriscus, a ˡ fellow of ᵐ mean birth, who ⁿ pretended to be ᵒ Philip the son of ᵖ Perseus, had ᑫ possessed himself of. He was conquered by ʳ Q. Cæcilius Metellus, with the ˢ slaughter of 25,000 of his ᵗ men. Metellus had ᵘ from thence ᵛ the sirname of ˣ Macedonicus.

At the time that the Romans were ʸ engaged in the ᶻ Numantine war, there was a ª rising of the ᵇ slaves in Sicily. A ᶜ Syrian, ᵈ by name Eunus, ᵉ pretending a ᶠ divine ᵍ inspiration, ʰ called the slaves to ⁱ arms and ᵏ liberty, ˡ as it were by the ᵐ order of the ⁿ gods; and having ᵒ raised a ᵖ vast ᑫ army, ʳ consisting of no less than 70,000 men, and ˢ vanquished four Roman prætors, he was ᵗ at last ᵘ routed by P. Rupilius the consul, in the year of the city 622.

Attalus son of ᵛ Eumenes, king of ˣ Phrygia, when the uncle ʸ Attalus was ᶻ dead, (who after

a *estrema disperazione*   b *uccidersi*   c *spianato*   d *sollevazione*   e *edificazione*   f *mentre*   g *ancora*   h *Acheani*   i *conquistato*   k *Andrisco*   l *uomo*   m *bassa nascita*   n *pretendere*   o *Filippo*   p *Perseo*   q *impadronito*   r *Q. Cecilio Metello*   s *Macello*   t *uomo*   u *da questo*   v *cognome*   x *Macedonico*   y *impegnato*   z *Numantino*   a *ribellione*   b *schiavo*   c *Siriano*   d *che si chiamava Euno*   e *pretendere*   f *divino*   g *ispirazione*   h *chiamare*   i *arma*   k *libertà*   l *come se fosse*   m *ordine*   n *nume*   o *levato*   p *ponderoso*   q *armata*   r *composto*   s *vinto*   t *alla fine*   u *sconfitto*   v *Eumene*   x *Frigia*   y *zio*   z *morto*.

Eumene's death had ª managed the ᵇ kingdom as his ᶜ guardian) ᵈ reigned five years, and dying about the year of the city 621, made the Roman people his ᵉ heir; which ᶠ Aristonicus, a son of Eumenes by one of his ᵍ mistresses, ʰ taking amiss, he ⁱ seizes upon Asia, and ᵏ cuts off the army of Crassus the prætor. Afterwards he was ˡ vanquished by the consul Peperna, and an ᵐ end was put to the war the year ⁿ following, 625, by M. Aquilius the consul. This was a ᵒ melancholy year for the ᵖ death of Scipio Africanus, who was ᑫ found dead in his ʳ bed, not without the ˢ suspicion of being ᵗ poisoned by his ᵘ wife.

The year in which Attalus ᵛ made the Roman people his ˣ heir, there was a ʸ terrible ᶻ sedition at Rome. For T. Gracchus, ª tribune of the ᵇ commons, having made the ᶜ Agrarian law, that ᵈ nobody should ᵉ possess above 500 ᶠ acres of ᵍ land, and ʰ proposing to have the ⁱ money of king Attalus ᵏ divided amongst the people, and ˡ likewise ᵐ suing for the ⁿ tribuneship against the year following, the senators being very much ᵒ disturbed at the ᵖ matter, he was, by the ᑫ procurement of P. Corn. Nasica, ʳ slain in the ˢ Capitol, ᵗ whither he had ᵘ fled for ᵛ refuge.

After the death of Tiberius, his ˣ brother Caius

a *governato*   b *regno*   c *curatore*   d *regnare*   e *erede*
f *Aristonico*   g *innamorata*   h *avendolo per male*   i *impadronirsi*   k *tagliare a pezzi*   l *vinto*   m *terminato*
n *seguente*   o *malinconico*   p *morte*   q *trovato*
r *letto*   s *sospetto*   t *avvelenato*   u *moglie*   v *fare*
x *erede*   y *terribile*   z *sedizione*   a *tribuno*   b *communi*   c *legge Agraria*   d *nissuno*   e *possedere*   f *jugero*   g *terra*   h *proporre*   i *danaro*   k *spartito*
l *parimente*   m *sollecitare*   n *l'ufficio del tribunato*   o *inquietato*   p *cosa*   q *intrapresa*   r *ucciso*   s *Campidoglia*   t *dove*   u *fuggito*   v *salvezza*.   x *fratello*.

ITALIAN EXERCISES. 131

ᵃ purfuing the fame ᵇ defign, was ᶜ taken off by Opimius the conful, and ᵈ together with him, Fulvius Flaccus, who had been conful.

In the year of the city 629, the Romans firſt made war upon the ᵉ Gauls ᶠ beyond the Alps. They ᵍ began with the Salii, and ʰ Allobroges, whom Fulvius Flaccus ⁱ fubdued. In the year 633, Fabius the conful, made an end of the war with the Allobroges. He ᵏ conquered Bituitus, king of the Arverni, in ˡ battle. The king himfelf ᵐ coming to Rome to ⁿ fatisfy the fenate, was ᵒ confined at Alba. Then Gallia Narbonenſis was made a ᵖ province, and a ᵠ colony ʳ fent to Narbon in the year 636.

The Romans were after this ˢ almoſt ᵗ perpetually at war with the Gauls, by whom they were ᵘ oftentimes ˣ foundly beat; but above all others the Cimbri and Teutones were ˣ terrible to them; who ʸ marching for Italy, and not ᶻ being able to ᵃ prevail with the fenate for ᵇ room to ᶜ fettle in, they ᵈ routed M. Silanus the conful: and the year following Scaurus was ᵉ defeated by the Cimbri, and L. Caffius by the Helvetii Tigurini the year after that. But the ᶠ overthrow of Q. Cæpio was more ᵍ memorable than all the ʰ reſt. He had ⁱ plundered ᵏ Tholoufe in the ˡ country of the Tectofagæ, and had ᵐ carried off an hundred thouſand ⁿ pounds of ᵒ gold, and fifteen hundred thouſand

 a *profeguire*   b *difegno*   c *ucciſo*   d *infieme*   e *Galli*
f *di là dall' Alpi*   g *principiare*   h *Allobrogi*   i *foggiogare*   k *conquiſtare*   l *battaglia*   m *venire*   n *foddisfare*   o *rilegato*   p *provincia*   q *colonia*   r *mandato*
s *quaſi*   t *perpetuamente*   u *ſpeſſo*   v *malmenato*
x *terribile* .   y *marciare*   z *potere*   a *ottenere*   b *ſito*
c *ſtabilirſi*   d *mettere in rotta*   e *ſconfitto*   f *rotta*
g *memorabile*   h *altro*   i *faccheggiare*   k *Toloufæ*
l *paeſe*   m *portare via*   n *libra*   o *oro.*

G 6   pounds

pounds of ᵃ silver. This was done in the year of the city 648. But the following, he, with C. Manilius, ᵇ paid for this ᶜ sacrilege, with the ᵈ utter ᵉ destruction of the Roman army. It is certain there were ᶠ slain in this ᵍ battle of the Romans and their ʰ allies, ⁱ fourscore thousand, and of ᵏ servants that ˡ followed the ᵐ camp ⁿ threescore thousand.

At length the Teutones and the ᵒ Ambrones were almost all ᵖ destroyed, two hundred thousand being slain, and seventy thousand ᑫ taken ʳ prisoners, by C. Marius the consul, in the year 652, and the following year, the same Marius, ˢ in conjunction with Catulus, defeated the Cimbri, that were ᵗ making their way through ᵘ Noricum ᵛ slew an hundred and twenty thousand, and took sixty thousand prisoners.

With so many ˣ victories did Marius ʸ consummate the ᶻ glory he had ᵃ got in the war with Jugurtha. For in the year of the city 643, a war was ᵇ undertaken against Jugurtha, king of Numidia, because he had ᶜ deprived his ᵈ cousins Hiempsal and Adherbal, the sons of Micipsa, and ᵉ grandsons of Masanissa, of their ᶠ lives and ᵍ kingdom. He ʰ prevailed against the Romans for some years, more by his gold than by his arms; but was at last ⁱ brought low by Metellus the consul, and ᵏ finally ˡ entirely ᵐ subdued by Marius, and ⁿ de-

a *argento*   b *pagare*   c *sacrilegio*   d *totale*   e *distruzione*   f *ucciso*   g *battaglia*   h *alleato*   i *ottanta*   k *servitore*   l *seguire*   m *campo*   n *sessanta*   o *Ambroni*   p *distrotto*   q *fatto*   r *prigioniero*   s *unitamente*   t *facendosi strada tra*   u *Norico*   v *uccidere*   x *vittoria*   y *terminare*   z *gloria*   a *acquistare*   b *intrappreso*   c *privato*   d *cugino*   e *nipotino*   f *vita*   g *regno*   h *prevalere*   i *abbassato*   k *finalmente*   l *affatto*   m *soggiogato*   n *tradito.*

livered

ITALIAN EXERCISES.

livered up by Bocchus, king of Mauritania, to whom he had ᵃ fled for refuge; after which he was ᵇ carried to Rome, to ᶜ grace the ᵈ triumph of Marius, and ᵉ put to death in ᶠ prison.

This ᵍ happy ʰ progress of the ⁱ empire ᵏ abroad, was ˡ interrupted by ᵐ frequent and ⁿ shameful ᵒ disorders at ᵖ home, which were ᑫ occasioned by the tribunes. Saturninus having ʳ got the Agrarian law ˢ passed, to ᵗ divide among the people the land which Marius had got, by ᵘ driving the Cimbri out of Gaul, ᵛ banished Metellus Numidicus who, ˣ opposed him; but at last was ʸ slain himself by Marius, then consul the sixth time, in the year 654; and the year following Metellus was ᶻ recalled from ᵃ banishment.

After Saturninus, Livius Drusus, tribune of the commons, but ᵇ favouring the senate, being ᶜ desirous to ᵈ restore them to their ᵉ ancient ᶠ splendor, and to ᵍ put the ʰ execution of their laws into their ⁱ hands, which C. Gracchus had ᵏ divided ˡ betwixt them and the ᵐ knights, he passed the same Agrarian laws, and put the ⁿ allies in ᵒ hopes of the ᵖ freedom of the city; which ᑫ being not able to ʳ bring about, he ˢ fell under an universal ᵗ odium, and was ᵘ stabb'd, no body ᵛ knew how, in the year 663.

After this, the Romans were ˣ engaged in two

a *fuggito per salvezza*   b. *condotto*   c *adornare*   d *trionfo*   e *messo*   f *prigione*   g *felice*   h *progresso*   i *imperio*   k *fuori*   l *interrotto*   m *frequente*   n *vergognoso*   o *disordine*   p *nel paese*   q *cagionato*   r *fatto*   s *passare*   t *spartire*   u *scacciare*   v *esiliare*   x *opporre*   y *ucciso*   z *richiamato*   a *esilio*   b *favoreggiare*   c *desideroso*   d *restituire*   e *antico*   f *splendore*   g *mettere*   h *esecuzione*   i *mano*   k *spartito*   l *frà*   m *cavaliere*   n *alleato*   o *speranza*   p *libertà*   q *non potere*   r *effettuare*   s *incorrere*   t *odio*   u *pugnalato*   v *sapere*   x *impegnato*.

most

moſt ª difficult and terrible wars, almoſt at the ſame time; one in Italy, and the other without. That was ᵇ called the ᶜ Social, or ᵈ Marſic war, becauſe the Marſi had been the firſt ᵉ beginners of it; for all the ᶠ Latins, and moſt of the people of Italy, being ᵍ diſguſted, that they who were ʰ ſharers in all the ⁱ hardſhips and ᵏ dangers of war, ſhould be ˡ excluded from the ᵐ honours and ⁿ dignities of the ᵒ ſtate; and being ᵖ balked in their hopes of ᑫ obtaining the ʳ freedom of the city by Druſus, ˢ endeavoured to ᵗ compaſs that by ᵘ force of arms which they could not get ᵛ by fair means. They firſt ˣ attempted in the Latin ʸ Feriæ to ᶻ aſſaſſinate both the conſuls, Philip and Cæſar; but the ª matter being ᵇ diſcovered, they ᶜ openly ᵈ revolted, ᵉ maſſacred Q. Servilius the proconſul, ᶠ Fonteius and all the Romans at ᵍ Aſculum. After this the war was ʰ carried on with ⁱ various ᵏ ſucceſs. Cn. ˡ Pompey Strabo, father of Pompey the ᵐ Great, ⁿ diſtinguiſhed himſelf upon this ᵒ occaſion. He ᵖ forced the Veſtini and Peligni to ᑫ ſubmiſſion, and ʳ triumphed upon that ˢ account. ᵗ Likewiſe L. Sylla Cæſar, the conſul's ᵘ lieutenant, did, by his great ſucceſſes againſt the enemy, ᵛ obtain the ˣ conſulſhip, in which he ʸ made an end of the war.

Soon after ᶻ broke out a war betwixt the Romans

a *faticoſo*　　　b *chiamato*　　c *Sociale*　　d *Marſico*
e *autore*　　f *Latino*　　g *diſguſtato*　　h *partecipante*
i *fatica*　k *pericolo*　l *eſcluſo*　m *onore*　n *dignità*　o *ſtato*
p *fruſtrato*　　q *ottenere*　　r *libertà*　s *procurare*　t *ſpuntare*　　u *forza*　　v *colle buone*　　x *tentare*　　y *Ferie*
z *aſſaſſinare*　　a *coſa*　　b *ſcoperto*　　c *apertamente*
d *rivoltarſi*　　e *uccidere*　　f *Fontejo*　　g *Aſculo* h *continuato*　　i *diverſo*　　k *ſucceſſo*　　l *Pompejo Strabone*
m *magno*　　n *diſtinguerſi*　　o *occaſione*　　p *forzare*
q *obbedienza*　　r *trionfare*　　s *cagione*　　t *parimente*
u *luogotenente*　v *ottenere*　x *conſolato*　y *terminare*
z *accenderſi*.

and

and ᵃ Mithridates, who having ᵇ taken off Ariarathes, king of Cappadocia, his ᶜ sister's ᵈ husband, together with his son of the same ᵉ name, had ᶠ seized upon the kingdom; but being forced to ᵍ forego what he had ʰ unjustly got, Ariobarzanes was ⁱ nominated king of Cappadocia by the senate, but forced out of his ᵏ dominions by Mithridates, and ˡ restored by Sylla. After this he was once more ᵐ driven out of Cappadocia, by Mithridates, as was ⁿ likewise Nicomedes out of Bithynia. But both ᵒ recovered their dominions again by a ᵖ decree of the senate; which Mithridates being ᑫ offended at, he ʳ invades Cappadocia and Bithynia, ˢ routs the Roman armies, and ᵗ massacred all the Italians ᵘ throughout Asia in one day; ᵛ reduced Macedonia, ˣ Thrace, ʸ Greece, and ᶻ Athens. The consul Sylla ᵃ marching against him, ᵇ takes Athens, and having ᶜ defeated his generals, forces him to a peace upon the ᵈ conditions of his ᵉ quitting Asia, Bithynia, and Cappadocia.

CHAP. VII.

MArius, ᶠ though now ᵍ broken with age and years, yet being very ʰ ambitious of getting ⁱ employed against Mithridates, could not ᵏ bear with patience the ˡ bestowing that ᵐ province upon Sylla. ⁿ Wherefore he ᵒ prevailed, by the ᵖ means

a *Mitridate*   b *ucciso*   c *sorella*   d *marito*   e *nome* f *impossessato*   g *abbandonare*   h *ingiustamente*   i *nominato*   k *dominio*   l *ristabilito*   m *scacciato*   n *parimente*   o *ricuperare*   p *decreto*   q *offeso*   r *invadere*   s *sconfiggere*   t *uccidere*   u *per tutta*   v *espugnare*   x *Tracia*   y *Grecia*   z *Atene*   a *marciare*   b *pigliare*   c *sconfiggere*   d *patto*   e *abbandonare*   f *benchè*   g *rotto*   h *vecchiaja*   i *ambizione*   k *impiegato*   l *tollerare*   m *concedere*   n *provincia*   o *perciò*   p *ottenere*   q *mezzo.*

of C. Sulpicius, the tribune of the commons, to have it [a] taken from Sylla, and bestowed upon himself. At which Sylla being [b] enraged, [c] seised upon the city, and having [d] slain Sulpicius, [e] obliges Marius to [f] fly. In his [g] absence, Cinna the consul, making a [h] disturbance, was [i] beaten out of the city, and being [k] joined by Marius, Carbo, and Sertorius, [l] assaults Rome; and having [m] taken it, [n] puts a great many of the Romans [o] to the sword. Marius [p] died a natural death the year following.

Sylla having made peace with Mithridates, [q] returned into Italy, and [r] made an end of the civil war in two years time, by the [s] defeat of Carbo, Norbanus, young Marius, and others; and being [t] declared [u] dictator, took off a great many of Marius's [v] party by a [x] proscription. Q. Sertorius [y] retired into Farther Spain, where he [z] held out for some years very [a] bravely.

Sylla having in the year 675 [b] laid down the [c] dictatorship, died the year following of the [d] lousy [e] disease, in the sixtieth year of his [f] age: after whose death, Lepidus the consul [g] endeavouring to [h] make void the [i] acts of Sylla, was [k] forced out of the city by his [l] colleague Catulus. And the year following, [m] advancing up to the city with an [n] army, he was defeated by the same Catulus and Cn. Pompey, and [o] fled into [p] Sardinia, where he [q] fell ill

a *levare*   b *sdegnato*   c *impossessarsi*   d *ucciso*   e *forzare*   f *fuggire*   g *assenza*   h *disturbo*   i *scacciato*   k *unito*   l *assaltare*   m *preso*   n *mettere*   o *a fil di spada*   p *morire*   q *tornare*   r *concludere*   s *rotta*   t *dichiarato*   u *dettatore*   v *partito*   x *proscrizione*   y *ritirarsi*   z *mantenersi*   a *coraggiosamente*   b *consegnato*   c *dettatura*   d *pidocchioso*   e *malattia*   f *età*   g *procurare*   h *annullare*   i *atto*   k *scacciato*   l *collega*   m *accostarsi*   n *armata*   o *fuggire*   p *Sardegna*   q *ammalarsi*.

and

ITALIAN EXERCISES. 137

and died. The same Pompey being ^a sent into Spain against Sertorius, ^b performed no great matter; but this being ^c treacherously ^d slain by his own men, he ^e easily ^f recovered that province in the year 681.

In the mean time the war with Mithridates ^g broke out again, while Sylla was yet living; and after Sylla's death, Mithridates having ^h entered into an ⁱ alliance with Sertorius, and ^k seised by force of arms upon Bithynia, which Nicomedes at his death in 679, had ^l left to the Roman people. L. Lucullus consul, in 680, ^m went against him, and being very ⁿ successful both by ^o sea and ^p land, he ^q obliged him to fly, first into ^r Pontus, and soon after to ^s Tigranes in Armenia. Lucullus ^t conquers Pontus, and defeats both the kings who ^u engaged him with an army of two hundred thousand ^v foot, and sixty thousand ^x horse, in the year of the city 685. After this, Tigranocerta, the capital of Armenia, and ^y Nisibis, two very great cities, were ^z taken. But this excellent general being ^a forsaken by his own men, was ^b obliged to ^c quit the ^d fruit of his ^e toil and ^f victories to Cn. Pompey, in the year 688; who having ^g forced Tigranes to ^h surrender himself obliged him to be ⁱ satisfied with Armenia; and whilst he ^k pursues after Mithridates, ^l adds the ^m Iberians and ⁿ Albanians to the Roman empire, in the year 689. ^o Finally, Mithridates

a *mandato* b *eseguire* c *perfidamente* d *ucciso*
e *facilmente* f *ricuperare* g *accendersi* h *entrato*
i *alleanza* k *impadronito* l *lasciato* m *andare* n *fortunato*
o *mare* p *terra* q *forzare* r *Ponto*
s *Tigrane* t *conquistare* u *attaccare* v *infanteria*
x *cavalleria* y *Nisibi* z *preso* a *abbandonato* b *obbligato*
c *lasciare* d *frutto* e *fatica* f *vittoria*
g *forzato* h *arrendersi* i *soddisfatto* k *incalzare*
l *aggiungere* m *Iberj* n *Albanesi*. o *finalmente*.

ITALIAN EXERCISES.

in the year 691, being ^a every where ^b beaten, ^c thought of ^d flying into ^e France, but being ^f discouraged by the ^g revolt of his son ^h Pharnaces and the army, he ⁱ slew himself.

Whilst the war with Mithridates was ^k warmly ^l carried on, there ^m broke out another with the ⁿ slaves, in the year of the city 681. One ^o Spartacus Ænomanus, and ^p Crixus, ^q gladiators, having ^r broken a ^s school of gladiators at Capua, ^t belonging to Lentulus, and ^u gotten together an army of ^v desperadoes, ^x routed the Roman armies several times, but at last were ^y vanquished by Crassus the prætor, and Pompey, in the year 685.

Pompey ^z likewise ^a subdued the ^b pirates, who, at the ^c instigation of Mithridates, ^d infested the seas, having an ^e extraordinary ^f commission ^g for that purpose by the ^h Gabinian law. Whilst Pompey is ⁱ enlarging the Roman empire ^k abroad, the ^l head of the empire was in no small ^m danger from a ⁿ conspiracy which ^o Catiline, ^p Lentulus the prætor, and ^q Cethegus, and other senators had ^r entered into, to ^s murder the consul ^t Cicero, and to ^u burn and ^v plunder the city. But their ^x designs were ^y prevented by the ^z vigilance of the consul. Cataline being ^a forced out of the city,

a *dappertutto* b *battuto* c *pensare* d *fuggire* e *Francia* f *scoraggito* g *rivolta* h *Farnace* i *ammazzarsi* k *vigorosamente* l *continuato* m *accentaersi* n *schiavo* o *Spartaco Enomano* p *Crisso* q *gladiatore* r *rotto* s *scuola* t *appartenere* u *radunato* v *disperato* x *sconfiggere* y *vinto* z *parimente* a *soggiogare* b *corsaro* c *instigazione* d *infestare* e *straordinario* f *commissione* g *a questo effetto* h *Gabiano* i *aggrandire* k *fuori* l *capo* m *pericolo* n *cospirazione* o *Catilina* p *Lentulo* q *Cetego* r *sare* s *uccidere* t *Cicerone* u *abbrucciare* v *saccheggiare* x *disegno* y *impedito* z *vigilanza* a *scacciato*.

repaired

ITALIAN EXERCISES.

ᵃ repaired to the army, which some of his ᵇ accomplices had ᶜ drawn together. Lentulus, and the rest of the ᵈ ringleaders of the ᵉ plot were put to death. This ᶠ happened in the year 691, and the following year Catiline was ᵍ defeated by ʰ Petreius, ⁱ Antony the proconsul's ᵏ lieutenant, and ˡ slain in the ᵐ fight.

The whole ⁿ world being now almost ᵒ subdued, the Roman empire was ᵖ arrived to that ᵠ grandeur, that it could ʳ hardly ˢ extend itself farther. No ᵗ outward ᵘ force was ᵛ sufficient to ˣ ruin it, it ʸ fell by its own ᶻ power, which was ᵃ occasioned by the ᵇ ambition of the ᶜ leading men, and the civil ᵈ jars that ᵉ arose from thence.

C. Cæsar, after the time of his ᶠ prætorship in the city was ᵍ expired, ʰ obtained the province of Lusitania; and by the great things he ⁱ performed there, ᵏ deserved well the honour of a ˡ triumph; but ᵐ postponed the ⁿ hopes of that to the ᵒ consular ᵖ dignity; for which, ᵠ while he made all ʳ possible ˢ interest, Pompey ᵗ unites with Cæsar and Crassus, Lucullus, and some others of the ᵘ grandees, ᵛ opposing his ˣ acts, which he ʸ desired might be ᶻ ratified by the senate. Thus Cæsar ᵃ carried the ᵇ consulship in the year 695, in which he ᶜ established the acts of Pompey by the senate, and

a *trasferirsi* b *complice* c *radunato* d *capo* e *congiura* f *succedere* g *sconfitto* h *Petrejo* i *Antonio* k *luogotenente* l *ucciso* m *battaglia* n *mondo* o *soggiogato* p *arrivato* q *grandezza* r *appena* s *estendersi* t *esterno* u *forza* v *bastante* x *rovinare* y *cadere* z *potere* a *cagionato* b *ambizione* c *principale* d *contesa* e *derivare* f *grado di pretore* g *espirato* h *ottenere* i *eseguire* k *meritare* l *trionfo* m *posporre* n *speranza* o *consolare* p *dignità* q *mentre* r *possibile* s *interesse* t *unirsi* u *grande* v *opporsi* x *atto* y *desiderare* z *ratificato* a *ottenere* b *consolato* c *stabilire*.

divided

^adivided the ^bpublic ^cland in Campania amongſt the ^dcitizens. He ^emarried his daughter Julia to Pompey, and ^ftook a ^gwife for himſelf Calphurnia, the daughter of ^hPiſo. Having by theſe ⁱarts, and a ^kboundleſs ^lgeneroſity, ^mgained the ⁿfavour of all ^oranks and ^pdegrees of men, he ^qprocured the province of Gaul, which he ^rgoverned for nine years; during that time he ^sreduced all Gaul, which is ^tcomprehended within the ^uPyrenæan mountains, the ^vAlps, the Rhone, and the ^xRhine, into the ^yform of a province, and ^zimpoſed a ^ayearly ^btribute upon it. He was the firſt of all the Romans that ^cattacked the ^dGermans ^ebeyond the Rhine. He likewiſe ^fviſited the ^gBritons, where ^hnone before him had ever ⁱcome. In this ^kinterval, in the year 698, he ^lentered into an ^maſſociation with Pompey and Craſſus; by ⁿvirtue of which he was to have France ^ocontinued to him. Pompey was to have ^pSpain, and Craſſus Syria, in order to a war againſt the ^qParthians; to which he ^raccordingly ^swent in the year 699, and the third year after, ^tperiſhed moſt ^umiſerably, with the greater ^vpart of his army; after which the Parthians made an ^xirruption into Syria, but were ^ybravely ^zrepulſed by Caſſius.

After the death of Craſſus, Pompey being not

a *dividere*   b *pubblico*   c *terra*   d *cittadino*   e *maritare*   f *prendere*   g *moglie*   h *Piſone*   i *arte*   k *immenſo*   l *generoſità*   m *guadagnare*   n *favore*   o *rango*   p *grado*   q *procurare*   r *governare*   s *debellare*   t *compreſo*   u *Pirenei*   v *Alpi*   x *Reno*   y *forma*   z *imporre*   a *annuale*   b *tributo*   c *attaccare*   d *Tedeſchi*   e *di là*   f *viſitare*   g *Britanno*   h *niuno*   i *venuto*   k *intervallo*   l *entrare*   m *confederazione*   n *virtù*   o *continuare*   p *Spagna*   q *Parti*   r *in conſequenza*   s *andare*   t *perire*   u *miſerabilmente*   v *parte*   x *incurſione*   y *coraggioſamente*   z *ripulſato*

able to [a] endure an [b] equal, nor Cæsar a [c] superior, the civil war broke out. Pompey's [d] party [e] endeavouring to [f] take away from Cæsar both his army and province, as soon as the time of his [g] government should [h] expire; whilst Cæsar's on the other [i] hand were for [k] serving Pompey [l] in like manner. At last in the year 705, in the [m] consulship of C. Claudius Marcellus, and L. Cornelius Lentulus, the senate, by a [n] vote, obliged Cæsar to [o] disband his army by a certain day. Antonius and Cassius, tribunes of the commons, [p] interposing their [q] authority in vain, [r] leave the town, and [s] repair to Cæsar, who [t] advancing his army towards the city, [u] struck such a [v] consternation into Pompey and the rest, that [x] leaving the city [y] without more ado, and [z] shortly after Italy, they [a] passed over into [b] Greece. Cæsar went for Spain, where he [c] vanquished Petreius and Afranius, and [d] forced their armies to [e] surrender [f] prisoners of war. In his [g] return he [h] took [i] Marseilles, and after that was made dictator, to which [k] office he was [l] chosen four times, and at last had it [m] given him for [n] life.

In the year 706, Pompey being [o] defeated by Cæsar in the [p] fields of [q] Pharsalia, went to [r] Egypt, where he was slain by the [s] order of [t] Ptolemy, in the 59th year of his [u] age. Hither Cæsar [v] likewise [x] came the following year, and after a very

   a *tollerare*   b *eguale*   c *superiore*   d *partito*   e *cercare*   f *levare*   g *governo*   h *spirare*   i *canto*   k *trattare*   l *nell' istesso modo*   m *consolato*   n *voto*   o *licenziare*   p *interporre*   q *autorità*   r *lasciare*   s *trasferirsi*   t *accostare*   u *mettere*   v *costernazione*   x *abbandonare*   y *senz' altro*   z *poco dopo*   a *passare*   b *Grecia*   c *vincere*   d *forzare*   e *arrendersi*   f *prigioniero*   g *ritorno*   h *prendere*   i *Marsiglia*   k *efficio*   l *scelto*   m *dato*   n *vita*   o *sconfitto*   p *campo*   q *Farsalia*   r *Egitto*   s *cenno*   t *Ptolemeo*   u *età*   v *parimente*   x *venire*.

142   ITALIAN EXERCISES.

ᵃ dangerous ᵇ rencounter, which he ᶜ happily ᵈ accomplished, ᵉ delivered the ᶠ kingdom of Egypt to Cleopatra and her brother. In the year following he vanquished Scipio and Cato, with king Juba, in Africa. Cato ᵍ laid violent hands upon himself at Utica. The year that ʰ followed was ⁱ remarkable for the ᵏ correction of the ˡ calendar and the year. The same year likewise he ᵐ conquered Pompey's sons; and the year after was ⁿ stabbed in the ᵒ senate-house, by a ᵖ conspiracy of Brutus and Cassius, and some others, in the 56th year of his age.

Besides these ᑫ convulsions, with which the whole ʳ world was ˢ shattered, there were some less ᵗ disturbances ᵘ happened a little before. ᵛ Clodius Pulcher being ˣ made tribune of the commons, ʸ banished Cicero, for having ᶻ condemned the ᵃ associates of Cataline to death without a ᵇ trial; which ᶜ calamity he ᵈ bore too ᵉ meanly, and ᶠ by no means ᵍ agreeably to the ʰ dignity of his life past. But he was ⁱ recalled the year after by the ᵏ procurement of Pompey, and Lentulus the consul, and ˡ received with the greatest ᵐ honour. The same Clodius ⁿ declared ᵒ Cyprus to ᵖ belong to the Roman people, and Cato being ᑫ sent to ʳ take possession of it, Ptolemy, king of the ˢ island, having first ᵗ thrown all his ᵘ money into the sea, ᵛ prevented his ˣ disgrace by a ʸ voluntary death. The se-

a *pericoloso*   b *scaramuccia*   c *fortunatamente*   d *compire*   e *consegnare*   f *regno*   g *uccidersi*   h *seguire*
i *segnalato*   k *correzione*   l *calendario*   m *conquistare*
n *pugnalato*   o *senato*   p *cospirazione*   q *convulsione*
r *mondo*   s *sconquassato*   t *disturbo*   u *succedere*   v *Clodio Pulcro*   x *fatto*   y *esiliare*   z *condennato*   a *collega*
b *processo*   c *calamità*   d *soffrire*   e *vilmente*   f *in nissun conto*   g *secondo*   h *dignità*   i *richiamato*   k *intrapresa*   l *ricevere*   m *onore*   n *dichiarare*   o *Cipro*
p *appartenere*   q *mandato*   r *impossessarsi*   s *isola*
t *gettato*   u *denaro*   v *avviare*   x *disgrazia*   y *volontaria*.

nate ᵃ beſtowed the ᵇ prætorſhip upon Cato at his
ᶜ return, by a ᵈ vote of the houſe, without any
ᵉ election; which honour he ᶠ refuſed, being ᵍ deſirous to ʰ obtain it rather by the ⁱ free ᵏ votes of
the people. But he was ˡ balked of his ᵐ hopes,
and Vatinius was ⁿ preferred before him.

ᵒ Bribery ᵖ ruling in ᵠ all ʳ elections, and the
ˢ candidates making a moſt ᵗ diſmal ᵘ confuſion,
after a long ᵛ interregnum, Pompey was made
conſul, without a ˣ colleague, a thing ʸ wholly
new, and never heard of before; in which office
he made a ᶻ ſevere ᵃ enquiry into all other ᵇ miſde-
meanours, as likewiſe into the death of Clodius,
whom Milo ᶜ killed the ſame year, for which he
was ᵈ baniſhed.

After the death of Cæſar, Antony the conſul ſo
ᵉ inflamed the people by a ᶠ ſeditious ᵍ harangue,
that they ʰ burnt his ⁱ body ᵏ publickly, and ˡ threatened to fire and ᵐ pull down the houſes of the ⁿ aſ-
ſaſſins. Octavius Cæſar, the ſon of Accia ᵒ Julius's
ſiſter, was his ᵖ adopted ſon by ᵠ will. He being
ʳ ſlighted by M. Antony, ˢ raiſed an army of ᵗ ve-
teran ſoldiers, and ᵘ oppoſed his ᵛ tyrannical ˣ pro-
ceedings. Antonius ʸ extorted from the people by
force the province of Gaul, but his ᶻ paſſage thi-

a *accordare* b *dignità di pretore*   c *ritorno*   d *voto*
e *elezione* f *rifiutare* g *deſideroſo* h *ottenere* i *li-
bero* k *voto* l *fruſtrato* m *ſperanza* n *preferito*
o *corruzione* p *dominare* q *tutto* r *elezione* s *can-
didato* t *terribile* u *confuſione* v *interregno* x *collega* y *affatto* z *ſevero* a *perquiſizione* b *delitto*
c *uccidere* d *bandito* e *accendere* f *ſedizioſo* g *ar-
ringa* h *incendiare* i *corpo* k *publicamente* l *minacciare* m *demolire* n *aſſaſſino* o *Giulio* p *adottato* q *teſtamento* r *ſprezzato* s *levare* t *vete-
rano* u *opporre* v *tirannico* x *portamento* y *ſtrap-
pare* z *paſſaggio*.

ther was opposed by D. Brutus at Modena, where he was [a] besieged by Antony.

In the [b] consulship of [c] Hirtius and Pansa, in the year of the city 711, by the [d] instigation of Cicero, Antony was [e] declared [f] enemy, and a war [g] undertaken against him, and Octavius [h] joined in [i] commission with the consuls, with the [k] power of proconsul, being then about the 20th year of his age. There was a [l] dreadful and [m] bloody [n] battle [o] fought near Modena, in which all Cæsar's [p] life-guards were slain; but Antony was routed, and the [q] siege [r] raised, yet both the consuls were killed.

In Macedonia, Brutus [s] took off C. Antonius, M. Antony's brother, who was [t] intriguing against him, and [u] got together a [v] formidable army. Upon which the senate [x] resolved by [y] degrees to [z] take down Octavius, [a] for fear of his [b] growing too [c] powerful; which he being [d] apprehensive of, [e] enters into an [f] association with Antony and Lepidus; and they were all three [g] consequently made [h] commissioners [i] for settling the [k] commonwealth; who having [l] divided the whole [m] empire into three parts, [n] proscribed a great many of the Romans, and amongst the rest M. [o] Tully Cicero, who, whilst he was [p] endeavouring to [q] make his escape into Greece, was killed by Pompilius, a [r] captain, whose [s] cause he had [t] pleaded in a capital [u] action. There

a *assediato* b *consolato* c *Irzio* d *instigazione*
e *dichiarato* f *inimico* g *intrapreso* h *unirsi* i *commissione* k *potere* l *spaventevole* m *sanguinoso* n *battaglia* o *dato* p *soldato di guardia* q *assedio* r *levato* s *uccidere* t *cospirare* u *radunare* v *formidable* x *risolvere* y *a poco a poco* z *abbassare* a *di paura che* b *doventare* c *potente* d *timoroso* e *entrare* f *lega* g *conseguentemente* h *commissionario* i *stabilire* k *republica* l *diviso* m *imperio* n *proscrivere* o *Tullio Cicerone* p *procurare* q *scampare* r *capitano* s *causa* t *litigare* u *processo*.

was

ITALIAN EXERCISES. 145

was a [a] dreadful [b] havoc made in this [c] proscription. The [d] Epitome of Livy speaks of no less than an hundred and thirty senators; the same year [e] gave [f] beginning to one of the finest cities of France, [g] Lyons.

The year following, Octavius and Antony [h] fought a battle with M. Brutus and the [i] principal of the [k] conspirators, near the city Philippi. The [l] right [m] wings were [n] victorious on both [o] sides, and on both sides the [p] camps were [q] plundered. But Cassius, who was in the wing that was [r] routed, [s] giving up all for gone [t] slew himself. Brutus being [u] defeated in another [v] engagement, likewise put an end to his own life, being then thirty-seven years of age, and none of Cæsar's [x] assassins [y] lived above three years after, being all [z] taken off by a [a] violent death, as [b] Suetonius says; some too [c] killed themselves with the same [d] dagger with which they had slain Cæsar.

After the [e] victory, Antony [f] went for Asia, and Octavius for Italy; where he was [g] engaged in war with L. Antony, the brother of the [h] triumvir, and his [i] wife Fulvia, a [k] woman of a [l] manly [m] spirit. He forced Lucius from the town; after which, being [n] declared an enemy, he [o] besieged him in Perusia, and obliged him to [p] surrender. In the mean time, the Parthians being [q] invited by Labienus, one of Pompey's party, made an [r] irruption into

a *orrendo* b *strage* c *proscrizione* d *sommario*
e *dare* f *principio* g *Lione* h *dare,* i *principale*
k *congiurato* l *ala* m *dritto* n *vittorioso* o *canto*
p *campo* q *saccheggiato* r *sconfitto* s *credere* t *ucciderſi*
u *rotti* v *conflitto* x *aſſaſſino* y *vivere*
z *morire* a *violente* b *Suetonio* c *ucciderſi* d *stiletto*
e *vittoria* f *partire* g *venire alle armi* h *triumviro*
i *moglie* k *donna* l *nobile* m *spirito*
n *dichiarato* o *aſſediare* p *arrenderſi* q *invitato*
r *scorreria.*

H
Syria,

Syria, whom Ventidius, after a very [a] signal [b] overthrow, in which the king was slain, [c] drove out again, and [d] recovered Syria.

S. Pompey, Cneius's son, having a [e] fleet at his [f] command, [g] infested the seas, with whom Cæsar made a peace, which was [h] quickly [i] broken. [k] An engagement [l] followed, wherein Pompey was [m] worsted, and [n] forced to [o] fly. He was soon after [p] put to death, by the [q] order of M. Antony, under whose [r] protection he had put himself. About this time Antony made an [s] attempt upon the Parthians, by whom he was most [t] shamefully [u] beaten. At last, Antony being [v] entirely [x] devoted to his Cleopatra, [y] divorced Octavia, Cæsar's sister, and [z] declared war against him, in which he was at last defeated by sea near [a] Actium, a [b] promontory of [c] Epire. Cæsar had upwards of 400 [d] ships, and Antony about 200, but so [e] prodigiously [f] large, that they [g] looked like [h] castles and cities [i] marching through the sea. The [k] fright of Cleopatra [l] turned the [m] fate of a [n] dubious [o] engagement to the [p] ruin of Antony; he followed her into Egypt, and being [q] besieged in Alexandria, slew himself, whom Cleopatra quickly followed.

  a *segnalato*   b *sconfitta*   c *scacciare*   d *ricuperare* e *flotta*   f *commando*   g *infestare*   h *presto*   i *rotto* k *combattimento*   l *seguire*   m *soprafatto*   n *forzato* o *fuggire*   p *messo*   q *cenno*   r *protezione*   s *intrapresa*   t *ignominiosamente*   u *battuto*   v *affatto*   x *dedicato*   y *ripudiare*   z *dichiarare*   a *Azio*   b *promontorio*   c *Epiro*   d *vascello*   e *prodigiosamente* f *grande*   g *rassomigliare*   h *castello*   i *marciare*   k *spavento*   l *cambiare*   m *sorte*   n *dubbioso*   o *battaglia* p *rovina*.   q *assediato*.

CHAP.

CHAP. VIII.

AFTER the death of Antony and Cleopatra, ᵃ Egypt was ᵇ reduced into the ᶜ form of a ᵈ province. Cæsar, in the year 725, ᵉ triumphed three times, for the ᶠ conquest of ᵍ Dalmatia, the victory at Actium, and the ʰ reducing of Egypt. After which he ⁱ advised with Agrippa and Mecænas, either ᵏ seriously, or ˡ pretendedly, about the ᵐ laying down of his ⁿ authority; Agrippa was for it, Mecænas against it, whose ᵒ advice he ᵖ resolved to follow; but ᵠ brought a ʳ bill ˢ nevertheless into the senate to ᵗ divest himself of his power, and by that ᵘ stratagem got it ᵛ secured 'to him by both senate and people, in the year 726.

ˣ Cornelius Gallus, a ʸ Roman ᶻ knight, ᵃ governor of Egypt, being ᵇ banished for his ᶜ insolence, slew himself. Augustus ᵈ carried on a war against the Cantabri and Austurs for some years, by his ᵉ lieutenants; that is to say, from the year 729 to 735, in which they were entirely ᶠ reduced by Agrippa; who, upon his ᵍ return ʰ refused a ⁱ triumph which was ᵏ offered him. ˡ Phraates, king of the Parthians, about this time, ᵐ restored the Roman ⁿ standards that had been ᵒ taken from Crassus.

Two of his ᵖ friends, Mecænas and M. Vipsanius Agrippa, he had a ᵖ particular ᵠ esteem for above

a *Egitto*   b *ridotto*   c *forma*   d *provincia*   e *trionfare*   f *conquista*   g *Dalmazia*   h *riducimento*   i *consigliarsi*   k *seriosamente*   l *fintamente*   m *deporsi*   n *autorità*   o *consiglio*   p *risolvere*   q *presentare*   r *supplica*   s *nonostante*   t *spogliarsi*   u *stratagemma*   v *assicurarsi*   x *Cornelio Gallo*   y *Romano*   z *cavaliere*   a *governatore*   b *esiliato*   c *insolenza*   d *fare*   e *luogotenente*   f *ridotto*   g *ritorno*   h *ricusare*   i *trionfo*   k *esibito*   l *Fraate*   m *restituire*   n *stendardo*   o *preso*   p *amico*   q *particolare*   r *stima*.

148   ITALIAN EXERCISES.

all others; the [a] former was a great [b] patron of [c] learning and [d] learned men: Augustus made Agrippa his [e] son-in-law, by [f] marrying his daughter Julia to him, whom he had by Scribonia. She had children, C. and L. Cæsars, Agrippa Posthumus, Agrippina married to Germanicus, Drusus's son, Livia's [g] grandson, and Julia, whom Æmilius married. He took Livia when she was [h] big with child from her former [i] husband Tiberius Nero, by whom he had no [k] issue, though she had by Nero, Tiberius, who was emperor afterwards, and Drusus who [l] died in Germany.

Tiberius having gotten the [m] tribunitial [n] power for five years, was [o] sent to [p] settle the [q] affairs of Armenia. Soon after he [r] returned to Rhodes, where, for fear of [s] falling under the [t] displeasure of his [u] step-sons, he [v] continued seven years. But the [x] occasion of his [y] retirement was his [z] aversion for his wife Julia, who [a] spent her time in all [b] manner of [c] debauchery; whom Augustus, upon a [d] discovery of her [e] pranks, [f] banished.

The [g] age of this emperor [h] produced several great [i] geniuses; amongst the [k] Greeks [l] Dionysius Halicarnassensis and [m] Nicholas Damascenus were [n] famous for their [o] talents in the writing of [p] history; and amongst the [q] Latins [r] Cornelius Nepos, Atticus's [s] son in-law, and Sallust, who died four years before the [t] fight at Actium.   In this age lived

    a *primo*   b *protettore*   c *scienza*   d *sapiente*   e *genero*   f *dare per moglie*   g *nipote*   h *gravida*   i *marito*   k *progenie*   l *morire*   m *tribunizio*   n *potere*   o *mandato*   p *regolare*   q *affare*   r *ritirarsi*   s *cascare*   t *dispiacere*   u *figliastro*   v *continuare*   x *cagione*   y *ritiratezza*   z *aversione*   a *passare*   b *sorta*   c *dissolutezza*   d *scoperta*   e *stravaganza*   f *bandire*   g *secolo*   h *produrre*   i *genio*   k *Greco*   l *Dionisio Alicarnassensi*   m *Nicola Damasceno*   n *celebre*   o *talento*   p *istoria*   q *Latino*   r *Cornelio Nepote*   s *genero*   t *battaglia*.

ITALIAN EXERCISES. 149

likewise those ^a celebrated ^b poets, ^c Virgil, ^d Horace, ^e Ovid, ^f Tibullus, and ^g Propertius.

Augustus died at Nola in Campania, in the 14th year of ^h Christ, and the 76th year of his age, having ⁱ held the empire by himself, from the death of M. Antony, three and forty years; he was an ^k excellent ^l prince, and ^m necessary for those times.

He was ⁿ succeeded by Tiberius, a prince of a ^o savage ^p disposition, and ^q given up to all manner of debauchery; he was the son of Livia by Nero. He ^r dissembled his ^s vices at the ^t beginning of his reign with ^u wonderful ^v art, out of fear of Germanicus his brother's son, whom he had ^x adopted, at the ^y command of his ^z father-in-law, who had ^a gained a great ^b reputation by his ^c virtues and ^d exploits in war, and was therefore ^e looked upon with a ^f jealous eye, as ^g fitter for the empire than himself. He ^h removed him from Germany, where he had ⁱ wonderful ^k success against the enemy, into the ^l East, to ^m fight against the Parthians, in the year 769, having sent at the same time Cn. Piso into Syria, betwixt whom and Germanicus was a ⁿ mortal grudge. Wherefore Germanicus died, not without the ^o suspicion of being ^p poisoned by him, for which being ^q prosecuted at Rome by Agrippina, Germanicus's lady, he ^r prevented his ^s sentence by a ^t voluntary death.

a *celebre*   b *poeta*   c *Virgilio*   d *Orazio*   e *Ovidio*   f *Tibullo*   g *Properzio*   h *Cristo*   i *tenuto*   k *eccellente*   l *principe*   m *necessario*   n *succeduto*   o *salvatico*   p *indole*   q *abbandonato*   r *nascondere*   s *vizio*   t *principio*   u *meraviglioso*   v *arte*   x *adottato*   y *commando*   z *suocero*   a *acquistare*   b *riputazione*   c *virtù*   d *fatto d'arme*   e *risguardato*   f *geloso*   g *proprio*   h *rimovere*   i *meraviglioso*   k *successo*   l *Levante*   m *battersi*   n *rancore mortale*   o *sospetto*   p *avvelenato*   q *proseguito*   r *prevenire*   s *sentenzia*   t *volontario*.

ITALIAN EXERCISES.

After that [a] Ælius Sejanus, a Roman [b] knight, was [c] raised by Tiberius, who after a great many [d] wicked [e] pranks, [f] aiming now, at no less than the empire itself, was by one [g] letter of Tiberius to the senate, [h] thrown from the [i] top of all his [k] grandeur, and died by the [l] hand of an [m] executioner, with all his [n] family, in the 18th year of Tiberius.

About the 13th year of his [o] reign, he [p] retired to Caprea, an [q] island on the [r] coast of Campania, with a [s] design never to come more at the town, where he [t] privately [u] wallowed in all manner of [v] debauchery, and died in the 23d year of his reign, to the great [x] joy of every body, being then in the 78th year of his age.

[y] *Jesus Christ*, the Son of God, was [z] born of the [a] Virgin Mary, in the reign of Augustus, and [b] crucified in that of Tiberius, being then four and thirty years of age.

Caius Cæsar Caligula, so [c] called from a [d] shoe [e] worn by the [f] soldiery, which, when a boy, he [g] used in the camp, [h] succeeded Tiberius, being the son of Germanicus and Agrippina, the daughter of M. Agrippa and Julia. He was then [i] entered into the five and twentieth year of his age. Great was the joy of the people upon his first [k] accession to the [l] throne, and no less were their [m] hopes that he would be [n] like Germanicus his father, who is said to have been [o] possessed of all the good [p] qualities

a *Elio Segiano* b *cavaliere* c *innalzato* d *cattivo*
e *tiro* f *aspirare* g *lettera* h *precipitato* i *colmo*
k *grandezza* l *mano* m *carnefice* n *famiglia* o *regno*
p *ritirarsi* q *isola* r *costa* s *intenzione* t *secretamente*
u *voltolare* v *dissolutezza* x *allegrezza*
y *Giesù Cristo* z *nato* a *Vergine Maria* b *crucifisso*
c *chiamato* d *scarpa* e *portato* f *soldatesca* g *portare* h *succedere* i *entrato* k *avvenimento* l *trono*
m *speranza* n *rassomigliare* o *dotato* p *qualità*

of ᵃ body and ᵇ mind. And indeed as the **worſt** of princes oftentimes ᶜ begin well, he gave not a few ᵈ tokens of his ᵉ moderation and ᶠ regard to the good of the public. But ſoon after, as if he had ᵍ put off all ʰ humanity, he ⁱ outſtripped the moſt ſavage ᵏ creatures in ˡ cruelty; and having made ᵐ havoc amongſt all ⁿ ranks and ᵒ degrees of men, he ᵖ killed likewiſe Macro, ᑫ commander of the ʳ prætorian ˢ bands, by whoſe ᵗ means he had been made emperor. He ᵘ committed ᵛ inceſt too with his ſiſters. Having ˣ exhauſted ʸ immenſe ᶻ treaſures that had been ᵃ left by Tiberius, in a year's time, he ᵇ fell to ᶜ proſcribing and ᵈ plundering. Among other tokens of his cruelty, he was ᵉ heard to ſay, I ᶠ wiſh the Roman people had but one ᵍ neck. In all his ʰ buildings, or public ⁱ works, he ᵏ effected what was ˡ looked upon to be impoſſible. He ᵐ ordered himſelf to be ⁿ worſhipped as a god throughout the ᵒ world, and ᵖ temples to be ᑫ erected to him. At laſt, he was ſlain by Chærea Caſſius, ʳ colonel of a ˢ regiment of his ᵗ guards, and ſome others, that had ᵘ entered into a ᵛ plot againſt him, after he had ˣ reigned three years, ten months, and eight days, and ʸ lived twenty-nine years.

Claudius Nero, Caligula's uncle, Druſus's ſon, ᶻ reigned after him, ᵃ naturally no ill man, but a

a *corpo*   b *mente*   c *principiare*   d *ſegno*   e *moderazione*   f *riſguardo*   g *ſpogliato*   h *umanità* i *ſuperare*   k *animale*   l *crudeltà*   m *ſtrage*   n *rango* o *grado*   p *uccidere*   q *capitano*   r *pretorio*   s *banda* t *mezzo*   u *commettere*   v *inceſto*   x *diſſipato*   y *immenſo*   z *teſoro*   a *laſciato*   b *cominciare*   c *proſcrivere*   d *saccheggiare*   e *ſentito*   f *vorrei*   g *collo* h *edifizio*   i *lavoro*   k *effettuare*   l *ſtimato*   m *farſi* n *adorare*   o *mondo*   p *tempio*   q *edificare*   r *colonnello*   s *reggimento*   t *guardia*   u *fatto*   v *coſpirazione*   x *regnato*   y *viſſuto*   z *regnare*   a *naturalmente*.

[a] senseless foolish fellow. Wherefore he was not of himself [b] cruel, but only as he was [c] put upon it by other people, [d] especially his [e] freedmen and his [f] wives, into whose hands he [g] gave himself up and his [h] affairs. His first lady was Messalina, whose [i] lewdness and [k] debaucheries every body [l] knew but himself; till at last [m] venturing to [n] marry one Silius, a knight, she was by her [o] husband's order slain, together with her [p] paramour, at the [q] instigation of [r] Narcissus, who with [s] Pallas, another of his [t] freedmen, [u] ruled him entirely.

Another [v] argument of his [x] folly is this, that after Messalina was [y] put to death, by whom he had his son [z] Britannicus, and Octavina, he married Agrippina, Germanicus his brother's daughter, the mother of Nero by [a] Domitius, in the ninth year of his reign, by the [b] advice of Pallas; at whose and Agrippina's [c] request, he [d] adopted Nero, and [e] passing by Britannicus, [f] designed him for his [g] successor. He [h] banished the [i] Jews from Rome, and the [k] mathematicians out of Italy: and [l] undertaking an [m] expedition into [n] Britain, he [o] subdued it all in sixteen days time, as Dio says, in the third year of his reign. He died in the year of Christ 54, by [p] poison [q] put in a [r] mushroom by Agrippina. He reigned thirteen years, eight months and twenty days, and lived sixty-four years.

a *insensato* b *crudele* c *instigato* d *sopratutto* e *liberto* f *moglie*, g *abbandonarsi* h *affare* i *sfrenatezza* k *dissolutezza* l *sapere* m *arrischiare* n *sposare* o *marito* p *drudo* q *instigazione* r *Narcisso* s *Pallade* t *liberto* u *governare* v *argomento* x *pazzia* y *messa* z *Britannico* a *Domizio* b *consiglio* c *richiesta* d *adottare* e *dimenticare* f *destinare* g *successore* h *bandire* i *giudeo* k *matematico* l *intraprendere* m *espedizione* n *Brettagna* o *soggiogare* p *veleno* q *messo* r *fungo*.

Domi-

ITALIAN EXERCISES. 153

Domitius Nero [a] mounted the throne after the death of his [b] step-father, being then seventeen years of age. He at first [c] behaved himself in such a manner, that he might be [d] reckoned among the best of [e] princes; that is, as long as he [f] listened to the [g] precepts of his [h] master Seneca. Afterwards, being [i] corrupted with [k] licentiousness and [l] flattery, he [m] became more like a [n] monster than a man. He [o] stopped the progress of the Parthians, who had [p] over-run Armenia, by Corbulo a [q] gallant [r] commander, and a person of great [s] virtue and [t] authority, who [u] recovered Armenia, in the ninth year of Nero, and [v] obliged [x] Tiridates Vologesis, the king of the Parthians brother, to [y] come to Rome, and to [z] beg his [a] crown of Nero, in the thirteenth year of Nero's reign; in which year he [b] recalled Corbulo, and put him to death. He [c] took off Britannicus by [d] poison, in the very [e] beginning of his reign. He likewise [f] ordered his mother Agrippina to be put to death, after having first [g] disgraced and [h] banished her from the [i] court. Which [k] parricide, that nothing might be [l] wanting to [m] complete the [n] unhappiness of the times, the senate [o] approved of. Afterwards having married Poppæa, whom he [p] took from Otho, he [q] banished Octavia, and at last put her to death. Upon the [r] discovery of a [s] plot, which Piso, and some

---

a *ascendere*   b *padrigno*   c *comportarsi*   d *annoverato*   e *principe*   f *ascoltare*   g *precetto*   h *maestro*   i *corrotto*   k *sfrenatezza*   l *adulazione*   m *doventare*   n *mostro*   o *arrestare*   p *trascorrere*   q *valoroso*   r *capitano*   s *virtù*   t *autorità*   u *ricuperare*   v *obbligare*   x *Tiridate Vologese*   y *venire*   z *domandare*   a *corona*   b *richiamare*   c *far morire*   d *veleno*   e *principio*   f *ordinare*   g *disgraziato*   h *bandito*   i *corte*   k *parricida*   l *mancare*   m *compire*   n *miseria*   o *approvare*   p *levare*   q *esiliare*   r *scoperta*   s *trama*.

others had ^a laid against him; he put to death the ^b poet Lucan, and Seneca the ^c philosopher, with several others, in the year of Christ 65, and the same year he ^d kicked his wife Poppæa, when ^e big with child, to death. He had the ^f impudence to ^g appear upon the ^h stage, and ⁱ act among the ^k players and ^l harpers, and ^m ride ⁿ chariot-races at the ^o Circensian games; and to ^p represent for his ^q diversion the ^r appearance ^s o' Troy in ^t flames, he ^u set fire to the city, and ^v laid it upon the ^x Christians. He ^y became so odious and ^z contemptible by his ^a villanies, that he was ^b forsaken by every body, and being ^c sought for in order to be ^d punished, he ^e executed the ^f hangman's ^g office upon himself, in the 14th year of his ^h reign, and 68th of our Lord.

A little before Nero's death, ⁱ C. Julius Vindex, who was ^k propraetor of Gaul, ^l openly ^m rebelled, and ⁿ persuaded Sergius Galba, ^o governor of Spain, to ^p set up for emperor, which he accordingly did, and ^q put Vindex to death presently after. He reigned about seven months, being very ^r old. He was slain together with Piso, whom he had ^s adopted, after M Silvius Otho was ^t proclaimed emperor; he reigned but about three months.

a *macchinato*   b *poeta Lucano*   c *filosofo*   d *dare dei calci*   e *gravida*   f *sfacciataggine*   g *comparire*   h *teatro*   i *recitare*   k *commediante*   l *suonatore d'arpa*   m *fare*   n *corse di carro*   o *giuochi circensi*   p *rappresentare*   q *spasso*   r *apparenza*   s *Troja*   t *fiamma*   u *incendiare*   v *imputare*   x *Cristiano*   y *doventare*   z *sprezzabile*   a *scelleratezza*   b *abbandonato*   c *cercato*   d *castigato*   e *eseguire*   f *carnefice*   g *ufficio*   h *regno*   i *C. Giulio Vindice*   k *propretore*   l *apertamente*   m *ribellarsi*   n *persuadere*   o *governatore*   p *farsi*   q *mettere*   r *vecchio*   s *adottato*   t *proclamato*.

ITALIAN EXERCISES. 155

In the mean time, Vitellius [a] trusting to the [b] legions of Germany, which he [c] commanded in [d] quality of a [e] consular [f] lieutenant-general, [g] took upon him the [h] name of emperor, and [i] defeated Otho's army in a [k] rencounter near [l] Bebriacum, who being [m] weary of a civil war, killed himself.

Vitellius reigned eight months after Otho, and was [n] succeeded by Vespasian, who had been [o] sent by Nero to [p] quell the [q] Jews. He reigned ten years with the greatest [r] justice and [s] clemency. He was a great [t] encourager of [u] learning and [v] learned men. The only thing that was [x] blamed in him, was his [y] covetousness, which he used to [z] excuse, by [a] alledging the [b] emptiness of the [c] Exchequer.

The war in [d] Judea was [e] finished in his time, to which he was sent by Nero, as we have [f] already [g] said. It was [h] begun by some [i] seditious [k] people that were [l] headed by Eleazar, the son of Ananias, the [m] high-priest, who [n] took up arms against the Romans, under the [o] pretence of [p] religion. Cestius Gallus, [q] lieutenant of Syria, [r] laid siege to [s] Jerusalem, but was [t] beaten off with great [u] slaughter in the 12th year of Nero. The [v] victorious Jews upon their [x] return to Jerusalem, amongst other generals, [y] made choice of [z] Josephus, the

a *confidare* b *legione* c *commandare* d *qualità*
e *consolare* f *luogotenente* g *prendere* h *nome*
i *sconfiggere* k *combattimento* l *Bebriaco* m *stanco*
n *succeduto* o *mandato* p *reprimere* q *Giudeo* r *giustizia*
s *clemenza* t *promotore* u *scienza* v *sapiente*
x *biasimato* y *cupidigia* z *scusare* a *allegare*
b *votezza* c *erario* d *Giudea* e *terminato*
f *già* g *detto* h *principiato* i *sedizioso*
k *gente* l *comandato* m *gran prete* n *prendere*
o *pretesto* p *religione* q *luogotenente* r *assediare*
s *Gierusalemme* t *rispinto* u *strage* v *vincitore*
x *ritorno* y *scegliere* z *Giuseppe*.

son of [a] Matthias for one. In the year of Christ 67, Vespasian [b] carrying his arms through Galilee and Judea, [c] took, besides most of their towns, Josephus their [d] commander, who [e] foretold his [f] rise. At last, he [g] fell upon Jerusalem, the [h] metropolis of the [i] nation, which was taken by his son Titus, in the second year of his reign.

This [k] proved the [l] ruin of the nation, and very name of the Jews. The [m] calamity was indeed so [n] violent, and the [o] miseries they [p] suffered so [q] various, that it was [r] visible they were [s] punished for the [t] horrid [u] murder of the [x] only begotten son of God; for a [y] dreadful [z] famine [a] forced the [b] besieged to [c] live on man's [d] flesh, and mothers to [e] eat up their own children; and eleven hundred thousand [f] people (a thing hardly ever [g] heard of before) [h] perished in that [i] siege. The city was [k] finally [l] razed to the ground. Vespasian, in the third year of his reign [m] triumphed with his son Titus, over the Jews; upon which he [n] shut up the [o] temple of [p] Janus He [q] died in his ninth [r] consulship, whilst he was [s] giving [t] audience to some [u] ambassadors, having lived sixty nine years, one month, and seven days, and reigned eight years.

Titus, who [v] succeeded his father, is [x] deservedly [y] ranked amongst the best [z] emperors, although

a *Mattia* b *portare* c *pigliare* d *commandante*
e *augurare* f *elevazione* g *cascare* h *metropoli*
i *nazione* k *ragionare* l *rovina* m *calamità* n *violento* o *miseria* p *soffrire* q *differente* r *visibile*
s *punito* t *orrendo* u *omicidio* x *unigenito* y *terribile* z *fame* a *forzare* b *assediato* c *vivere*
d *carne* e *mangiare* f *persona* g *sentito* h *perire* i *assedio* k *finalmente* l *spianato* m *trionfare*
n *chiudere* o *tempio* p *Giano* q *morire* r *consolato* s *dare* t *audienza* u *ambasciadore* v *succedere* x *meritamente* y *annoverato* z *imperatore*.

before

ITALIAN EXERCISES. 157

before he ᵃ came to the ᵇ empire, he was ᶜ thought to be of a ᵈ cruel ᵈ temper, ᵉ covetous and ᶠ luſtful. But upon his ᵍ advancement, he was ſo much ʰ altered for the better, that he ⁱ deſerved the ᵏ title of the ˡ delight of ᵐ mankind. He was ⁿ remarkable for his great ᵒ mildneſs, and ᵖ eaſy temper, and never ᑫ ſent any body away ʳ diſſatisfied; and ˢ remembering once at ᵗ ſupper that he had ᵘ done nobody any ᵛ kindneſs that day, he told all thoſe who were about him that he had ˣ loſt a day. In his reign, in the year of Chriſt 80, there was a ʸ dreadful ᶻ irruption of ᵃ flames and ᵇ aſhes out of ᶜ mount Veſuvius, which ᵈ flew as far as Africa, Syria, and Egypt; and the two towns of Pompeii and ᵉ Herculaneum were ᶠ utterly ᵍ ruined by it. This good emperor died in the year of Chriſt 81, two years and three months after he had ʰ ſucceeded his father, and in the one and fortieth year of his ⁱ age, not without the ᵏ ſuſpicion of being ˡ poiſoned by his ᵐ brother Domitian.

Titus was very much ⁿ lamented both by the ſenate and people; and their ᵒ concern for his death was very much ᵖ encreaſed by his brother and ᑫ ſucceſſor Domitian, the worſt prince of all that ʳ came before, or ˢ followed after him. At firſt he made ſome ᵗ ſhew of ᵘ clemency and ᵛ juſtice, but ſoon ˣ diſcovered his ʸ temper, and ᶻ imitated Nero in

a *arrivare*   b *imperio*   c *creduto*   d *natura*   e *avaro* f *ſenſuale*   g *avanzamento*   h *cambiato*   i *meritare* k *titolo*   l *delizia*   m *genere umano*   n *notabile*   o *benignità*   p *piacevolezza*   q *licenziare*   r *malcontento* s *ricordarſi*   t *cena*   u *fatto*   v *beneficio*   x *perduto*   y *ſpaventevole*   z *ſcorrimento*   a *fiamma*   b *cenere*   c *Monte Veſuvio*   d *ſcorrere*   e *Ercalano*   f *affatto*   g *diſtrotto*   h *ſucceduto*   i *età*   k *ſoſpetto* l *avvelenato*   m *fratello*   n *lamentato*   o *afflizione* p *accreſciuto*   q *ſucceſſore*   r *venire*   s *ſeguire*   t *moſtra*   u *clemenza*   v *giuſtizia*   x *ſcoprire*   y *natura*   z *imitare.*

cruelty,

[a] cruelty, [b] rapine, and [c] luxury. He [d] ordered himself to be [e] called god, and was at last [f] taken off by a [g] plot, in the year of Christ 96, after he had reigned fifteen years.

CHAP. IX.

[h] COcceius Nerva succeeded Domitian in the empire. He reigned but a year, four months, and eleven days; an [i] excellent prince, but [k] despised for his age. He [l] made void all the [m] acts of Domitian, and [n] restored what had been [o] taken from the people by [p] violence and [q] injustice; but he [r] wanted [s] authority to [t] keep the soldiers within [u] due bounds: wherefore those who were [v] concerned in the death of Domitian, from whom he had [x] received the empire, were [y] killed by the [z] guards, [a] in spite of all he could do to [b] prevent it. He made Trajan, [c] lieutenant of Germany, his [d] adopted son, with whom he lived three months.

Trajan [e] took upon him the [f] government of the empire at [g] Cologn, being then in the 42d year of his age; and a man [h] excellently [i] skilled in the [k] military art. He was likewise a person of great prudence, [l] moderation, and [m] meekness of [n] temper; so that he was thought by all to [o] deserve the [p] sir-

a *crudeltà*   b *rapina*   c *lussuria*   d *farsi*   e *chiamare*   f *ucciso*   g *cospirazione*   h *Coccejo Nerva*   i *eccellente*   k *sprezzato*   l *annullare*   m *atto*   n *restituire*   o *preso*   p *violenza*   q *ingiustizia*   r *mancare*   s *autorità*   t *tenere*   u *dovere*   v *aver parte*   x *ricevuto*   y *ucciso*   z *guardia*   a *ad onta di*   b *impedire*   c *luogotenente*   d *adottato*   e *pigliare*   f *governo*   g *Colgna*   h *ottimamente*   i *versato*   k *arte militare*   l *moderazione*   m *dolcezza*   n *natura*   o *meritare*   p *cognome*,

name

ITALIAN EXERCISES. 159

firname of [a] Optimus. He [b] added Dacia to the empire, and [c] marching into tne [d] East, [e] fubdued the [f] Armenians, the [g] Iberians, the [h] Colchians, the [i] Sarmatians, the [k] Ofrhoenians, the [l] Arabians, and the [m] Bofphoranians. He likewife [n] fell upon the Parthians, and [o] took the cities, Seleucia, [p] Ctefiphon, and [q] Babylon, with feveral others. But upon his [r] taking a voyage in the [s] Red Sea, almoft all thofe nations [t] rofe in rebellion; but he [v] quickly [u] reduced them, either in perfon, or by his [x] lieutenants. There was in his time a great [y] earthquake, which [z] ruined the city of [a] Antioch: it [b] happened in the year of Chrift 115, in the [c] confulfhip of Meffala, and Pedo, the latter of whom was [d] buried in the [e] ruins of the [f] place, and Trajan was [g] drawn through a [h] window, and had [i] much ado to [k] efcape. The Jews of [l] Syrene [m] took up arms, and [n] exercifed all manner of [o] cruelty upon the Romans and Greeks throughout all [p] Egypt and [q] Cyprus, whom Trajan [r] fuppreffed with infinite [s] flaughter, by his lieutenant Martius Turbo. [t] Whilft he was [u] preparing to march againft the Parthians, who were in arms, having [v] forced from amongft them the king that had been [x] given them by the Roman emperor; this excellent prince [y] fell ill, and [z] died at [a] Selinus in Cilicia.

a *Ottimo* b *aggiungere* c *marciare* d *Levante* e *foggiogare* f *Armeniani* g *Iberj* h *Colchi* i *Sarmati* k *Ofroeni* l *Arabi* m *Bofforani* n *attaccare* o *prendere* p *Ctefifone* q *Babilonia* r *fare un viaggio per il mare roffo* s *ribellarfi* t *prefto* u *ridurre* x *luogotenente* y *terremoto* z *rovinare* a *Antioco* b *fuccedere* c *confolato* d *feppellito* e *rovina* f *piazza* g *tirato* h *fineftra* i *molta difficoltà* k *fcappare* l *Sirene* m *prender l'armi* n *efercitare* o *crudeltà* p *Egitto* q *Cipro* r *fopprimere* s *ftrage* t *mentre* u *prepararfi* v *forzato* x *dato* y *ammalarfi* z *morire* a *Selino*.

He

He reigned nineteen years, six months, and fifteen days.

^a Ælius Adrianus, Trajan's ^b cousin and ^c countryman, ^d obtained the empire after him, by the ^e favour of Plotina, Trajan's lady, a man of a great deal of ^f variety in his ^g temper and ^h genius, ⁱ equally ^k cut out for virtue and ^l vice. He ^m went through all the ⁿ provinces of the empire, so that no body ever ^o travelled over so much of the ^p world as he did. After the death of Trajan, he ^q quitted Armenia, Syria, and Mesopotamia, to the Parthians, and ^r intended likewise to ^s leave Dacia, had he not been ^t afraid of ^u ruining the many thousands of Romans that were there.

He ^v rebuilt Jerusalem, which he ^x called Ælia Capitolina, and ^y settled a colony there; and in the same place where the ^z temple had ^a stood, ^b built another in ^c honour of ^d Jupiter; which thing so ^e provoked the Jews, that ^f taking up arms, they ^g carried on the war with more ^h fury than ever, under the ⁱ conduct of Barcochebas; against whom, amongst others ^k skilful generals that he ^l employed, Adrian ^m sent for Julius Severus out of ⁿ Britain, by whom the Jews were by ^o degrees ^p suppressed and utterly ^q destroyed; there being no less than 50,000 slain in that war, besides an ^r innumerable ^s multitude that were ^t consumed by ^u famine, ^v pes-

a *Elio Adriano*   b *cugino*   c *compatriotto*   d *ottenere*   e *favore*   f *varietà*   g *natura*   h *genio*   i *ugualmente*   k *nato*   l *vizio*   m *andare*   n *provincia*   o *viaggiare*   p *mondo*   q *cedere*   r *disegnare*   s *lasciare*   t *temuto*   u *rovinare*   v *redificare*   x *chiamare*   y *stabilire*   z *tempio*   a *situato*   b *edificare*   c *onore*   d *Giove*   e *irritare*   f *pigliar l'armi*   g *fare*   h *furia*   i *condotta*   k *sperimentato*   l *impiegare*   m *far venire*   n *Brettagna*   o *gradualmente*   p *soppresso*   q *distrotto*   r *innumerabile*   s *moltitudine*   t *consumato*   u *fame*   v *pestilence,*

ITALIAN EXERCISES.

tilence, and ᵃ fire ; fo that ᵇ Paleſtine was almoſt made a ᶜ wildernefs. After that time, the Jews were ᵈ forbid, ᵉ under pain of death, to come to Jerufalem, unlefs one day in a year to ᶠ lament their ᵍ mifery.

At laſt Adrian ʰ growing old and ⁱ infirm, having no ᵏ children of his own, ˡ adopted ᵐ Arrius Antoninus, who was afterwards ⁿ furnamed ᵒ Pius, ᵖ upon condition that he ſhould adopt Annius Verus, fon of Ælius Verus, and ᑫ M. Aurelius Antoninus. After which he died at Baiæ, in the year of Chriſt 138, having lived fixty-two years, and reigned twenty-one and eleven months.

Antoninus Pius, adopted by Adrian, ʳ governed the Roman empire with fo much virtue and ˢ goodnefs, that he ᵗ outdid all ᵘ example ; for he ˣ managed the ʸ commonwealth rather with the ᶻ affection of a father, than that of a prince, and ᵃ kept the world in ᵇ peace during his whole reign, for which ᶜ reaſon he was ᵈ compared to Numa. ᵉ Foreign and ᶠ remote princes and ᵍ nations ʰ feared him to that degree, that they ⁱ referred the ᵏ deciſion of their ˡ controverſies to him. He ᵐ forbad any ⁿ ſcrutiny to be made after thoſe, who had ᵒ entered into a ᵖ plot againſt his ᑫ life. He died in the feventieth year of his age, and twenty-fourth of his reign.

ſilenza   a fuoco   b Paleſtina   c deſerto   d proibito e ſotto pena di morte   f compiangere   g miſeria   h divenire vecchio   i infermo   k figliuolo .   l adottare   m Arrio Antonino   n cognominato   o Pio   p con patto   q M. Aurelio Antonino   r governare   s benignità   t forpaſſare   u eſempio   x maneggiare   y republica   z affezione   a tenere   b pace   c ragione d comparato   e ſtraniero   f remoto   g nazione   h temere   i rimettere   k deciſione   l controverſia   m proibire   n ſcrutinio   o entrare   p coſpirazione   q vita.

After

ITALIAN EXERCISES.

After him reigned M. Antoninus Verus, Pius's *son-in-law; for he had married his daughter Valeria Fauſtina. He had from his *b* youth been *c* educated as well in the *d* knowledge of other *e* arts as the *f* ſtudies of *g* wiſdom; which he made *h* appear no leſs in his life and *i* conduct, than in his *k* words and *l* profeſſion. In the *m* beginning of his reign, he made L. Ælius Verus his *n* partner of the empire, to whom he married his daughter Lucilla. They reigned together eleven years, being of very *o* different *p* inclinations; for Verus was of a *q* liſtleſs, *r* luxurious, and *s* moroſe temper, but was *t* kept within ſome *u* bounds by the *v* reſpect he had for his brother; by whom he was *x* ſent againſt the Parthians, and *y* carried on the war *z* ſucceſsfully for four years, by his lieutenants; wherefore they both *a* triumphed over the Parthians. Afterwards they *b* undertook an *c* expedition againſt the Marcomanni, but upon their *d* march Verus was *e* ſeiſed with an *f* apoplexy, between Concordia and *g* Altinum, and died. M. Aurelius carried on the war for three years againſt the Marcomanni, to whom the Quadi, *h* Vandals, *i* Sarmatians, and Suevi *k* joined themſelves. His army in *l* want *m* of water, was *n* relieved by a *o* legion of *p* Chriſtians that was in it, who, by their *q* prayers *r* procured *s* rain from *t* heaven, as *u* Euſebius *v* tells us. The

a *genero* b *gioventù* c *educato* d *conoſcenza*
e *arte* f *ſtudio* g *ſapienza* h *comparire* i *condotta* k *parola* l *profeſſione* m *principio* n *compagno* o *differente* p *inclinazione* q *pigro* r *luſſurioſo* s *faſtidioſo* t *tenuto* u *moderazione* v *riſpetto* x *mandato* y *fare* z *fortunatamente* a *trionfare* b *intraprendere* c *eſpedizione* d *marcia* e *aſſalito* f *apopleſſia* g *Altino* h *Vandali* i *Sarmati* k *unirſi* l *neceſſità* m *acqua* n *aſſiſtito* o *legione* p *Criſtiano* q *preghiera* r *procurare* s *pioggia* t *cielo* u *Euſebio* v *raccontare*.

ITALIAN EXERCISES. 163

a exchequer being quite b exhausted by the great c expence of the war, that he might not d burden the people with e taxes, he f produced all the imperial g furniture and h sold it; and after the victory i restored the k price to those l chapmen that m were willing to n part with what they had o bought. Avidius Cassius, upon p false advice that he was q dead, r seised the s government, and was three months after slain. M. Aurelius died at Vienna, after a reign of nineteen years and eleven months.

He was t succeeded by his u wicked son Aurelius Commodus Antoninus, who v resembled Nero for x cruelty, y lust, z avarice, and such arts as are a scandalous in an emperor. Having b settled his affairs with the c Germans, he triumphed at Rome. He put to death his sister Lucilla, who, with d several others, had e conspired against his life. He f used to g fight among the h gladiators in the i public games. He was at last, after an k infamous life, l taken off by the m contrivance of a n mistress, and the captain general of his o life-guards, whom he had p determined to q put to death. He reigned twelve years, nine months, and fourteen days.

After Commodus was r taken off in the year of Christ 193, P. s Helvius Pertinax, was t declared emperor, by the same that had u dispatched Com-

a *erario*   b *votato*   c *spesa*   d *caricare*   e *tassa*
f *produrre*   g *formimento*   h *vendere*   i *restituire*
k *prezzo*   l *compratore*   m *volere*   n *disfarsi*   o *comprato*
p *falso avviso*   q *morto*   r *usurpare*   s *governo*
t *succeduto*   u *malvagio*   v *rassomigliare*   x *crudeltà*
y *sensualità*   z *avarizia*   a *scandaloso*   b *regolàto*
c *Germani*   d *parecchi*   e *cospirato*   f *solere*
g *battersi*   h *gladiatore*.   i *giuochi publici*   k *infame*
l *ucciso*   m *arte*   n *amorosa*   o *guardie del corpo*
p *risoluto*   q *mettere*   r *ammazzato*   s *Elvio Pertinace*
t *dichiarato*   u *spacciato*.

modus,

modus, who ᵃ endeavouring to ᵇ reduce the ᶜ commonwealth into better ᵈ order, and to ᵉ curb the ᶠ licentiousness of the ᵍ soldiery, was, within eighty days after his coming to the empire ʰ murdered by his own guards. The empire after this, was by the soldiers ⁱ exposed to ᵏ sale, and Didius Julianus, ˡ coming up to their ᵐ terms, was ⁿ accepted of, and ᵒ proclaimed emperor accordingly. But ᵖ being not able to ᵠ make up the ʳ promised donative, he was ˢ forsaken by them, and slain by the ᵗ order of Septimius Severus, after he had reigned two months and five days.

This Severus, a ⁿ native of Africa, was at that time lieutenant of Pannonia, and ᵒ took upon him the government, under the ᵖ pretence of ᵠ revenging Pertinax's death. He first of all ʳ disbanded the guards for that ᵃ abominable ᵇ murder. Then he ᶜ fell upon Pescennius Niger, lieutenant of Syria, and Clodius Albinus of ᵈ Britain, his ᵉ competitors for the empire. Niger was ᶠ conquered, and Antioch, into which he ᵍ threw himself, was taken; after which, ʰ flying towards the ⁱ river Euphrates, he was ᵏ taken and slain. After the ˡ taking off of Niger, Severus ᵐ took ⁿ Byzantium, which had ᵒ declared for him, after a ᵖ siege of three years.

ᵠ Matters being ʳ brought to a ˢ peaceable ᵗ settle-

a *procurare*   b *ridurre*   c *repubblica*   d *ordine*
e *reprimere*   f *licenza*   g *soldatesca*   h *assassinato*
i *esporre*   k *vendita*   l *venire*   m *patto*   n *accettato*   o *proclamato*   p *potere*   q *fare* ·   r *donativo promesso*   s *abbandonato*   t *ordine*   u *nativo*   v *prendere*   x *pretesto*   y *vendicare*   z *licenziare*   a *abbominevole*   b *assassinamento*   c *attaccare*   d *Brettagna*
e *competitore*   f *vinto*   g *gettarsi*   h *fuggire*   i *fiume Eufrate*   k *preso*   l *assassinamento*   m *prendere*   n *Bisanzio*   o *dichiarato*   p *assedio*   q *le cose*   r *condotto*
s *pacifico*   t *accommodamento*.

ment

tlement in the ᵃ East, he ᵇ turned his arms ᶜ westward against Clodius Albinus, and ᵈ engaged him at ᵉ Lyons in ᶠ France; where many being slain on both ᵍ sides, and amongst others, Albinus, he was ʰ left sole ⁱ possessor of the empire. The city was ᵏ plundered and ˡ burnt, Albinus's ᵐ head ⁿ sent to Rome, and ᵒ dreadful ᵖ havoc made among those who had been his ᵠ favourers and ʳ friends.

After this, he ˢ marched ᵗ eastward again, and ᵘ conquered the Parthians, the ᵛ Adiabenians, and Arabians, whilst Plotianus, in the mean time, ˣ governed all at Rome, whose daughter Plotilla was ʸ contracted to Antoninus, Severus's son, and the ᶻ nuptials ᵃ celebrated in the tenth year of Severus's reign. But not long after, Plotianus being ᵇ engaged in a ᶜ plot against the emperor, was slain by his ᵈ son-in-law, and a great many that had been in his ᵉ interest, killed after him.

Severus ᶠ undertook an ᵍ expedition into Britain, with his two sons, in the 15th year of his reign, where he ʰ continued three years, being very ⁱ successful, and ᵏ drew a ˡ wall ᵐ across the ⁿ island for its ᵒ security. He died at York, after he had reigned seventeen years, eight months, and three days.

ᵖ Antoninus Caracalla and Geta, the two sons of Severus, were after him ᵠ advanced to the empire,

   a *Levante*   b *voltare*   c *verso l'occidente*   d *attaccare*   e *Lione*   f *Francia*   g *canto*   h *lasciato*   i *possessore*   k *saccheggiato*   l *abbrucciato*   m *testa*   n *mandato*   o *orribile*   p *strage*   q *favoreggiatore*   r *amico*   s *marciare*   t *verso il levante*   u *conquistare*   v *Adiabeniani*   x *governare*   y *fidanzato*   z *nozze*   a *celebrato*   b *impegnato*   c *cospirazione*   d *genero*   e *interesse*   f *intraprendere*   g *spedizione*   h *continuare*   i *fortunato*   k *tirare*   l *muro*   m *attraverso*   n *isola*   o *sicurezza*   p *Antonino Caracalla*   q *alzato*.

in the year of Christ 211. But the [a] difference of their [b] humour and [c] manners were such, that they were [d] perpetually [e] at variance. Geta was of a [f] mild and civil [g] temper, the other [h] cruel and [i] boisterous, who, in the second year of his reign, [k] slew his brother in his [l] mother's [m] bosom. After him, a great many of his friends and [n] favourers were [o] put to death, amongst whom the [p] famous [q] lawyer [r] Papinian, because he would not [s] justify his [t] parricide. After this, he [u] marched into the [x] East. At Alexandria he made a [y] shocking [z] massacre of the [a] inhabitants, for having some time before made some [b] jests upon him. He [c] invaded after that [d] Artabanus, king of the Parthians, and [e] laid waste his [f] dominions. He was [g] taken off by the [h] contrivance of Opilius Macrinus after he had reigned six years and two months.

Macrinus [i] enjoyed the empire but a short time; for he and his son were slain by the [k] soldiers within a year and two months after he came to it; and was [l] succeeded by [m] Antoninus Heliogabalus, [n] supposed, but [o] falsely, to be the son of Caracalla. He was the [p] vilest [q] wretch that ever lived, [r] given up to all manner of [s] debauchery. Wherefore, after a reign of three years and nine months, he was slain by the [t] soldiery, with his mother Julia, or Semiamira.

a *differenza*   b *umore*   c *costume*   d *perpetuamente*
e *in lite*   f *benigno*   g *disposizione*   h *crudele*   i *impetuoso*   k *uccidere*   l *madre*   m *in seno*   n *favoreggiatore*   o *messo*   p *celebre*   q *avvocato*   r *Papiniano*
s *giustificare*   t *parricidio*   u *marciare*   x *levante*
y *orribile*   z *strage*   a *abitante*   b *burla*   c *invadere*   d *Artabano*   e *desolare*   f *dominio*   g *ucciso*
h *arte*   i *godere*   k *soldato*   l *succeduto*   m *Antonino Eliogabalo*   n *supposto*   o *falsamente*   p *vile*
q *scellerato*   r *abbandonato*   s *sfrenatezza*   t *soldatesca*.

After this, [a] M. Aurelius Alexander [b] mounted the throne, having been [c] created Cæsar the year before, an [d] extraordinary prince; and well [e] instructed in all the [f] arts of [g] peace and war. He [h] carried a strict hand over the [i] judges, and was very [k] severe upon all those that by [l] favour or [m] bribery [n] transgressed the [o] bounds of [p] justice. He [q] banished from his [r] person all [s] flatterers, [t] buffoons, and such as are a [u] scandal to the [v] court. He [x] forbad the [y] sale of [z] offices, saying, that what was [a] bought would be [b] sold again. He [c] allowed the [d] deputies of the [e] provinces all their [f] furniture out of the [g] exchequer, that they might not be [h] burdensome to the people. He was [i] successful against the Persians, but at last slain in a [k] sedition of his army.

In the fifth year of his reign, [l] Artaxerxes, [m] the Persian, having [n] defeated the Parthians in three [o] battles, and slain their king, Artabanus, [p] raised anew the empire of the Persians in the East. He made an [q] excursion too into the Roman [r] territories, but was defeated by Alexander. After which he [s] undertook an [t] expedition against the Germans, in which he was slain by Maximinus, together with his mother, after a reign of thirteen years.

Maximinus was made emperor after the [u] murder of Alexander, and [v] put a happy end to the German

a *M. Aurelio Aleſſandro* b *aſcendere* c *creato* d *ſtraordinario* e *iſtruito* f *arte* g *pace* h *comportarſi rigoroſamente* i *giudice* k *ſevero* l *favore* m *corruzione* n *uſcire* o *termine* p *giuſtizia* q *bandire* r *perſona* s *adulatore* t *buffone* u *ſcandalo* v *corte* x *proibire* y *vendita* z *uffizio* a *comprato* b *rivenduto* c *concedere* d *deputato* e *provincia* f *mobili* g *erario* h *incomodo* i *fortunato* k *ſedizione* l *Artaſarſe* m *il Perſiano* n *ſconfitto* o *battaglia* p *rialzare* q *ſcorreria* r *territorio* s *intraprendere* t *eſpedizione* u *aſſaſſinio* v *terminare*

war.

war. In the mean time he made a ª dreadful ᵇ havoc at Rome, by his governor there, and killed a great many of the ᶜ nobility. During this, the two ᵈ Gordians, father and son, while at ᵉ Carthage, ᶠ laid claim to the empire. The Romans, being ᵍ headed by the senate, ʰ declared against Maximinus; and ⁱ persons were ᵏ dispatched away to ˡ secure the provinces for the senate. At home twenty ᵐ commissioners are ⁿ nominated for the ᵒ management of public ᵖ affairs. The Gordians being ᑫ taken off in Africa, after a year and a few days, by ʳ Capelian, Maximinus's general, ˢ Balbinus and ᵗ Maximus Pupienus, two of the ᵘ twenty ᵛ commissioners, were ˣ advanced to the empire by the senate in the year of Christ 237; in which Maximinus, as he was ʸ besieging Aquileia, was slain by the ᶻ soldiers with his son that was but a ª boy, after a reign of two years and ten months.

Balbinus and Pupienus, with Gordian, a boy, whom we have ᵇ already ᶜ told you, ᵈ perished in Africa, reigned together for a year. But afterwards being ᵉ desirous to ᶠ get rid of Gordian, who was more in ᵍ favour than themselves, they were slain by the soldiers in the year of Christ 238; from which time Gordian ʰ enjoyed the empire by himself, a ⁱ youth of an ᵏ extraordinary ˡ genius, and ᵐ turned to all manner of virtue; which was ⁿ improved by the ᵒ prudence of Militheus, a very ᵖ learned and

felicemente   a *spaventevole*   b *strage*   c *nobiltà*   d *Gordiani*   e *Cartagine*   f *aver pretensione*   g *comandato*   h *dichiararsi*   i *persona*   k *spedito*   l *assicurarsi*   m *commissario*   n *nominato*   o *condotta*   p *affare*   q *ucciso*   r *Capelliano Massimino*   s *Balbino*   t *Massimo Pupieno*   u *ve..t:*   v *commissario*   x *alzato*   y *assediare*   z *soldato*   a *ragazzo*   b *già*   c *detto*   d *perire*   e *desideroso*   f *disfarsi*   g *grazia*   h *godere*   i *giovine*   k *straordinario*   l *genio*   m *inclinato*   n *coltivato*   o *prudenza*   p *sapiente*.

eloquent

ᵃ eloquent man, whofe daughter he ᵇ married; with whom he ᶜ marched at the ᵈ head of a great army againſt the Perſians, and ᵉ recovered from them ᶠ Carræ, ᵍ Niſibis, and other towns, and ʰ forced them back into their own ⁱ country. The year ᵏ following, Miſitheus being ˡ taken off by the ᵐ contrivance of ⁿ Philip the Arabian, Gordian himſelf was ſoon after ſlain in a ᵒ tumult, which the ſame Philip ᵖ raiſed by the ᵠ help of ſome ſoldiers he had ʳ corrupted, after he had reigned ſix years, in whoſe ˢ place the ᵗ parricide ᵘ ſucceeded.

In the fourth year of this Philip's reign, the ᵛ ſecular games were ʷ celebrated at Rome, in the ˣ thouſandth year of the city. He was ʸ at laſt ᶻ ſlain at Verona, by the ſoldiers, in the ſixth year of his ᵃ reign.

Decius, ᵇ born in ᶜ Lower Pannonia, a man of great ᵈ courage and ᵉ experience in war, ᶠ ſucceeded him. He ᵍ periſhed in a ʰ morafs in a battle againſt the ⁱ Barbarians. This ᵏ defeat was ˡ occaſioned by the ᵐ treachery of Gallus, who ⁿ ſecretly ᵒ caballed with the enemy after he had reigned thirty months. This Gallus being made emperor by the ᵖ choice of the ᵠ ſoldiery, and having ʳ taken his ſon as a ˢ partner in the ᵗ government, was ſlain together with him by the ſoldiers, two years and four months after, at Interamna, as he was ᵘ march-

---

a *eloquente*   b *ſpoſare*   c *marciare*   d *teſta*   e *ricuperare*   f *Carrea*   g *Niſibi*   h *riſpignere*   i *paeſe*   k *ſeguente*   l *ucciſo*   m *invenzione*   n *Filippo l' Arabo*   o *tumulto*   p *ſuſcitare*   q *aſſiſtenza*   r *corrotto*   s *luogo*   t *parricida*   u *ſuccedere*   v *giuochi ſecolari*   w *celebrato*   x *milleſimo*   y *finalmente*   z *ammazzato*   a *regno*   b *nato*   c *baſſo*   d *coraggio*   e *ſperienza*   f *ſuccedere*   g *perire*   h *palude*   i *barbaro*   k *ſconfitta*   l *cagionato*   m *perfidia*   n *naſcoſtamente*   o *congiurare*   p *ſcelta*   q *ſoldateſca*   r *preſo*   s *compagno*   t *governo*   u *marciare*.

ing against Æmilian, who was ᵃ raising a ᵇ rebellion in Mœsia.

Æmilian did not reign long, being slain three months after his ᶜ advancement, and was ᵈ succeeded by Valerian, with his son Gallienus, who reigned six years together; during which time the Roman empire was ᵉ miserably ᶠ rent by the Barbarians. Thirty ᵍ tyrants ʰ started up in several ⁱ places, as ᵏ Trebellius Pollio tells us. Wherefore Valerian ˡ marching against the ᵐ Scythians, who had ⁿ taken ᵒ Chalcedon, ᵖ burnt Nice, and the ᑫ temple of the ʳ Ephesian Diana, and from thence ˢ advancing against Sapores, that was very ᵗ troublesome to the ᵘ Eastern ᵛ borders, he ˣ took him ʸ prisoner, and ᶻ treated him like a vile ᵃ slave; for when he ᵇ mounted his ᶜ horse, he ᵈ set his ᵉ foot upon his ᶠ neck, who ᵍ bowed himself ʰ for that purpose. At last he ⁱ ordered him to be ᵏ flead and ˡ salted. This ᵐ victory over the Romans ⁿ happened in the year of Christ 260. After which Odenatus, a senator of the ᵒ Palmyrenians, whom Zenobia had ᵖ married, ᑫ bravely ʳ repulsed the Persians, that still ˢ harassed the ᵗ borders.

ᵘ In the mean time Gallienus, ᵛ given up to nothing but ˣ luxury and ʸ debauchery, ᶻ suffered the empire to be ᵃ torn to pieces by the Barbarians and

a *suscitare*   b *ribellione*   c *avanzamento*   d *succeduto*   e *miserabilmente*   f *lacerato*   g *tiranno*   h *sollevarsi*   i *luogo*   k *Trebellio Pollione*   l *marciare*   m *sciti*   n *preso*   o *Calcedonia*   p *abbrucciato*   q *tempio*   r *Efesiano*   s *avanzare*   t *fastidioso*   u *orientale*   v *frontiere*   x *fare*   y *prigioniero*   z *trattare*   a *schiavo*   b *montare*   c *cavallo*   d *porre*   e *piede*   f *collo*   g *abbassarsi*   h *a questo effetto*   i *fare*   k *scorticare*   l *salare*   m *vittora*   n *succedere*   o *Palmireniani*   p *sposato*   q *coraggiosamente*   r *rispignere*   s *rovinare*   t *confine*   u *nell' istesso tempo*   v *abbandonato*   x *lussuria*   y *dissolutezza*   z *lasciare*   a *lacerare in pezzi*.

tyrants.

ITALIAN EXERCISES. 171

[a] tyrants. Odenatus, after the [b] taking of Nisibis and Carræ, and [c] recovery of Mesopotamia, [d] upon routing of the king of the Persians, having [e] sent the great [f] lords of the Persians to him in [g] chains, he was [h] not ashamed to [i] triumph, as if he had [k] conquered them himself. Odenatus was [l] murdered by his [m] cousin, together with his son Herod, whose [n] wife Zenobia, being a [o] woman of a [p] manly spirit, [q] undertook the government. Gallienus was slain with his brother Valerian at [r] Milan, as he was marching against Aureolus the tyrant. He reigned almost seven years with his father, and eight alone.

Claudius [s] succeeded him, a [t] frugal and [u] moderate prince, and very [v] serviceable to the public, who having [x] taken off the tyrant Aureolus, was very [y] successful against the [z] Goths, of whom he [a] slew 320,000, and [b] sunk 200 of their [c] ships. The rest of the Barbarians were [d] consumed at [e] Hæmimontium by [f] famine and [g] pestilence; and soon after Claudius [h] died of the same [i] plague, after a reign of one year and nine months.

His brother Quintilius [k] usurping the empire, was slain by the soldiers ten days after, who had now [l] made choice of Aurelian, a person of [m] mean birth, but [n] reckoned amongst the most [o] glorious princes, only a little too [p] cruel. He [q] subdued the Alemanni and Marcomanni, from whom the Ro-

a *tiranno*   b *presa*   c *ricoveramento*   d *dopo la sconfitta*   e *mandato*   f *signore*   g *catena*   h *vergogna*   i *trionfare*   k *conquistato*   l *assassinato*   m *cugino*   n *moglie*   o *donna*   p *animo coraggioso*   q *intraprendere*   r *Milano*   s *succedere*   t *frugale*   u *moderato*   v *servizievole*   x *ucciso*   y *fortunato*   z *Gotti*   a *uccidere*   b *affondare*   c *nave*   d *distrutto*   e *Hemimonzio*   f *fame*   g *pestilenza*   h *morire*   i *peste*   k *usurpare*   l *fare scelta*   m *bassa nascita*   n *annoverato*   o *glorioso*   p *crudele*   q *soggiogare*.

mans had before [a] received a [b] signal [c] overthrow. After their victory he [d] came to Rome, and [e] put several of the [f] senators to death, and [g] enlarged the [h] walls of the city. Then marching [i] eastward, he conquered Zenobia, whom with the tyrant [k] Tetrichus, he [l] led in [m] triumph. [n] Aurelius Victor tells us, he was the first of the Roman emperors that [o] wore a [p] diadem on his [q] head, or [r] used [s] jewels and [t] cloth of [u] gold. He was [v] taken by [x] Mnestheus, a [y] notary to the [z] secretaries at [a] Cænophrurium, [b] betwixt [c] Byzantium and Heraclea. After his [d] death there was an [e] interregnum of about seven months, [f] occasioned by a [g] dispute between the senate and the army, about the [h] choice of an emperor; at length Tacitus was [i] chosen by the senate, a person of [k] excellent [l] morals, and very [m] fit for the [n] government, who was [o] descended from Tacitus the [p] historian; but he [q] died of a [r] fever six months after at Tarsus. His brother Florianus [s] succceded him; but Probus being [t] set up by a [u] majority of the army, Florianus [v] bled himself to death, two months after his brother died, in the year of Christ 276.

This Probus was [x] born in Pannonia Sirmiensis, a very fine man, and an excellent [y] soldier of [z] unspotted morals. [a] As soon as he was [b] made em-

a *ricevuto*   b *segnalato*   c *sconfitta*   d *venire*   e *mettere*
f *senatore*   g *allargare*   h *mure*   i *verso l'oriente*   k *Tetrico*   l *condurre*   m *trionfo*   n *Aurelio Vittore*   o *portare*   p *diadema*   q *capo*   r *servirsi*
s *gioja*   t *panno*   u *oro*   v *preso*   x *Mnesteo*   y *notaro*   z *secretario*   a *Cenofrurio*   b *trà*   c *Bisanzio*.
d *morte*   e *interregno*   f *cagionato*   g *disputa*   h *scelta*
i *scelto*   k *eccellente*   l *costume*   m *capace*   n *governo*.   o *disceso*   p *istorico*   q *morire*.   r *febbre*.
s *succedere*   t *innalzato*   u *pluralità*   v *fare sangue*
x *nato*   y *soldato*   z *intatta probità*   a *subito che*.
b *fatto*.

peror,

ITALIAN EXERCISES. 173

·peror, he [a] punished all those that [b] had a hand in the death of Aurelian. After that he [c] marched for [d] France, and [e] recovered several towns out of the [f] hands of the [g] Barbarians, and [h] slew almost 70,000 of them. After the [i] reducing of [k] Gaul, he recovered [l] Illyricum, and [m] subdued the people [n] called the [o] Getæ; then going into the [p] East, he [q] fell upon the [r] Persians; and having [s] defeated them, and [t] taken several towns, he was [u] slain in his [v] return to Italy by the soldiers at [w] Sirmium, who [x] hated him for his great [y] severity. This [z] happened in the seventh year of his [a] reign, and the 282d of Christ.

Probus was [b] succeeded by M. Aurelius Carus, [c] born at [d] Narbon in France, who [e] immediately [f] made his sons Carinus, and Numerianus, [g] Cæsars; and having [h] sent Carinus to [i] take care of France, he [k] marched into the [l] East against the Persians with Numerianus; where after he had [m] reduced Mesopotamia, and marched as far as [n] Ctesiphon, he was [o] struck dead with [p] thunder, having [q] reigned about a year. Numerianus being much [r] concerned for his father's death, [s] contracted a [t] weakness in his [u] eyes with [v] weeping, and was [w] slain by the [x] contrivance of Aper his [y] father-in-law.

Carinus was nothing [z] like his father and brother,

a *punire* b *essere complice* c *marciare* d *Francia* e *ricuperare* f *potere* g *barbaro* h *ammazzare* i *riduzione* k *Gallia* l *Illirico* m *soggiogare* n *chiamato* o *Geti* p *Levante* q *attaccare* r *Persiano* s *sconfitto* t *preso* u *ucciso* v *ritorno* w *Sirmio* x *odiare* y *severità* z *succedere* a *regno* b *successo* c *nato* d *Narbone* e *subito* f *fare* g *Cesare* h *mandato* i *aver cura* k *marciare* l *Levante* m *ridotto* n *Ctesifone* o *ammazzato* p *fulmine* q *regnato* r *afflitto* s *acquistare* t *debolezza* u *occhio* v *piangere* w *ucciso* x *invenzione* y *suocero* z *rassomigliare*.

being

being ^a guilty of all ^b manner of ^c wickedness; ^d wherefore he was ^e odious to all ^f ranks of ^g people. He was ^h betrayed by his own army at ⁱ Margum in Mœsia, and ^k killed by the soldiers of Dioclesian, who, as soon as Numerian was ^l dead, ^m accepted of the ⁿ scarlet ^o offered him by the army, being born of ^p mean parents in ^q Dalmatia, (for ^r he is said to have been the ^s slave of ^t Anulinus the senator) but a ^u gallant soldier. He ^v took his ^x oath in an ^y assembly of the soldiers, that he ^z had no hand in the death of Numerian, and upon that ^a slew Aper with his own ^b hand; and so ^c fulfilled the ^d prophecy of him, that he should be emperor, when he had killed a ^e boar with his own hand; for which reason ^f as often as he ^g met with a boar, he ^h used to kill him. After he had killed Aper, he said he had ⁱ found the fatal boar. He ^k suppressed the ^l boors that made an ^m insurrection in Gaul, and ⁿ called themselves Bacaudæ, by ^o Maximianus, Herculius, whom he ^p sent thither ^q for that purpose in the year 285, in which this Herculius was first made Cæsar, and the year ^r following he was made Augustus. About the same time Carausius having ^s seised upon ^t Britain, and Achilleus in ^u Egypt, ^v pretended to the empire; and in the ^x East, Narses, king of Persia being ^y ready to ^z fall upon the Ro-

a *colpevole* b *sorta* c *scelleratezza* d *perciò* e *odioso* f *grado* g *gente* h *tradito* i *Margo* k *ammazzato* l *morto* m *accettare* n *scarlatto* o *offerto* p *bassi parenti* q *Dalmazia* r *si dice che* s *schiavo* t *Anulino* u *bravo* v *pigliare* x *giuramento* y *Assemblea* z *essere complice* a *uccidere* b *pugno* c *adempire* d *profezia* e *cignale* f *ogni volta che* g *rincontrare* h *solere* i *trovato* k *sopprimere* l *Villano* m *rivolta* n *chiamarsi* o *Massimiano Erculio* p *mandare* q *a questo effetto* r *seguente* s *impadronito* t *Brettagna* u *Egitto* v *pretendere* x *Levante* y *pronto* z *attaccare*.

mans

ITALIAN EXERCISES. 175

mans, and Africa being [a] wasted by the [b] Quinquegentians; the better to [c] deal with all these wars at once, he [d] created Constantius Chlorus, and Galerius Maximian, Cæsars. This latter was [e] born in Dacia, not far from Sardica, and was [f] sirnamed [g] Armentarius because he had been a [h] herdsman. Dioclesian [i] gave his daughter Valeria to Armentarius, and Maximianus Herculius [k] disposed of his step-daughter Theodora to Constantius. After this Dioclesian [l] went to Egypt, Herculius into Africa, Armentarius into the East, and Constantius into Britain. Alexandria was [m] taken by Dioclesian, after a [n] siege of eight months, in the twelfth year of his reign. Cerausius was [o] killed by his friend [p] Alectus, eight years after his [q] revolt. At the same time the Quinquegentians were [r] reduced by Maximianus Herculius; and Galerius Armentarius [s] defeated by Narsus, being [t] haughtily [u] received by Dioclesian, did the year following 297, [v] revenge this [x] disgrace, by [y] routing the Persian army, and [z] taking the [a] wives, [b] sisters, and [c] children of Narses, prisoners; upon which Dioclesian received him [d] honourably in Mesopotamia.

At last, after a [e] splendid [f] triumph, Dioclesian and Herculius [g] laid down their [h] authority; the former did it [i] out of choice, and [k] retired to Salonæ; the other was [l] prevailed upon more by the [m] authority of his [n] colleague, than that he had any

a *desolato* b *Quinquegenziani* c *fare* d *creare* e *nato*
f *cognominato* g *Armentario* h *pastore* i *dare* k *disporre* l *andare* m *preso* n *assedio* o *ammazzato* p *Aletto* q *rivolta* r *ridotto* s *sconfitto*
t *alteramente* u *ricevuto* v *vendicare* x *disgrazia*
y *sconfiggere* z *fare* a *moglie* b *sorella* c *figliuolo* d *onoratamente* e *splendido* f *trionfo* g *rinunziare* h *autorità* i *spontaneamente* k *ritirarsi*
l *disposto* m *autorità* n *collega*.

incli-

ᵃ inclination for it. This ᵇ fell out in the 20th of Dioclesian, and 304th year of Christ; upon which ᶜ Constantius Chlorus, and ᵈ Galerius Maximianus Armentarius, were ᵉ proclaimed emperors; Severus, and Galerius Maximianus, the ᶠ nephew of Armentarius by a sister, were ᵍ declared Cæsars. Constantius ʰ divided the Roman empire with Maximian, ⁱ keeping to himself Gaul, Italy, and Africa; but the two ᵏ last he afterwards ˡ quitted to his colleague, who had besides ᵐ Illyricum, Asia, and the ⁿ East. Of this he made Maximinus ᵒ governor, and ᵖ placed Severus in Italy.

CHAP. X.

COnstantius Chlorus having ᑫ enjoyed his ʳ dignity one year, or two, as most ˢ will have it, ᵗ died at York. He was of a ᵘ mild and ᵛ civil ˣ disposition; he would ʸ suffer no ᶻ enquiry to be made after the ᵃ Christians, and ᵇ preferred such of his ᶜ servants as he ᵈ knew to be of that ᵉ profession before the ᶠ rest.

Constantine, his son, ᵍ began his ʰ reign in the year of Christ 306, being 32 or 33 years of age, ⁱ born of ᵏ Helen of Bithynia, which, most ˡ authors say, was Constantius's concubine; but some will have her to have been his ᵐ lawful ⁿ wife, but of ᵒ mean ᵖ birth.

a *inclinazione*   b *succedere*   c *Costanzio Cloro*   d *Galerio Massimiano Armentario*   e *proclamato*   f *nipote*   g *dichiarato*   h *spartire*   i *tenersi*   k *ultimo*   l *lasciare*   m *Illirico*   n *Levante*   o *governatore*   p *collocare*   q *goduto*   r *dignità*   s *volere*   t *morire*   u *affabile*   v *civile*   x *disposizione*   y *soffrire*   z *inchiesta*   a *Cristiano*   b *preferire*   c *servitore*   d *sapere*   e *professione*   f *altro*   g *principiare*   h *regno*   i *nato*   k *Elena*   l *autore*   m *concubina*   n *legittimo*   o *moglie*   p *basso*   q *nascita*.

ITALIAN EXERCISES.

r At Rome, [a] Maxentius, [b] Herculius's son, was [c] proclaimed emperor, by the [d] prætorian [e] bands; who, at first, to [f] gain the [g] people, [h] seemed to [i] favour the [k] Christians; but [l] presently after [m] wallowed in all [n] manner of [o] wickedness and [p] cruelty. Galerius Maximianus [q] sent Severus against him, who, being [r] forsaken by his men, [s] fled to Ravenna; Galerius, upon this, [t] marching for Rome, with his [u] army, was [v] likewise forsaken by his men, and went into [w] Illyricum, where he [x] made Licinius Cæsar. Upon which Herculius [y] being now in hopes of [z] recovering the empire which he had [a] quitted against his [b] will, [c] returned from Lucania to Rome, and [d] advised [e] Dioclesian, [f] living at Carnus in Pannonia, by his [g] letters to him, to [h] do the like, which he [i] refused. He [k] trapanned Severus by [l] perjury, and [m] slew him. Then [n] laying a plot for his son, he was [o] forced to [p] fly from Rome to Constantine in Gaul, to whom he [q] gave his daughter Faustina in [r] marriage. But some time after, having [s] entered into a [t] wicked [u] design against his [v] son-in-law, Constantine, (which was [w] discovered by his daughter) he [x] fled to [y] Marseilles, and there [z] suffered the [a] punishment of his [b] treachery. About this time Galerius Maximianus [c] died

---

a *Masenzio* b *Erculio* c *proclamato* d *pretoriano* e *truppa* f *guadagnare* g *popolo* h *parere* i *favoreggiare* k *Cristiano* l *poco dopo* m *voltolarsi* n *sorta* o *dissolutezza* p *crudeltà* q *mandare* r *abbandonato* s *rifugiarsi* t *marciare* u *armata* v *parimente* w *Illirico* x *fare* y *sperare* z *ricuperare* a *lasciato* b *volontà* c *ritornare* d *consigliare* e *Diocleſiano* f *dimorare* g *lettera* h *fare* i *ricusare* k *adescare* l *spergiuro* m *uccidere* n *fare una congiura* o *forzato* p *fuggire* q *dare* r *matrimonio* s *entrato* t *cattivo* u *disegno* v *genero* w *scoperto* x *rifugiarsi* y *Marsiglia* z *soffrire* a *castigo* b *tradimento* c *morire.*

178 ITALIAN EXERCISES.

of a ^a filthy ^b difeafe, whom his fon-in-law Maxentius ^c enrolled amongſt the ^d gods.

In the year 312, ^e Conſtantine ^f marched againſt ^g Maxentius, and was ^h encouraged to it by the ⁱ prodigy of a ^k crofs he ^l faw in the ^m heavens. Having ⁿ paſſed the ^o Alps, and ^p defeated his generals near Verona, he ^q routed Maxentius himſelf not far from Rome, who ^r flying over a ^s bridge he had ^t laid upon the ^u Tyber, which ^v broke under him, was ^x drowned.

^y Affairs being ^z fettled in the city, Conſtantine in his ^a way to Germany, at Milan ^b married his fiſter ^c Conſtantia to Licinius, who had now been ^d made emperor. The fame year Galerius Maximinus, a cruel ^e enemy of the ^f Chriſtians, ^g undertaking a war againſt both the emperors, was ^h beaten by Licinius. in ⁱ Illyricum, and ^k fled into Aſia, where he ^l died a ^m horrible death at Tarfus in Cilicia. Nor did the ⁿ agreement betwixt the two ^o princes ^p laſt long; their firſt ^q rencounter was at Cibalis, a town in Pannonia; after which they had another ^r battle in the ^s plains of Mardia; in both which the ^t Licinians were ^u entirely defeated. At laſt a ^v peace was ^x made, and the empire ^y divided again.

In the year 324, Licinius ^z taking up arms againſt Conſtantine, ^a upon a pretence that he

a *fporco*   b *malattia*   c *arrolare*   d *nume*   e *Coſtantino*   f *marciare*   g *Maſenzio*   h *incoraggito*   i *prodigio*   k *croce*   l *vedere*   m *cielo*   n *traverſato*   o *Alpi*   p *ſconfitto*   q *mettere in rotta*   r *fuggire*   s *ponte*   t *meſſo*   u *Tevere*   v *romperſi*   x *affogato*   y *aſfare*   z *regolato*   a *viaggio*   b *maritare*   c *Coſtanzia*   d *fatto*   e *inimico*   f *Criſtiano*   g *intraprendere*   h *battuto*   i *Illirico*   k *fuggire*   l *morire*   m *orribile*   n *patto*   o *prencipe*   p *durare*   q *combattimento*   r *battaglia*   s *pianura*   t *Liciniani*   u *affatto*   v *pace*   x *fatto*   y *diviſa*   z *prendere*   a *ſotto preteſto*.

went

ᵃ went beyond his ᵇ bounds, and had ᶜ broken into his ᵈ dominions, received a great ᵉ overthrow near Hadrianople. ᶠ From thence flying into ᵍ Byzantium, he was again ʰ defeated by ⁱ fea; and being ᵏ routed in another ˡ battle near ᵐ Chalcedon, he was ⁿ taken prifoner by Conftantine, from whom he ᵒ procured his life by the ᵖ interpofition of hᵢs fifter, and was ᵠ banifhed to ʳ Theffalonica, where ˢ endeavouring to make a new ᵗ infurrection, he was ᵘ put to death.

After this, ˣ Crifpus Cæfar, his fon, by a former ʸ wife Minervina, a ᶻ youth of an extraordinary ᵃ genius, was put to death upon ᵇ fufpicion of ᶜ attempting to ᵈ debauch his ᵉ ftep-mother; and the year ᶠ following Faufta, being ᵍ found ʰ guilty of ⁱ falfly ᵏ accufing him, was ˡ ftifled to death in a hot ᵐ bath, by ⁿ order of her ᵒ hufband Conftantine.

In this emperor's time Byzantium was ᵖ rebuilt, and ᵠ enriched with the ʳ fpoils of almoft the whole ˢ world; fo that it ᵗ equalled Rome, and ᵘ took its ˣ name from the ʸ founder, being ᶻ called ᵃ Conftantinople.

After this, having ᵇ fubdued the ᶜ Sarmatians, and ᵈ difpofed of them in feveral ᵉ places of the

a *paffare*   b *limiti*   c *sforzato*   d *flato*   e *fconfitta Adrianopoli*   f *di là fuggire*   g *Bifanzio*   h *fconfitto*   i *mare*   k *meffo in rotta*   l *battaglia*   m *Calcedone*   n *fatto prigioniero*   o *ottenere*   p *interpofizione*   q *bandito*   r *Teffalonica*   s *cercare*   t *follevazione*   u *meffo*   x *Crifpo Cefare*   y *moglie*   z *giovine*   a *ftraordinario*   a *genio*   b *fofpetto*   c *tentare*   d *fedurre*   e *matrigna*   f *feguente*   g *trovato*   h *colpevole*   i *falfamente*   k *accufare*   l *foffogato*   m *bagno*   n *ordine*   o *marito*   p *rifabbricato*   q *arricchito*   r *fpoglia*   s *mondo*   t *ugguagliare*   u *prendere*   x *nome*   y *fonditore*   z *chiamato*   a *Coftantinopoli*   b *foggiogato*   c *Sarmati*   d *mandato*   e *luogo.*

Roman [a] empire: he died in the [b] suburbs of Nicomedia, where, most of the [c] ancients say he was [d] baptised a little before his [e] death.

He [f] left by Fausta, Maximianus's daughter, three children, [g] heirs of the empire, who [h] divided it amongst them. Constantine the [i] eldest had [k] Gaul, and all [l] beyond the [m] Alps. [n] Constans the [o] youngest had Rome, Italy, Africa, Sicily, and the rest [p] of the [q] islands, Illyricum, [r] Thracia, Macedonia, and [s] Greece. Constantius, the [t] middlemost, Asia, and the [u] East, with [v] Egypt.

But the brothers did not long [x] agree; four years after their father's [y] death, Constantius making war upon his brother Constans, and [z] invading his [a] territories, was [b] slain near Aquileia. Constans himself was slain ten years after by [c] Magnentius's general Gaison, nigh the [d] Pyrenæan mountains. Constantius was [e] engaged in a [f] dangerous war with this Magnentius. In the [g] battle [h] fought at Morsa in Pannonia, Constantius's army was [i] worsted in the first [k] assault, but [l] came off [m] victorious at last. Two years after this, Magnentius slew himself at Lyons in [n] despair.

Gallus was [o] declared Cæsar, and [p] governor of the East; but [q] abusing his [r] authority, he was [s] sent for by Constantius, and [t] put to death in Illyricum. [u] Julian, his brother was [v] saved by the [x] interpo-

a *imperio*   b *sobborgo*   c *antico*   d *battezzato*   e *morte*
f *lasciare*   g *erede*   h *dividere*   i *primogenito*   k *Gallia*
l *oltre*   m *Alpi*   n *Constante*   o *giovine*   p *resto*
q *isola*   r *Tracia*   s *Grecia*   t *secondogenito*   u *Levante*
v *Egitto*   x *accordarsi*   y *morte*   z *invadere*
a *territorio*   b *ucciso*   c *Magnenzio*   d *Pirenei*   e *impegnato*
f *pericoloso*   g *battaglia*   h *dato*   i *sopraffatto*
k *assalto*   l *essere*   m *vittorioso*   n *disperazione*
o *dichiarato*   p *governatore*   q *abusare*   r *autorità*
s *mandato a cercare*   t *messo*   u *Giuliano*
v *salvato*   x *interposizione*.

ITALIAN EXERCISES. 181

sition of Eusebia, Constantius's ᵃ lady, and sent to Athens, to ᵇ study there. Afterwards he was ᶜ advanced to the ᵈ dignity of Cæsar, ᵉ married to the emperor's sister ᶠ Helen, and was ᵍ made governor of ʰ Gaul, where he was very ⁱ successful against the ᵏ Germans, ˡ Franks, and ᵐ Alemans; he ⁿ sent the ᵒ king of the Alemans a ᵖ prisoner to Rome to Constantius, who ᑫ envying his ʳ success, ˢ endeavoured to ᵗ draw his soldiers from him, and ᵘ send them into the ᵛ East against the Persians. But they ˣ proclaimed Julian emperor at ʸ Paris, ᶻ whilst Constantius was ᵃ preparing for a war against the Persians. ᵇ As soon as he ᶜ understood this, he ᵈ marched against Julian, but died on the ᵉ road near Tarsus.

Julian, after the death of Constantius, was sole ᶠ master of the empire. He ᵍ killed, or ʰ banished all the ⁱ friends of Constantius, ᵏ opened the ˡ temples of the ᵐ idols, and ⁿ abjuring the ᵒ Christian ᵖ faith, was ᑫ consecrated ʳ high-priest, ˢ according to the ᵗ rites of the ᵘ pagan ᵛ religion. He made war against the Persians, and was ˣ slain in it. They tell you that, when he ʸ perceived his ᶻ wound to be ᵃ mortal, he ᵇ received the ᶜ blood in his ᵈ hand, and ᵉ threw it up ᶠ towards ᵍ heaven, with these

a *consorte*   b *studiare*   c *promosso*   d *dignità*   e *maritato*   f *Elena*   g *fatto*   h *Gallia*   i *fortunato*   k *Tedeschi*   l *Franchi*   m *Alemanni*   n *mandare*   o *Rè*   p *prigioniero*   q *invidiare*   r *successo*   s *procurare*   t *tirare*   u *mandare*   v *Levante*   x *proclamare*   y *Parigi*   z *mentre*   a *prepararsi*   b *subito che*   c *intendere*   d *marciare*   e *strada*   f *padrone*   g *uccidere*   h *bandire*   i *amico*   k *aprire*   l *tempio*   m *idolo*   n *abjurare*   o *Cristiano*   p *fede*   q *consacrato*   r *gran prete*   s *secondo*   t *rito*   u *pagano*   v *religione*   x *ucciso*   y *accorgersi*   z *ferita*   a *mortale*   b *ricevere*   c *sangue*   d *mano*   e *gettare*   f *verso*   g *cielo*.

words;

ITALIAN EXERCISES.

[a] words; "Thou hast [b] conquered me, O [c] Galilæan!" [d] meaning [e] Christ, whose religion he had [f] abjured.

After the death of Julian, [g] Jovian, a [h] native of Pannonia, was [i] proclaimed emperor by the [k] soldiers. He [l] ordered the temples of the idols to be [m] shut up, and their [n] sacrifices to be [o] abolished. He made an [p] inglorious peace with Sapores, king of the Persians, for thirty years, by which he [q] yielded up Nisibis, and the greatest [r] part of Mesopotamia to him. He died in his [s] return to Constantinople, in the [t] confines of Galatea and Bithynia.

In the year of Christ 364, [u] Valentinian was [v] chosen emperor at Nice, and not long after [x] gave the [y] title of [z] Augustus to his brother [a] Valens; and [b] leaving him in the East, [c] came into the [d] West himself. He had a great many good [e] qualities, but was [f] particularly [g] famous for his [h] love of [i] justice. He made war against the Alemanni [k] Saxons, Quadi, and other [l] nations. He [m] died of an [n] apoplexy in Pannonia, in the 55th year of his [o] age, and the 12th of his [p] reign.

His brother Valens [q] suppressed Procopius, a [r] relation of [s] Julian's, who had [t] assumed the [u] scarlet at Constantinople. After which he had a war with the [x] Goths; but upon the [y] suit of their king

a parola   b vinto   c Galileo   d voler dire   e Cristo
f Abjurare   g Gioviano   h nativo   i proclamato   k soldato
l fare   m chiudere   n sacrifizio   o abbolire
p infame   q cedere   r parte   s ritorno   t confini
u Valentiniano   v eletto   x dare   y titolo   z Augusto
a Valente   b lasciare   c venire   d Occidente
e qualità   f particolarmente   g illustre   h amore
i Giustizia   k Sassoni   l nazione   m morire   n apoplessia
o età   p regno   q sopprimere   r parente
s Giuliano   t arrogato   u scarlatto   x Gotti   y solle-

Atha-

ITALIAN EXERCISES. 183

[a] Athanaricus, [b] granted them a [c] peace in the year 369. Ten years after this, Athanaricus, with Fritigernes were [d] driven out of their [e] country by the [f] Huns, and were [g] kindly [h] received by Valens, and [i] settled with their Goths in [k] Thrace. They afterwards made an [l] insurrection against the Romans, and Valens being [m] wounded in a [n] battle against them, near [o] Hadrianople, was [p] burnt [q] alive by the barbarians, in a [r] cottage he [s] fled to. He reigned fourteen years and four months.

The emperor Valentinian had two sons, [t] Gratian and Valentinian. The former he [u] declared Augustus in Gaul, in the year 367; and his other son was [v] immediately after the death of his father [x] advanced to the same [y] dignity by the soldiers, in the year 375, and the 10th year of his age. Gratian had an [z] aversion to [a] public [b] business. After the death of Valens, the Goths [c] over-running Thrace, and other [d] provinces of the Roman empire, [e] being not able to [f] bear the [g] burden alone, he [h] sent for [i] Theodosius out of [k] Spain, and made him his [l] partner, who was then in the 33d year of his age.

Theodosius having [m] conquered the barbarians, [n] restored the public [o] peace. At last the whole [p] nation of the Goths, with their king, [q] delivered themselves up to the Romans, to whom the emperor [r] assigned [s] lands. After these things, Maximus

citazione   a *Atanarico*   b *accordare*   c *pace*   d *scacciato*   e *patria*   f *Unni*   g *cortesemente*   h *ricevuto*   i *stabilirsi*   k *Tracia*   l *rivolta*   m *ferito*   n *battaglia*   o *Adrianopoli*   p *bruciato*   q *vivo*   r *capanna*   s *rifuggiarsi*   t *Graziano*   u *dichiarare*   v *subito*   x *promosso*   y *dignità*   z *aversione*   a *pubblico*   b *affare*   c *inondare*   d *provincia*   e *non potere*   f *sopportare*   g *peso*   h *far venire*   i *Teodosio*   k *Spagna*   l *compagno*   m *conquistato*   n *ristabilire*   o *pace*   p *nazione*   q *arrendersi*   r *assegnare*   s *terra*.

ᵃ seised the ᵇ government in ᶜ Britain, in the year 382; and having ᵈ fixed his imperial ᵉ seat at Tryers, ᶠ basely killed Gratian at Lyons, after he had been ᵍ forsaken by his army; but Theodosius ʰ revenged his death, and ⁱ likewise ᵏ re-established Valentinian the ˡ younger, who had been ᵐ obliged to ⁿ quit Italy. This ᵒ happened in the year 388, in which he ᵖ overthrew and killed Maximus near Aquileia. Theodosius had all the ᑫ accomplishments ʳ becoming a Christian emperor, ˢ inferior to none of the ᵗ foregoing or ᵘ following princes, a ᵛ consummate general, never ˣ undertook any wars but such as were ʸ necessary; of ᶻ singular ᵃ clemency and ᵇ humanity, yet a little ᶜ inclined to ᵈ passion.

In the year 391, Eugenius, ᵉ supported by the ᶠ power of Arbogastes comes, ᵍ sets up for emperor, and in the following year, Valentinian was slain at Vienne in Gaul, by the same Arbogastes. Two years after ʰ Eugenius was ⁱ routed, ᵏ taken prisoner, and put to ˡ death by Theodosius. Arbogastes was his own ᵐ executioner. The year following, 395, this excellent emperor died at Milan, after a reign of sixteen years.

Theodosius ⁿ left two sons, ᵒ Arcadius and ᵖ Honorius; to the ᑫ former he ʳ gave the ˢ East, to the ᵗ latter the ᵘ West. Arcadius, ᵛ immediately after his father's death, ˣ married Eudoxia, which

a *usurpare*   b *governo*   c *Brettagna*   d *fissato*
e *seggio*   f *bassamente*   g *abbandonato*   h *vendicarsi*
i *parimente*   k *ristabilire*   l *giovine*   m *obbligato*
n *lasciare*   o *succedere*   p *sconfiggere*   q *compimento*
r *convenevole*   s *inferiore*   t *precedente*   u *seguente*
v *consumato*   x *intraprendere*   y *necessario*   z *singolare*
a *clemenza*   b *umanità*   c *inclinato*   d *collera*
e *sopportato*   f *potenza*   g *farsi*   h *Eugenio*
i *sconfitta*   k *fatto*   l *morte*   m *carnefice*   n *lasciare*
o *Arcadio*   p *Onorio*   q *primo*   r *dare*   s *Levante*
t *ultimo*   u *Occidente*   v *subito*   x *sposare*.

match

ITALIAN EXERCISES.

a match was b brought about by Eutropius, c for fear of his d taking to wife Ruffinus's daughter. This Ruffinus in the East, and Stilicho in the West, were at that time, two men of the greatest e eminence and f power in the empire. Stilicho, after the death of Theodosius, g laying claim to the h management of both the Eastern and Western empires, and i marching k eastward, Ruffinus l endeavoured m to hinder him, by n posting his o troops in all the p passages into q Greece, and r sending for Alaricus, king of the Goths, who s over-run Greece, but was t defeated by Stilicho. At last, Ruffinus was u slain by the y soldiers, the same year in which Theodosius died. After his death Eutropius x became very great with Arcadius, but was at last y disgraced and slain, in the very year in which he was z consul. In 403, died Arcadius, a prince of a a peaceable, but b indolent c temper, and too much d governed by his e wife. He left the f guardianship of his son, by g will, to Jezdegirdes, king of the h Persians, who i faithfully k executed that l trust, and m committed the n care of his o pupil to Antiochus, a very p learned man, and q threatened to make war upon any that should r offer to s disturb him.

In the west, the t frequent u invasions of the barbarians were almost v fatal to the Roman x state.

a *matrimonio*　　b *fatto*　　c *di paura che*　　d *pigliare*
e *eminenza*　　f *potere*　　g *pretendere*　　h *condotta*　　i *marciare*　　k *verso il levante*　　l *cercare*　　m *impedire*　　n *collocare*　　o *truppa*　　p *passaggio*　　q *Grecia*　　r *fare venire*　　s *trascorrere*　　t *sconfitto*　　u *ucciso*　　v *soldato*
x *doventare*　　y *disgraziato*　　z *console*　　a *pacifico*　　b *indolente*　　c *natura*　　d *governato*　　e *moglie*　　f *tutela*
g *testamento*　　h *Persiano*　　i *fedelmente*　　k *eseguire*
l *deposito*　　m *rimettere*　　n *cura*　　o *pupillo*　　p *sapiente*
q *minacciare*　　r *tentare*　　s *molestare*　　t *frequente*
u *invasione*　　v *fatale*　　x *stato*.

Radagisus king of the Goths, with four, or as [a] others [b] say, two hundred thousand men, [c] invaded Italy; which were very [d] happily [e] cut off by Stilicho, the general himself being [f] taken and [g] slain. After him, Alaricus, a king of the [h] Goths, having [i] wasted [k] Greece, and [l] continued a long time in [m] Epire, at the [n] instigation of Stilicho, who was [o] desirous to [p] take [q] Illyricum from Arcadius, in order to [r] annex it to the [s] dominions of Honorius, afterwards [t] penetrated into Italy. To [u] get rid of him, Honorius [v] gave him [x] Spain, and Gaul to [y] live in, because he was not in a condition to [z] keep those [a] provinces. As Alaricus was [b] marching thither, Saul, a [c] pagan general, whom Stilicho had [d] placed at the [e] head of an army, [f] falling upon the Barbarians, was [g] defeated by them. This [h] success did so [i] elevate Alaricus, that [k] quitting his [l] former [m] design, he [n] over-run Italy, and [o] took Rome; but before he did it, Stilicho was [p] put to death by the [q] order of Honorius. For after the death of Theodosius, [r] designing to get the empire to himself, and to make his son [s] Eucherius, who was a [t] pagan, and an enemy to the [u] Christians, emperor; the better to [v] accomplish his [x] design, he [y] resolved to [z] throw all things into a [a] confusion. [b] Wherefore he sent for the Barbarians to [c] ravage

a *altro*   b *dire*   c *invadere*   d *fortunatamente*
e *tagliato a pezzi*   f *preso*   g *ucciso*   h *Gotti*   i *desolato*   k *Grecia*   l *continuato*   m *Epiro*   n *istigazione*   o *desideroso*   p *prendere*   q *Illirico*   r *aggiungere*   s *stato*   t *penetrare*   u *disfarsi*   v *dare*   x *Spagna*   y *istato*   z *mantenere*   a *provincia*   b *marciare*   c *pagano*   d *messo*   e *testa*   f *attaccare*   g *sconfitto*   h *successo*   i *elevare*   k *desistere*   l *primo*   m *disegno*   n *trascorrere*   o *prendere*   p *messo*   q *ordine*   r *proporsi*   s *Eucherio*   t *pagano*   u *Cristiano*   v *compire*   x *disegno*   y *risolvere*   z *mettere*   a *confusione*   b *perciò*   c *saccheggiare*.

the empire, and ᵃ let the Alans, the Vandals, the Suevans, and the Burgundians, loofe upon France and Spain. His ᵇ relation to the emperor ᶜ encouraged him in it ; for he had Serena, the daughter of Theodofius's brother in ᵈ marriage, and had ᵉ difpofed of the two daughters he had by her, firſt, ᶠ Mary, and after her death, ᵍ Termantia, in marriage to Honorius. But thefe ʰ intrigues being ⁱ difcovered by ᵏ Olympius, in the year of Chriſt 408, he was flain by the ˡ hands of ᵐ Heraclius. The year following, Eucherius was ⁿ put to death, with his mother Serena. After Stilicho was ᵒ taken off, Alaricus was ᵖ defirous to ᑫ come to an ʳ accommodation with Honorius, but was ˢ foolifhly ᵗ rejected. Wherefore, with a ᵘ body of ᵛ Goths, and ˣ Huns, in ʸ conjunction with his wife's brother ᶻ Athaulfus, he ᵃ laid fiege to Rome, and ᵇ carried it in the year 410. The ᶜ plunder of it he ᵈ gave to his foldiers, but gave orders that all fuch as ᵉ fled to the ᶠ churches, ᵍ efpecially thofe of ʰ Peter and ⁱ Paul, fhould have ᵏ quarter given them. Then he ˡ went to ᵐ Rhegium, in order to ⁿ pafs over into Sicily and Africa, but ᵒ died there. He was ᵖ fucceeded by Athaulfus, who ᑫ plundered Rome again, ʳ carried off Placidia the emperor's fifter, and ˢ married her.

During this ᵗ ſtorm in Italy, the fame ᵘ calamity

a *fcatenare*   b *affinità*   c *incoraggire*   d *matrimonio*   e *difpoſte*   f *Maria*   g *Termanzia*   h *maneggio*   i *fcoperto*   k *Olimpio*   l *mano*   m *Eraclio*   n *meſſo*   o *ucciſo*   p *defideroſo*   q *venire*   r *accommodamento*   s *fcioccamente*   t *rigettato*   u *corpo*   v *Gotti*   x *Unni*   y *congiunzione*   z *Ataulfo*   a *aſſediare*   b *vincere*   c *bottino*   d *dare*   e *rifuggiarſi*   f *chieſa*   g *fpecialmente*   h *Pietro*   i *Paolo*   k *quartiere*   l *andare*   m *Reggio*   n *paſſare*   o *morire*   p *ſucceſſo*   q *faccheggiare*   r *portare via*   s *ſpoſare*   t *tempeſta*   u *calamità.*

fell

ᵃ fell upon Gaul and Spain. The Alans, Vandals, Suevans, ᵇ laid waste Gaul, passed the ᶜ Pyrenæan mountains, and ᵈ made themselves ᵉ masters of Spain in the year 409. The Vandals and Suevans ᶠ seised upon Galæcia; the Alans, Lusitania and the ᵍ province of ʰ Carthage; the ⁱ Silingans, which was another ᵏ branch of the Vandals, Bœtica.

After the ˡ breaking in of the Goths in 410, ᵐ divers ⁿ pretenders to the empire ᵒ started up in ᵖ several ᑫ places. First Attalus was ʳ made emperor by the ˢ senate, at the ᵗ command of Alaricus. He ᵘ proudly ᵛ rejected Honorius, that ˣ offered by his ʸ ambassadors to ᶻ receive him as his ᵃ partner in the empire, but was ᵇ obliged by Alaricus to ᶜ return to a ᵈ private ᵉ condition, and was afterwards ᶠ put up, and ᵍ down again several times. At last, ʰ renewing his ⁱ pretensions in Gaul, but being not ᵏ supported by the ˡ Goths, he was ᵐ taken ⁿ prisoner, and ᵒ put into the ᵖ hands of Honorius, who ᑫ spared his ʳ life, but ˢ cut off one of his hands.

ᵗ Marcus Gratianus, and Constantine in ᵘ Britain, ᵛ usurped the ˣ supreme ʸ power, and were ᶻ taken off. Then ᵃ Jovin and ᵇ Sebastian, two brothers, ᶜ pretended to the empire; but were ᵈ taken and

a *attaccare*   b *desolare*   c *Pirenei*   d *rendersi*
e *padrone*   f *impossessarsi*   g *provincia*   h *Cartagine*
i *Silingani*   k *ramo*   l *incursione*   m *diverso*   n *pretendente*
o *levarsi*   p *diverso*   q *luogo*   r *fatto*
s *senato*   t *commando*   u *superbamente*   v *rigettare*
x *offerire*   y *ambasciadore*   z *ricevere*   a *compagno*
b *obbligato*   c *ritornare*   d *privato*   e *stato*   f *esaltato*   g *deposto*   h *rinnovare*   i *pretensione*   k *sopportato*   l *Gotti*   m *fatto*   n *prigioniero*   o *messo*
p *mano*   q *risparmiare*   r *vita*   s *tagliare*   t *Marco Graziano*   u *Brettagna*   v *usurpare*   x *supremo*
y *potere*   z *ucciso*   a *Giovino*   b *Sebastiano*   c *pretendere*   d *preso*.

slain

ᵃ slain by ᵇ Athaulfus, king of the Goths. ᶜ Heraclianus was set up in Africa, and ᵈ venturing over into Italy against Honorius, was ᵉ routed by Marinus at ᶠ Utriculum; and ᵍ returning into Africa, was slain at ʰ Carthage.

In the year 415, Athaulfus was slain by a Goth, and ⁱ succeeded by Sigericus, who was taken off seven days after; and succeeded by Vuallia, who ᵏ made peace with the Romans, and ˡ restored Placidia to Honorius; after which he made war against the Alans, Vandals, Suevans, and other ᵐ nations, who had ⁿ settled in Spain. Honorius ᵒ married Placidia against her ᵖ will to ᵠ Constantius Comes, who ʳ confirmed the peace with Vuallia, ˢ sent for him back into Gaul, and ᵗ gave him that part of ᵘ Aquitain which ᵛ lies betwixt Tholouse and the ˣ sea, to ʸ dwell in. Upon this, Tholouse ᶻ became the ᵃ capital of the ᵇ Gothic, or ᶜ Visigothic ᵈ kingdom in Gaul. This ᵉ happened in the year 419. In the year following, Honorius, against his ᶠ will, made Constantius his ᵍ partner in the empire, who died seven months after, as did Honorius himself in the year 423.

He was ʰ succeeded by Valentinian his sister's son. In his reign the Vandals, whom Boniface had hitherto ⁱ repulsed from the ᵏ shores of Africa, ˡ entered it from Spain, under the ᵐ command of Geisericus. For Boniface being ⁿ impeached by

a *ucciso*   b *Ataulso*   c *Eracliano*   d *avventurare*
di *passare*   e *sconfitto*   f *Utriculo*   g *ritornare*   h *Cartagine*   i *successo*   k *far pace*   l *restituire*   m *nazione*   n *stabilito*   o *maritare*   p *volontà*   q *Costanzio Comete*   r *confermare*   s *far ritornare*   t *dare*   u *Aquitana*   v *giace*   x *mare*   y *dimorare*   z *doventare*   a *capitale*   b *Gotico*   c *Visigotico*   d *regno*   e *succedere*   f *volontà*   g *compagno*   h *successo*   i *ripulsato*   k *costa*   l *entrare*   m *commando*   n *accusato*.

Ætius,

ᵃ Ætius of ᵇ high-treason, and ᶜ Sigisvultus being ᵈ sent against him, ᵉ finding himself not a ᶠ match for the Romans, ᵍ fled to the Vandals for ʰ assistance, with whom he had ⁱ contracted an ᵏ affinity before. Wherefore in the year 427, Geisericus, with 80,000 Vandals and Alans, ˡ passed over into Africa, and ᵐ made himself master of it. In the mean time, Boniface being ⁿ reconciled to Placidia, and not ᵒ being able to ᵖ persuade the Barbarians to ᑫ go home again, ʳ endeavoured to ˢ oblige them to it, by ᵗ force of arms, and was ᵘ routed. He ᵛ went to Rome upon it, and died there soon after.

Ætius in Gaul ˣ played his part pretty well for the Romans against the Franks, Goths, Burgundians, Huns, and other Barbarians. Ætius had ʸ sent for the Huns to his assistance against the Goths. In the year 434, Honoria, Valentinian's sister, being ᶻ banished the ᵃ court for ᵇ lewdness with her ᶜ steward, and sent to Theodosius, emperor of the ᵈ East, ᵉ engaged Attila, king of the Huns, to make war upon the ᶠ West. ᵍ Litorius, a Roman general, having the ʰ command of them, whilst he ⁱ endeavoured to ⁱ outstrip the ˡ glory of Ætius, and was so ᵐ foolish as to ⁿ regard the ᵒ answers of ᵖ soothsayers and ᑫ dæmons, ʳ rashly ˢ engaged ᵗ Theodoricus, king of the Goths, who by the

a *Ezio* b *delitto di lesa maestà* c *Sigisvulto* d *mandato* e *trovarsi* f *uguale* g *ricorrere* h *assistenza* i *contrattato* k *affinità* l *passare* m *impadronirsi* n *riconciliato* o *potere* p *persuadere* q *ritornare* r *procurare* s *obbligare* t *forza d'armi* u *sconfitto* v *andare* x *sostenere* y *mandato a cercare* z *banditα* a *corte* b *disonestà* c *maggiordomo* d *Levante* e *impegnare* f *Occidente* g *Litorio* h *commando* i *procurare* k *eclissare* l *gloria* m *stolto* n *badare* o *risposta* p *indovino* q *demonio* r *temerariamente* s *attaccare* t *Teodorico*.

most

ITALIAN EXERCISES.

moſt ᵃ abject ᵇ ſubmiſſion ᶜ declined the war, and after a great ᵈ overthrow was ᵉ taken and ᶠ ſlain in the year 439, in which ᵍ Carthage was ʰ ſurpriſed by the Vandals. At laſt, in the year 442, Valentinian ⁱ renewed the peace with Geiſericus, and Africa was ᵏ divided betwixt them.

In the year 450, Attila ˡ marched into Gaul, which at that time the ᵐ Viſigoths, Franks, Burgundians, Alans, and other Barbarians, were in ⁿ poſſeſſion of. Part of the Romans ᵒ reluctantly ᵖ ſtaid under the ᵠ command of Ætius, who alone at that time ʳ kept the ˢ weſtern ᵗ empire from ᵘ falling to ᵛ utter ˣ ruin. Attila ʸ laid ſiege to Aurelia, but Ætius ᶻ coming upon him, ᵃ obliged him to ᵇ raiſe the ᶜ ſiege, and ᵈ purſued him into Gallia Belgica, and ᵉ overthrew him, in a great ᶠ battle that was ᵍ fought in the ʰ plains of Catalonia. There were ⁱ ſlain on both ᵏ ſides at leaſt 170,000, and amongſt them Theodoricus king of the Goths. It is ˡ certain the Huns might have been ᵐ utterly ⁿ deſtroyed, if Ætius had not been ᵒ afraid, that in caſe the Huns ſhould be ᵖ entirely ᵠ cut off, the Goths would be ʳ inſupportable in Gaul.

Attila having ˢ unexpectedly ᵗ eſcaped, ᵘ poured his ᵛ troops into Italy, where he laid ſiege to Aquileia, and ˣ levelled it with the ground. After that

a *abbietto*   b *ſommeſſione*   c *ſfuggire*   d *ſconfitta*   e *preſo*   f *ucciſo*   g *Cartagine*   h *ſorpreſo*   i *rinnovare*   k *ſpartito*   l *marciare*   m *Viſigotti*   n *poſſeſſo*   o *malvolentieri*   p *rimanere*   q *commando*   r *impedire*   s *occidentale*   t *imperio*   u *caſcare*   v *totale*   x *rovina*   y *aſſediare*   z *venire addoſſo*   a *forzare*   b *levare*   c *aſſedio*   d *incalzare*   e *rompere*   f *battaglia*   g *dato*   h *pianura*   i *ucciſo*   k *banda*   l *certo*   m *affatto*   n *diſtrotto*   o *paura*   p *interamente*   q *ſconfitto*   r *inſopportabile*   s *impenſatamente*   t *ſcappato*   u *inondare*   v *truppa*   x *ſpianare*.

he ᵃ laid waste ᵇ Milan, ᶜ Ticinum, and other ᵈ towns; and ᵉ marching for Rome, was so ᶠ wrought upon by an ᵍ ambassy from ʰ Leo, who ⁱ met him at the ᵏ river Mincius, that he ˡ went into his own ᵐ country; afterwards ⁿ returning into Gaul against the Alans, who had ᵒ posted themselves beyond the Loire, he was again ᵖ defeated by ᵠ Thorismundus, as he had been in the ʳ plains of Catalonia; and in the year 454, after a ˢ debauch with ᵗ wine, died of ᵘ a vomiting of ᵛ blood.

They ʷ say the city of ˣ Venice ʸ owes its ᶻ origin to that ᵃ inroad of the Barbarians, most of the Italians, ᵇ especially those of ᶜ Patavium, ᵈ flying from the ᵉ fire and ᶠ ruins of their cities to some ᵍ rocks and ʰ desert ⁱ islands in the ᵏ sea for ˡ refuge.

Valentinian, upon the death of his mother Placidia, ᵐ let loose the ⁿ reins of ᵒ licentiousness and ᵖ abused his ᵠ authority, for the ʳ satisfaction of his ˢ lust and ᵗ cruelty. He ᵘ debauched the ᵛ wife of Maximus the senator, ʷ put Ætius to death, after Maximus had by his ˣ crafty ʸ contrivances ᶻ rendered him ᵃ suspected, in the year 454; and the year following, by the contrivance of the same Maximus, he was ᵇ stabbed by Ætius's ᶜ life-guard

a *desolare*   b *Milano*   c *Ticino*   d *città*   e *marciare*   f *toccato*   g *ambasciata*   h *Leone*   i *rincontrare*   k *fiume Mincio*   l *ritirarsi*   m *patria*   n *ritornare*   o *messo*   p *sconfitto*   q *Torismondo*   r *pianura*   s *stravizzo*   t *vino*   u *vomito*   v *sangue*   w *dire*   x *Venezia*   y *dovere*   z *origine*   a *incursione*   b *specialmente*   c *Patavio*   d *fuggire*   e *fuoco*   f *rovina*   g *scoglio*   h *disabitato*   i *isola*   k *mare*   l *rifugio*   m *sciogliere*   n *redine*   o *dissolutezza*   p *abusare*   q *autorità*   r *soddisfazione*   s *sensualità*   t *crudeltà*   u *sedurre*   v *moglie*   w *mettere*   x *astuto*   y *invenzione*   z *reso*   a *sospetto*   b *pugnalato*   c *guardia di corpo*

in the [a] field of [b] Mars, being thirty-fix years of age, and in the 31ſt of his reign. [c] Eudoxia, Valentinian's [d] lady, to [e] revenge the death of her [f] huſband, [g] ſent for Genſericus out of Africa, into Italy. Maximus, upon his [h] arrival, [i] endeavoured to [k] ſave himſelf by [l] flight, but was [m] torn in pieces by his own men, and [n] thrown into the [o] Tiber, after a [p] reign of [q] hardly two [r] months. Genſericus, after he had [s] taken the city, was ſo [t] affected by an [u] addreſs of [v] pope Leo's, that he did not [x] ſet it on fire, or [y] put any to the ſword; but [z] made plunder of all the [a] wealth of the [b] place, both [c] ſacred and [d] profane, for fourteen days together, and [e] carried off Eudoxia, with her two daughters, Eudocia and Placidia, into Africa; the [f] former of which he [g] married to his ſon [h] Hunericus.

In the mean time, [i] Avitus Gallus being [k] proclaimed emperor by the Gallic [l] army at Tholouſe, made peace with the Goths; at whoſe [m] perſuaſion, Theodoric [n] entering Spain, [o] conquered the Suevans, and [p] killed their king [q] Rechiarius in the year 456.

After him [r] Majorianus [s] took the [t] government upon him at Ravenna; a [u] prince of a [v] great [x] ſoul, who being [y] deſirous to [z] recover Africa, was going

a *campo*   b *Marte*   c *Eudoſſia*   d *conſorte*   e *vendicare*   f *marito*   g *far venire*   h *arrivata*   i *procurare*   k *ſalvarſi*   l *fuga*   m *ſbranato*   n *gettata*   o *Tevere*   p *regno*   q *appena*   r *meſe*   s *preſo*   t *toccato*   u *ſupplica*   v *papa Leone*   x *mettere il fuoco*   y *mettere a filo di ſpada*   z *predare*   a *ricchezza*   b *piazza*   c *ſacra*   d *profano*   e *portare via*   f *primo*   g *maritare*   h *Unerico*   i *Avito Gallo*   k *gallico*   l *armata*   m *perſuaſione*   n *entrare*   o *conquiſtare*   p *uccidere*   q *Rechiario*   r *Maggioriano*   s *prendere*   t *governo*   u *principe*   v *valoroſo*   x *anima*   y *bramoſo*   ricuperare.

to Genericus, under the ^a title of an ^b ambassador; but being ^c seized by Ricimer at Dertona, and ^d obliged to ^e resign, was ^f put to death in the year 461, after a reign of four years and four months.

Ricimer ^g set up Severus for emperor, ^h according to an ⁱ agreement betwixt them, and ^k poisoned him in the fourth year of his reign.

After this, there was an ^l interregnum of a year, and some months, 'till Anthemius was ^m sent into the West by ⁿ Leo, emperor of the ^o East, between whom and ^p Ricimer it had been ^q agreed he should be ^r declared emperor, and his daughter should ^s marry Ricimer. Thus the barbarian being ^t made Anthemius's ^u son-in-law, with his ^v wonted ^x perfidiousness, first ^y raised a civil war against him, and then ^z put him to death at Rome, after he had ^a reigned five years and some months.

^b Olybrius was after this ^c put up in the ^d room of Anthemius by Ricimer, who ^e died forty days after Anthemius's death; nor was he long ^f survived by Olybrius, for he died the same year, about seven months after his ^g promotion.

He was ^h followed by ⁱ Glycerius, who ^k took the ^l government upon him at Ravenna, in the year 473, and reigned a year and four months. He was ^m succeeded by ⁿ Julius Nepos, who was ^o taken off in about five years after his ^p advancement.

a *titolo* b *ambasciadore* c *preso* d *obbligato* e *rassegnare* f *messo* g *alzare* h *secondo* i *patto* k *avvelenare* l *interregno* m *mandato* n *Leone* o *Levante* p *Ricimero* q *convenuto* r *dichiarato* s *sposare* t *fatto* u *genero* v *solito* x *perfidia* y *suscitare* z *mettere* a *regnato* b *Olibrio* c *messo* d *luogo* e *morire* f *sopravvissuto* g *promozione* h *seguito* i *Glicerio* k *prendere* l *governo* m *successo* n *Giulio Nepote* o *ucciso* p *elevazione*.

Momyl-

ᵃ Momyllus, who was ᵇ likewise ᶜ called ᵈ Auguſtulus, was ᵉ ſet up by his father ᶠ Oreſtes, being the ᵍ laſt of all the emperors in the ʰ Weſt; for ⁱ Odouacer, king of the ᵏ Turcilingans, with the ˡ Scyrans, and ᵐ Herulans, ⁿ ſeized Italy, and after he had ᵒ ſlain Oreſtes and his brother ᵖ Paul, ᑫ baniſhed Auguſtulus into Campania. Thus ʳ ended the ˢ empire of the Weſt, in the year of ᵗ Chriſt 476.

a *Momillo* b *parimente* c *chiamato* d *Auguſtolo* e *innalzato* f *Oreſte* g *ultimo* h *Occidente* i *Odouacero* k *Turcilingani* l *Scirai* m *Erulani* n *uſurpare* o *ucciſo* p *Paolo* q *bandire* r *finire* s *imperio* t *Criſto.*

F I N I S.

BOOKS printed for J. Nourse, in the Strand, Bookseller to his Majesty.

1. THE Complete Italian Master: containing the best and easiest Rules for attaining that Language. By Signor Veneroni, Italian Secretary to the late French King. Translated into English, and compared with the last Lyons Edition. A new Edition, with considerable Additions and Improvements by the Translator. 5s.

2. The New Italian, English, and French Pocket Dictionary. Carefully compiled from the Dictionaries of La Crusca, Dr. S. Johnson, the French Academy, and from other Dictionaries of the best Authorities. In which the Parts of Speech are properly distinguished, and each word accented according to its true and natural pronunciation. To which is prefixed, a New Compendious Italian Grammar. By F. Bottarelli, A. M. in three vols. Price 18s.

3. Lettere d'una Peruviána tradótte dal Francése in Italiáno, di cúi si sóno accentáte tutte le vóci, per facilitár ágli straniéri il módo d'imparar la prodia di quésta língua. Dal Signór Deodati. Nuóva edizióne. In fine si aggiúnge úna raccolta di favole r uso de' fanciúlli. 12mo. 3s. 6d.

4. Istoria critica della vita civile, scritta da Vinzio Martinelli. Terza edizione emendata ed a esciuta dall' Autore. 2 vols. 8vo. 12s.

5. Lettere familiari e critiche di Vincenzio Martini. 8vo. 6s.

6. A Dictionary of the English and Italian Languages; 1. Italian and English; 2. English and Italian. By Joseph Baretti. A New Edition improved. 2 vols 4to. 2l. 2s.

7. Commedie scelte di Carlo Goldoni. 3 vols. 12mo. 10s. 6d.

www.ingramcontent.com/pod-product-compliance
Lightning Source LLC
Chambersburg PA
CBHW020914230426
43666CB00008B/1448